bonjour
kale

a MEMOIR of PARIS,
LOVE & RECIPES

KRISTEN BEDDARD

Published by Sourcebooks, Inc.
P.O. Box 4410, Naperville, Illinois 60567-4410
(630) 961-3900
Fax: (630) 961-2168
www.sourcebooks.com

Library of Congress Cataloging-in-Publication Data

Names: Beddard, Kristen, author.
Title: Bonjour kale : a memoir of Paris, love, and recipes / Kristen Beddard.
Description: Naperville, Illinois : Sourcebooks, [2016]
Identifiers: LCCN 2015047465 | ISBN 9781492630043 (pbk.)
Subjects: LCSH: Cooking (Kale) | Cooking, French. | Beddard, Kristen--Travel.
   | Paris (France)--Description and travel. | LCGFT: Cookbooks.
Classification: LCC TX803.G74 B429 2016 | DDC 641.6/5347--dc23 LC record available
at http://lccn.loc.gov/2015047465

Printed and bound in the United States of America.
VP 10 9 8 7 6 5 4 3 2 1

Praise for

"As someone who roamed the streets and markets of Paris in search of the elusive kale, I (and many others) have Kristen to thank for revolutionizing the city for *légume*-lovers. *Bonjour Kale* is a charming tale of how she found her place in Paris, becoming a tireless advocate for the leafy green that we all now know, and love...in abundance!"

—David Lebovitz, author of *My Paris Kitchen*

"Every time I spot a crate of kale in a store near me, I whisper a prayer of thanks to Kristen, patron saint of leafy greens in Paris. Beyond the culinary gratitude, hers is an inspiring tale of finding an identity and a purpose in a foreign city—one you are bound to relate to if you've ever sought a home away from home."

—Clotilde Dusoulier, author of *Chocolate & Zucchini*

"A triumphant story of finding love, moving to Paris, and overcoming that one little French word: 'impossible.' Kristen's tenacity on the trail to bringing kale to Paris is deliciously inspiring."

—Amy Thomas, author of *Paris, My Sweet: A Year in the City of Light (and Dark Chocolate)*

"Of the great kale heroes, none rival kale crusader Kristen Beddard. Beyond the kale, read this book for the inspiring tale of love, Paris, and how the tenacity of one woman changed French food."

—Drew Ramsey, MD, author of *Eat Complete* and *50 Shades of Kale* and co-founder of National Kale Day

"Kristen Beddard's approachable voice is filled with passion and heart in a tale that goes well beyond that signature leafy green. *Bonjour Kale* has it all: love, loss, and hope, with wonderful recipes to extend the experience at home."

—Lindsey Tramuta, journalist
and creator of *Lost in Cheeseland*

"*Bonjour Kale* is an endearing love letter to leafy greens as well as the story of a dedicated woman bravely making a home for herself in Paris. Kale lovers, Francophiles, and adventurous souls will enjoy following Kristen as she introduces kale to Paris and encounters both heartbreaking and hilarious obstacles along the way."

—Emily Dilling, author of *My Paris Market Cookbook*

"*Bonjour Kale* made me nostalgic for life in Paris, with all its elegance and eccentricity. With warmth and wit, Kristen Beddard has written a charming story of perseverance and fresh produce!"

—Ann Mah, author of *Mastering the Art of French Eating*

To my mom, for giving me kale.
And to Philip, for giving me France.

Recipes

A Note about the Recipes

As my life has changed since moving to Paris, so has my cooking. The recipes in this book are influenced by France's culinary tradition, colorful produce, and—of course—a little butter and cream.

And while this is a memoir about kale and living in France, the recipes are not *only* kale or *only* French. There are other books out there that can guide you to a perfect *coq au vin* or *croque monsieur*, and the Internet is an encyclopedia of kale ideas. So I've chosen to give you a little bit of both—some kale, some French—many of which are inspired by each other.

Others are recipes that were part of my childhood, remind me of my mother, or are now a staple in my own kitchen. And while there are exact measurements in this book, many of them are meant to be prepared, as the French say, *au pif*, by the nose. You can add a little more kale, a little less garlic, or an extra stalk of rhubarb. Most recipes have an exact measurement for how much kale to include, but it will not make or break a dish if you use less or add a little more. I only hope that these encourage you to head to the kitchen and cook!

Keeping a Kale Kitchen

Kale comes in many different shapes, sizes, and weights. Some leaves are big, some are small. Some bunches are one pound, some are only one-quarter pound. In France, kale is sold by the kilogram and rarely bunched. Sometimes it is sold as tiny, baby leaves in plastic containers or bags. This makes it a little more difficult to measure out the exact amount of kale for a recipe. In the majority of recipes, it's not a problem if you have a little less or a little more than what is called for. Unless a recipe calls for a larger quantity, I've chosen to measure out kale in cups and grams, already chopped. The measurements are not much different if it is destemmed or if the stems are intact.

Buying Kale

Look for leaves that are a deep green color and avoid leaves that are brown or yellow or extremely tough. Tough kale means it is the end of the season. Kale is a heavily sprayed crop, so if possible, try to buy organic. If not, thoroughly wash each leaf.

Washing Kale

Take each leaf individually and run under water. Move your fingers through each fold and crevice to remove any excess dirt or, if organic, any potential pest.

Destemming Kale

It sounds difficult but destemming kale is easy and quick. After washing each leaf, take both sides of the leaf, fold them together, and rip the stem away from the leaf. Save stems for juicing.

Massaging Kale

The key to any good kale salad is a good kale massage. On already washed and dried kale, add the dressing of your choice and massage the kale with your hands for a minute or so. The dressing will marinate the leaves, slightly wilting them and making them softer to eat and enjoy.

These are a few ingredients and kitchen tools I recommend you keep on hand to complete your kale kitchen:

Lemons, garlic, shallots, olive oil, sherry vinegar, and sea salt: Whether making dressings or sautéing, these ingredients are commonly used.

Lemon squeezer: This is something I take away on vacation with me—especially if I know we will be making a lot of salads. It's quick, easy, and efficient. I've never found anything that juices a lemon as well as this—and it ensures no seeds accidentally fall into the juice.

Tongs: Another item I have a hard time cooking without, tongs are a great tool to use to sauté and serve kale.

Salad spinner: I had a friend who once admitted to using a hair dryer to dry the kale she was going to use for kale chips—I bought her a salad spinner for her birthday. Like lettuce, a salad spinner will dry the kale well enough for either storing or immediate use.

Plastic freezer bags: If you buy a lot of greens but want them to last through the week, wash them right away, dry them, and store them in plastic freezer bags in the refrigerator. The leaves will keep longer, and it will be that much easier to cook with the greens throughout the week because the hard work of cleaning and destemming is already done.

Chapter I

The regional RER train sat on the track at the Gare du Nord station, stripping the romance out of double-decker transportation. It loomed over me, covered in city soot, and let out a big sigh of dirt. A dramatic, French sigh—if it could have shrugged, it would have. I walked into the carriage, searching for a seat that wasn't torn or already taken over by French youths eating McDonald's, or as the French say, *McDo*. I could *not* handle that greasy fast-food smell for the next forty-five minutes.

I found a window seat, and an older woman who seemed to have a gentle spirit sat next to me. We politely and quickly said, "*Bonjour*," rearranged our belongings so they wouldn't touch, and settled in for the journey. My tense body sank into the seat back of springs, broken from the daily grind of commuters, living their lives of *métro, boulot, dodo*—subway, work, sleep.

As the train pulled out, I cocked my head and looked out the window into the never-ending Paris gray. I was no longer in the postcard version of the city, with the enchanting Louvre and the immaculate gardens. Instead, I was surrounded by graffiti-stained walls, electrical wires crisscrossing overhead, and building after building dissolving into a gray, concrete blur. If I closed my eyes, I could at least block out the somber colors outside, if not the noise of the train and the smell of *Le Big Mac*.

The RER slowly picked up speed. I was headed to the airport for the second time that week. Four days ago, my husband, Philip, and I had returned from the States after visiting for Thanksgiving. We'd only lived in France for three months, and coming back to our new home after the holiday was a lot more difficult than I had anticipated. I told everyone back in America, "Yes, things in Paris are great. I love it!" But was I lying to myself? To them? After spending only a few days in New York City, I was reminded how desperately I missed it. I missed after-work drinks with my girlfriends and the energy of the city. I missed being understood while ordering coffee to go and knowing where to find things in the grocery store. And, most of all, I felt sad that even though we'd only been away for a few months, the city was obviously no longer our home.

I *lived* in Paris, but the problem was that my *life* was not in Paris yet. After visiting New York, I realized that it was going to take more than a few months for the City of Lights to feel like it was where Philip and I actually belonged. And now our new home, after a beautiful Indian summer, was dark, cold, and rainy—weather that I would soon learn was more typical than not. My mood followed suit. If Paris wanted to be consistently cold and depressing, then so would my disposition.

The reason I was returning to the airport didn't help my mood either. I needed to recuperate our, or should I say my, lost luggage. Philip's bag had arrived safe and sound, but mine had not. And I had a sneaking suspicion why.

Kale.

I had yet to find the leafy green in Paris. Not at a single market or at any grocery store. Farmers and *maraîchers* who sold a wide variety of vegetables didn't even seem to know what it was, and after an extensive Internet search, I'd come to the conclusion that kale was nearly impossible to find.

So while I was in New York, stocking up on the vegetable at Whole Foods seemed like a great idea. If I couldn't find kale in Paris, then I would bring kale *to* Paris. I reveled in the shopping trip, patting myself on the back for buying bunches of it—grown by my own uncle's farm no less—to take back with us. I chose several varieties of the cabbage, from curly to lacinato to red Russian, filling the shopping cart with glorious shades of green. The height of foliage rose tall, allowing me to breathe in the earthy scent that was not so familiar anymore. I packed each bunch carefully in Ziploc bags, sealing them tight for the twelve-hour journey. I was already dreaming of the salad I would prepare for our first dinner back in Paris. What could go wrong?

The train slowed, about to arrive at the airport, and my palms began to sweat. I could see Philip, a few days earlier, standing next to the baggage claim conveyor belt, his suitcase next to him. After what felt like an eternity, the belt slowed to a stop.

"You had to pack all that kale, didn't you?" he asked, trying unsuccessfully to maintain his cool.

He had a right to be irritated. Even though he would have enjoyed the soup, salad, and smoothies that were floating around on the menu in my head, he was the fluent French speaker, which meant that he was the one who would have to deal with the airline staff—and the line for lost baggage was not getting any shorter.

A phone call from the airline had triggered this journey back to the airport, and this time the responsibility was all mine, regardless of whether I spoke the language—which I did not. Philip told me it was my "French homework" for the day, but I was in no position to navigate this situation. It wasn't just the speaking that made me apprehensive; I knew why my bags were stalled and almost a week late, and I still didn't have my *carte de séjour* to legally stay in the country. Would a few bags of soggy kale get me kicked out of France?

By the time I reached the airline desk, I was so nervous I could practically smell the incriminating scent of spoiled cabbage. "*Oui,* Madame Heimann," the woman said, pronouncing my married name without the *H*. I handed her the paperwork and boarding pass. She stared at the papers, at me, and back at the papers.

"*Ah, oui,*" she said, a long, exasperated sigh bubbling at her lips. "There it is," she pointed to her left, turning up her nose with a look of disgust.

I smiled at her sheepishly, signed a form, and, relieved that nothing worse had happened, quickly rolled my luggage into the main hall. I couldn't handle the putrid smell for the taxi ride home, so I opened my bag and discarded the soggy leaves and warm kale juice into a nearby garbage can.

I had a serious problem on my hands. Kale was impossible to find in Paris, and we would be living there for the next *five years*. Could I go that long without my favorite vegetable? Clearly, my smuggling plan was not going to work. There had to be another solution.

·· HOW TO GROW ··
YOUR OWN KALE

If you ever find yourself in the same situation as I did and want to stay away from smuggling in bunches of kale in your suitcase, you can always try to grow your own. Traditionally kale is a cold-weather vegetable, and seeds are sown in mid to late July for an autumn harvest that can last through the winter. The vegetable is resistant to frost, although temperatures well below freezing will eventually make the leaves too tough to enjoy (even with a hearty kale massage!). Aside from when you're "supposed" to grow kale, it is an easy plant to cultivate. The seeds germinate quickly, and sprouts will pop up only a few days after being planted. Within sixty days, the plants will be mature and ready for harvest.

Kale prefers a fertile, well-drained soil high in organic matter with a pH range of 6.0–7.5. Consistent moisture will produce the best quality and highest yields. Ideal daytime temperatures are in the 70s °F (low 20s °C) and night temperatures in the high 40s °F (8–12 °C). Pests are mainly worms, cabbage loopers, and flea beetles. It is recommended to germinate seeds in a seed tray.

PREPARATION

Place seeds ½ inch (1 cm) below soil and water daily. Sprouts should appear in about a week. When plants are about 5 inches (12 cm) high, replant them to the ground about 20 inches (50 cm) apart. You can also keep in a planter or a large pot, and the vegetable will produce smaller leaves. Water daily, and keep an eye out for pests like caterpillars! To harvest, pick leaves off the stalk. Leaves typically grow back one more time.

Chapter 2

To a lot of people, the fact that what I missed the most as an expat was kale seemed ridiculous. And until living in France, I never gave much thought to the vegetable. I never thought that someday I would think, talk, and write about it on a daily basis. Kale is just a cabbage after all! But it's almost like I had no choice. Kale has always been a part of my life because of my mother—she set me up for this. As she liked to say, "You've been eating kale since conception." In the diary she kept during my first year, she clearly wrote out at around nine months, "Kristen tried kale today. She loved it!"

She was macrobiotic at the time, following a strict diet that was high in whole grains—like brown rice, quinoa, and millet—and vegetables—like leafy greens, beans, and sea vegetables—and that restricted animal proteins and processed foods. So kale was not the only leafy green that held a prominent role in our meals. All vegetables were created equal, and did we ever eat our vegetables. Our dinner plates included baked varieties of squash and beets in winter, crisp cucumbers and lightly simmered green beans in summer, and steamed broccoli and cauliflower almost year-round, paired with brown rice or millet and sprinkled with toasted sesame seeds.

On my first day of third grade, while playing a game to introduce ourselves, we had to choose a noun corresponding to the first letter of our first name. I casually chose "kale," not thinking twice about it, until I realized that none of my classmates knew what it was. This was when I began to understand that my mother and I ate differently than the majority of Americans, and that experiencing the flavors, aromas, and textures of different vegetables was something unique we shared.

The summer I turned five was the summer my mother finally left my father. Married almost twelve years, unhappy for most of them, she'd had enough of the affairs, the late nights at bars with his band members, the excessive drinking of Rolling Rock. She was tired of being the only person supporting our family. She didn't need to be with someone who was taking advantage of her, someone who thought her only worth was her money, which was ironic since she wasn't earning much money to begin with. When I thought back over those years, I realized that everything came down to her. *She* worked two jobs to put him through school, *she* was at home every day with a newborn but without access to a car, and *she* kept the family afloat while my father aimed to set up his recording-studio business. I never doubted that he loved me, but he was not there day after day.

Eventually, enough was enough. Gathering all of her strength, my mom moved us away from the post-steel-mill south side of Pittsburgh that lined the Monongahela River. We left the remnants of what the city used to be: yellow factories, empty, dead, and rusting. In 1989, there was nothing clean or respectful about Pittsburgh, and the same went for my parents' marriage. I'm sure my father would say it all differently, and there are always two sides to every story, but that is what *I* remember.

And then it was just the two of us. We were headed to the quaint, almost country-like village of Sewickley, northwest of the city along the Ohio River. It was in the school district where my mom taught kindergarten. I remember the big evergreen-colored truck from the day of the move. My grandmother unpacked all of our kitchen stuff. My great-aunt wore one of my tutus on her head to keep me entertained. My mom cried. We drove the thirty minutes to our new home in her silver Camry. The stick shift churned as each emotion pulsed from her heart to her limbs: anger—*shift*—despair—*shift*—exhaustion—*neutral*.

We settled into a duplex apartment not far from the train tracks. I had a bike and a backyard with a new swing set. I met a few neighborhood friends, and we built a clubhouse in an old garage. I remember being happy and well fed. To this day, I don't know how she did it. The strength hidden behind her eyes, bloodshot from crying, still astounds me.

My mother never stopped cooking. She never stopped nourishing me. On Sundays, her face would disappear into steam from simmering carrots, celery, and onions, as she prepped our soup for the week. Her food processor held a prominent spot on the kitchen counter, mixing homemade sauces. The kitchen always smelled of tahini. She showed me, leading by example, that real food is the right food. It is the only food. No matter what my mother went through emotionally, I never felt it. She pushed everything negative aside, especially when it came to cooking for us.

My mother's devotion to healthy living and eating began in 1977, two years into her marriage, when she took her first yoga class at a local YMCA. She immediately felt different. Yoga led to yoga friends, which led to vegetarian cooking classes, which led to a deep interest in and practice of macrobiotics.

The purpose of macrobiotics is based on the Chinese philosophy of keeping the yin and yang of the body in balance, and certain foods are better at balancing each. Kale happens to be one of the best foods for balancing the yang and detoxifying the blood.

Now, thirty years later, a lot of people consider macrobiotics a crazy food fad for the rich and famous, like Gwyneth Paltrow and Madonna. And rightly so, considering how much time, effort, and energy goes into doing it right. My mom did it all herself, without a personal chef, grocery shopper, or food delivery service. She was that passionate.

Although she never admitted it, I think a big part of her devotion to living such a clean life was about control. While the rest of her life with my father was in flux, she could at least control everything she put into her body. Spending hours in the kitchen was her escape. It distracted her from the real issue at hand.

It wasn't just squash and cruciferous vegetables that my mom and I shared together. As a young child, during her daily yoga practice, I would sit on her back while she relaxed in child's pose or make my own attempt at cat-cow pose. We took summer trips to visit one of her yoga friends in Rockport, Massachusetts, where I spent my days climbing over rocks and searching for mussels in the Atlantic. We took impromptu weekend drives to my uncle's organic vegetable farm in Selinsgrove, Pennsylvania. He and my aunt would be out in the fields before sunrise and back after sunset—early pioneers of the organic food movement. I'd tiptoe behind my cousins as they ran through the greenhouses barefoot, my soft "city mouse" feet, as they called them, unable to keep up on the sharp gravel. We made sure to pick the sweetest blackberries and find the crispest green beans for our midday snacks, which we ate sitting in the kale fields.

My mom and I also spent hours at the East End Food Co-op, one of the only places in Pittsburgh where you could buy organic produce in the nineties. Crunchy, granola-type customers would wear tie-dye and overalls. The entire store always smelled of wheatgrass, and the scent of wet, fragrant dirt would grow stronger as we made our way to the glistening produce at the back of the store. I snacked on fruit leather while my mother bagged greens. I watched her pick and choose between collards, swiss chard, and dandelion greens. I laughed as she shook the condensation off the bouquet of curly kale into my face.

So even though I knew it sounded silly, not being able to find kale in Paris really did affect me, so much more than I could have expected. It had nothing to do with not being able to recreate a trendy New York City restaurant's kale salad or make a homemade green elixir. Kale was comfort. Kale was my childhood. Kale was my mom.

In Paris, as an adult and a wife with a kitchen of my own, what and how I cook is very much the same as what and how my mom has always cooked in hers. Like her, I keep my pepper next to the stove, bag my carrots the same way, and flick water off my fingertips in a similar quick motion. But without kale, something was missing. I could not imagine building a healthy kitchen—or home—without it.

·· SHARZIE'S SECRET SAUCE ··

My mom's name is Sharon, but her brothers and my stepfather, John, call her Sharzie, which is why we named her special sauce "Sharzie's Secret Sauce." A Sharzie dinner wouldn't be complete without leafy greens, like kale or collards, and broccoli sautéed in a cast-iron skillet. Rarely does a dinner go by where she hasn't made some variation of this. When she met John, a lot of her healthy cooking was new to him, and while he was open-minded about trying things like seaweed and miso soup, one thing he couldn't get enough of was this dressing, which goes with many different dishes. Like a magic potion, this sauce stayed a mystery for a long time—until now.

INGREDIENTS

- ⅜ CUP OR 6 TABLESPOONS (90 ML) OLIVE OIL
- 3 TABLESPOONS UMEBOSHI* VINEGAR
- 1 TEASPOON DILL

PREPARATION

Combine the olive oil and Umeboshi vinegar in a medium-size jar (you can use an old mustard or mayonnaise jar, 7.3 ounces or 203 g). Sprinkle the dill into the jar, covering the liquid mixture. Shake vigorously. Taste. If desired, add more dill. Serve on salads, grains, or sautéed greens. Dressing will keep for 2 to 3 weeks.

YIELD

- ¾ JAR OF DRESSING—ENOUGH TO DRESS THE BROCCOLI, CORN, AND TOFU RECIPE ON PAGE 12

*Umeboshi vinegar, also called ume vinegar, is made from pickled ume fruits, which are Japanese salt plums. In Japan, they are commonly served with rice as a side dish during breakfast. The ume fruit is believed to be good for digestion. You can easily find this vinegar at Whole Foods Markets and other natural food stores.

SUMMERTIME ROASTED GREEN VEGGIES

Another way to use Sharzie's Secret Sauce is with roasted summer vegetables like green beans, asparagus, broccoli, or even cauliflower.

INGREDIENTS

- Fresh vegetables, such as green beans, asparagus, or broccoli
- Sharzie's Secret Sauce, divided

PREPARATION

Put the vegetables in an 8 x 8-inch (21 x 21-cm) roasting pan. Pour half the sauce over the vegetables, and mix together with your hands. Roast at 350°F (180°C) for 20 to 25 minutes. Pour the remaining sauce over the vegetables, mix, and serve.

YIELD

- 3 to 4 servings

BROCCOLI, CORN, AND TOFU

This dish, which also uses Sharzie's Secret Sauce, is best made when you have access to fresh corn from a farmer's market. When I was growing up in the early nineties, my mom would always bring this to summer picnics. It definitely stuck out next to the green bean casseroles, hot dogs, and sauerkraut, but we always went home with an empty bowl.

INGREDIENTS

- 4 ears corn, shucked

- 2 HEADS BROCCOLI, CHOPPED
- 1 (14-OUNCE/400-G) PACKAGE FIRM TOFU, DRAINED* AND CUT INTO 1-INCH CUBES
- SHARZIE'S SECRET SAUCE (SEE RECIPE ABOVE)

PREPARATION

Bring a large pot of water to boil. Boil the corn for 5 to 8 minutes, remove from the pot, and set aside. When cool, cut the corn off the cob into a large bowl. Lightly steam the broccoli for 2 to 3 minutes, so that it is still a vibrant green and not too soft.* Remove and set aside. When cool, add the broccoli to the bowl. Lightly steam the tofu in the boiling water for 4 minutes. Drain,** and run cold water over the tofu. When cool, add the tofu to the bowl. Add the sauce to the bowl, and mix all the ingredients with a large spoon. Cover, and refrigerate for 2 to 3 hours. Serve slightly chilled or at room temperature.

YIELD

- 4 SERVINGS

* To steam vegetables, I do not use steamers or colanders because that creates one more dish to wash. My preferred method is to fill a medium-size saucepan three-quarters full with water. Cover with lid and place on high heat until the water is boiling. Add the vegetables and cover with lid again, leaving a small opening between the pot and the lid. Steam in the boiling water for 3 to 4 minutes or until al dente. Hold the pot lid over the pot and drain the water into the sink. Place vegetables in a bowl and add desired sauce or seasoning.

** To drain the tofu, place a paper towel on top of a plate, then put the tofu on the paper towel. Place another paper towel and plate on top of the tofu, to add pressure. The paper towels will absorb the water. Allow one hour for tofu to drain.

·· WINTRY SEAWEED ··

During my childhood, if I was sick and staying home from school, I was only allowed to eat a few things: brown rice, kale, and miso soup. But a few bites of this seaweed recipe were mandatory. Another dish from my mother's macrobiotic years, it might not be the most obvious choice for a sick day, but seaweed is filled with vitamins and minerals.

INGREDIENTS

- 1 CUP (15 TO 20 G) OF ARAME SEAWEED
- 1 TEASPOON SESAME OIL
- 1 MEDIUM ONION, SLICED
- 1 MEDIUM CARROT, MATCHSTICK-CUT
- 1 TEASPOON OF TAMARI
- 1 TEASPOON OF GINGER JUICE OR LEMON JUICE

PREPARATION

Soak the arame in lukewarm water for 10 minutes. Heat the oil in a pan, and sauté onions until soft, about 5 to 6 minutes. Add the carrots, and continue to sauté until tender, about 6 to 7 minutes. Drain the soaked arame, and chop. Add the arame to the onions and carrots, add enough water to barely cover, and simmer for 20 to 30 minutes. Watch carefully, and allow the liquid to boil down but not burn. Season with tamari and ginger or lemon juice.

YIELD

- 1 SERVING

Chapter 3

P hilip and I moved to Paris at the end of August 2011. The plane had barely touched ground at Charles de Gaulle when I started asking when we would be able to take our first trip to an outdoor market. As with most cultures, in France, the market began as a common place for people to buy and sell various goods, from produce, meat, and fish to housewares, clothing, and more. It was the original third space for people to congregate, share ideas, and spend time together. The first market in Paris dates back to the fifth century, when the city, then occupied by the Romans and called Lutetia, was located on the Île de la Cité in the middle of the River Seine. Today there are roughly eighty outdoor and covered market destinations in the city, most open from eight thirty in the morning to one thirty in the afternoon. They are still packed with people sharing their love for fresh food and ideas. If there was one thing I was most excited about for our new life in France, *le marché* was it.

On our second day, we needed food, so I grabbed my straw *panier*—my bag for shopping—and dragged Philip out the door. Everyone says the best way to tackle jet lag is by getting outside, right?

Our temporary apartment, where we lived for a month while we looked for more permanent accommodations, was located on the border of the Seventeenth and Eighth arrondissements, and only a five-minute walk from the neighborhood market, Marché Poncelet.

Walking down boulevard de Courcelles toward place des Ternes, the Arc de Triomphe peeked out in the distance. The avenue des Ternes was a busy main road, with noisy traffic and chain stores, and was a stark contrast to the small, pedestrian-only rue Poncelet. As if I'd pulled back a curtain and gone back in time, the modern city rush dissipated behind me as I walked Poncelet's quaint village *tableau.*

The corner broke into two streets, rue Poncelet to my right and rue Bayen to my left, encompassing more than a dozen small shops. The grocer on the corner featured the in-season *cèpes*, large fairy-tale-like porcini mushrooms. Sold by the container, their fat tops and thick trunks (which are sometimes filled with insects) were cut in half to display clean insides. The mushroom halves were lined up next to a matrix of dark purple figs, so tender and ripe their skin was beginning to split near the tops. Bumblebees swarmed over each fig tip, hoping for a tiny taste of the gooey, pink fruit.

Taking in the warming scents and rowdy noises, I noticed a *boucherie* with cow tongues and hooves in the front window case. A rabbit with its brown fur sticking out hung from the ceiling, with a sign clipped to its foot, "Sold." Men behind the counter wore bloodstained white aprons and worked on wooden counters, dented from years of pounding meat. A handwritten chart hung on the wall, outlining where each cut of meat came from and they rung up every purchase on an antique cash register.

Beads of sweat dripped from the *poulet* man's brow as he placed chickens, pink with goose-bump skin, onto rotating roasting spits. They revolved in rows of eight, attached to a large wall of flames, while potatoes, onions, and peppers cooked below, soaking up the juices dripping from the birds.

Young men outfitted in knee-high, rubber rain boots and bright blue jackets and aprons circled the outside tables of the *poissonnerie*, shoveling ice chips onto trays of *crevette rose* (pink shrimp), *oursin* (sea urchin), and *bulot* (whelk) that spiraled like the turret of a castle. As each fish was filleted, the heads collected in buckets on the ground, wet from melted ice.

Vendors hollered playfully to each other and at passersby, shouting reasons to buy *their* bright red strawberries or crisp, green-tipped endive over anyone else's. Being in this market was magical, like I was part of a sacred daily ritual. We were all there with the same goal in mind: to decide what we would take home that day to nourish ourselves and our families. It felt more real than going to a supermarket and thoughtlessly dumping king-size packages into a shopping cart. The purchases at this market were deliberate and intentional.

Old French grandmas, or *bonne-mamans* as they are affectionately called, impeccably dressed with not a strand of hair out of place, toddled past, inspecting each piece of produce.

"*Monsieur*, I would like some mirabelles, please," a *bonne-maman* said, asking for the small, golden plums that are ripe every September. Dressed in a fur coat with an elegant walking stick at her side, she stood her ground at the front of the stand, making sure no one cut in front of her.

"*Bonjour, madame*, of course, but today we are selling them on special," he exclaimed, hoping that his special price was better than the other man's price a few stands away.

"That's wonderful, *monsieur*," she replied, moving her cane a centimeter to the right, maintaining her balance against the rush of shoppers behind her. "But it is just me and my husband. It is not possible to eat all of these in only a few days!"

"Why, of course, *madame*. I will give you a *poignée*, a handful for today, they will be ripe and sweet, and then you will have another handful for later this week, which will ripen over time," he explained, feeling through the mound of yellow-green fruits, searching for the perfect pieces for today and for later. The sweet granny was satisfied.

The *maraîcher* knew best. Initially, not being able to pick out my own produce stressed me out. I didn't know all the words for everything or how to ask for what I wanted—at least not clearly and succinctly. And when you have a line of anxious and impatient French women sighing behind you, it becomes even harder to speak correctly without a frog in your throat. But I learned to let the market men and women choose. After all, it is their *métier*, profession. They know better than I do when a peach will be ripe or which apples have a sweeter bite.

Our first market excursion was exciting. I loved the energy, the options, and the smiling people, laughing and so joyful to share their food with you. For my first cooking effort in Paris, I decided not to be very adventurous, but I did want to prepare something using fresh ingredients: salmon, roasted potatoes, and a kale salad. And that's when it hit me.

"Philip, do you know what I haven't seen yet?" I asked, stopping midstep by the last vegetable stand on the street. "Kale. Not one leaf."

Philip, still dreaming of the gooey Saint-Félicien Tentation double-cream cheese we'd just purchased at the *fromagerie*, turned. "You're right. And I don't know how to say 'kale' in French." He took out his phone and used Google Translate. That was the first time I saw the name *chou frisé*. *Chou* translates to cabbage and *frisé* translates to curly. That is what kale is and what it looks like, so the translation made sense to me.

We approached the last vegetable stand and asked for *chou frisé*.

The man listened, walked into the shop, and came out with a green, crinkly, and round…savoy cabbage.

"No, Philip," I whispered, trying to hide that I was, clearly, the new American on the market block. "That's not it. That's not kale. You know that."

"*Monsieur*, yes that is *chou*, but do you have one that is just the leaves? A darker color and curly?" Philip asked in French.

The man stared at us and tore off the outer leaf of the savoy cabbage. "*Voici*. Here, this is just the leaf. It is curly and *chou*," he replied, deadpan.

Not wanting to frustrate or insult the man, we paid for the cabbage, and I dumped it into my bag, knowing it would not be part of that evening's meal. I moped off to the lettuce man and would make a regular salad instead. While waiting in line for the lettuce, I did a reverse Google Translate. "Savoy cabbage" in French was *chou de Savoie*. Something did not make sense. So what was the real French translation for kale?

My second search for *chou frisé* happened a few days later. With Philip at work, I forced myself out of the apartment to the grocery store. I had seen a small organic shop near the Poncelet market and decided to check it out, hoping they had kale.

The shop, a small, dingy, rectangular space smelling of damp cardboard, was a time warp, taking me back to the co-op days with my mother. The only difference was that there wasn't a back shelf filled with leafy greens. Instead, I was met with crates of wilted chard with thick, chalky stems; celery branches with browned leaves; and soft, wrinkled beets, turnips, and potatoes that were all a few days past their prime. The options, and their freshness, left a lot to be desired.

I didn't see any kale, but I still wanted to ask. Maybe they had some in the back? Approaching the storekeeper, I timidly whispered to him, "*Bonjour, monsieur. Est-ce que vous voulez le chou frisé?*" He stared at me, his blond goatee twitching, with a confused look on his face. He didn't understand me. I asked him again if he had any kale. Or at least, that's what I thought I was asking. In fact, what I actually asked was if he *wanted* any kale. Of course the storekeeper didn't want any *chou frisé*!

Rightfully confused, he walked with me to the back of the depressing store and handed me a dry, yellow...savoy cabbage. Not to be discouraged, this time I was prepared with a photo of kale. With just one quick look, his face lit up. "*Mais oui! C'est la,*" he said, pointing to...broccoli.

It wasn't until my third attempt to find kale that I realized that perhaps the situation was dire. OK, not dire—that's a little dramatic—but by the third attempt, I realized that I might not find any kale in Paris. At *all*.

Since the local outdoor market and organic grocery store only served up savoy cabbage, I decided to dig a little deeper, and I discovered that Paris has three organic markets each week. Seeing this as an opportunity to explore the Left Bank together, Philip and I set out for the Marché Raspail the following Sunday. The market spans two blocks along the wide boulevard Raspail, and we started near the Rennes *métro* station, entering the market's canopy of green-and-white awnings that protected us from the sun. It was bursting with people, everyone waiting in lines at their favorite stands. We passed a loud fishmonger, yelling out to customers while holding an entire fish in his hand and cutting it around the head, preparing it for his customer. Below, chilling on beds of ice, were salmon, sea bass, and scallops still attached to their palm-sized, cream-colored shells. Mackerel shimmered, their long, black-and-gray stripes standing out from the other, plainer fish.

Farm-fresh, cage-free eggs with brown shells were carefully stacked on handfuls of hay, the small, medium, and large eggs each in their own baskets. People waited in line holding their empty egg cartons from the week before, ready to refill them with this week's dozen.

A woman, her hair tied back in a bandanna, piled whole-wheat English muffins into wooden baskets and warmed up thick, creamy hot chocolate, and across the narrow path a man juiced oranges into glass bottles. Bees flew along his feet, landing on the deflated oranges, dipping in and out of the small puddles of sweet liquid. The aroma of potato, onion, and cheese pancakes, fried in front of us, wafted through the air, leaving our stomachs grumbling.

Finding the produce stand with the longest line, we took a red plastic basket and waited. When our turn came, one of the stand's employees followed us along the stand, picking out lettuce, roots, and allium vegetables, and then fruits and different herbs. The stand had a chalkboard at the front of the line, listing everything that they had produced themselves. Everything we needed was at this market: bread, butter, cheese, fish, meat, and vegetables—everything except kale.

Armed this time with both the photo and Philip's fluency, we began approaching different vendors and producers. Like going door-to-door raising money, we went stand to stand, showing the photo and asking the same question: "Do you have any *chou frisé* or do you know where we can find some?" And each time we were met with raised eyebrows, quizzical reactions, and a lot of *nons*, and every person handed us...savoy cabbage.

Kale was nowhere to be found, and no one could lead us in the right direction. Philip, sensing my disappointment, put one arm around me, the other weighed down by the large, green *chou*, and tried to make me feel better. "Don't worry, darling. I'm sure we will find it. After all, it's just a cabbage."

·· *CHOU FRISÉ* CURRY ··

I'll be honest. I gave the chou frisé a try. I really did. I started with the basic technique that I had done with kale my entire life—steaming and adding umeboshi vinegar. But it didn't work. The leaves were too tough, much more so than kale leaves, and they lacked the earthy and fresh taste. Even more of a letdown was that after peeling back the first two layers of the savoy cabbage, its leaves weren't even green anymore; they just looked like the light green or white flesh of regular cabbage. But savoy cabbage was the closest I was going to get to kale, so I had no choice. I had to adapt and finally found a way to make it work. Every cabbage has a calling in life, and the calling for savoy cabbage includes curry and coconut milk.

INGREDIENTS

- 2 TABLESPOONS SESAME OIL
- 3 MEDIUM SPRING ONIONS (3 TO 4 OUNCES/100 G), CHOPPED
- 15 MEDIUM BUTTON OR CREMINI MUSHROOMS, SLICED
- 1 RED PEPPER, SLICED
- 2 TABLESPOONS CURRY POWDER
- 1- TO 2-INCH (2½- TO 5-CM) PIECE GINGER, FINELY CHOPPED
- 1 TEASPOON CUMIN
- 1 TEASPOON GARLIC POWDER
- 1 (13.5-OUNCE/400 ML) CAN COCONUT MILK
- 1 (14.5-OUNCE/400 G) CAN DICED TOMATOES, DRAINED
- ¼ CUP (60 ML) WATER
- 2 TABLESPOONS TAMARI OR SOY SAUCE
- ½ HEAD (1½ POUNDS OR 700 G) SAVOY CABBAGE, WASHED AND FINELY CHOPPED*

PREPARATION

Heat the sesame oil in a wok or large pan over low heat. Add the spring onions, and cook, stirring occasionally, for 3 to 4 minutes, until translucent. Add the mushrooms and red pepper, and cook, continuing to stir, for 4 to 5 minutes, until they start to release juice. Add the curry powder, ginger, cumin, and garlic powder, and stir for another 3 to 4 minutes. Add the coconut milk, tomatoes, water, and tamari. Simmer on low heat for 10 minutes, stirring every minute or so. Add the chopped greens, and stir for about 1 minute, until they are lightly cooked. Serve over brown rice or quinoa.

YIELD

- 4 SERVINGS

* When working with savoy cabbage, only use the outer leaves if they're in good condition (not yellow, brown, or too dry with holes). For this dish, I like to use leaves from all different layers; the changing shades of green and white bring nice variety.

Chapter 4

I should confess something here. I'm not a Francophile. I know, hate me. I'm not a lover of all things French, and *I live in France*.

My dream was always to get out of Pittsburgh and head to New York City. I was fifteen the first time I saw New York, and like many people, I fell in love at first sight. I went with my high school drama group during a frigid January weekend in 2000, and even the temperature couldn't keep me from being enamored with the city's energy. It took only a glimpse as we made our way out of the Lincoln Tunnel for me to know that New York was where I wanted to be. It was the cold air mixed with the scent of roasted street-corner nuts. It was the subway grit and the sound of the train thundering into the station—always moving, going somewhere. It was the diner with the blinking sign where I had a bowl of not very special but for some reason memorable vegetable soup. It was my first meal in the city, and my first meal out in the world without an adult looking over me. It was my first taste of independence. I ate each salty spoonful, sinking deeper into the cracked leather booth, watching condensation drip down the front windows, rosy from flashing lights outside. I could tell that things happened in New York. I only hoped that one day I would be there.

Four years later, as a sophomore in college, I was back in the city for a two-month summer internship at a small public relations firm specializing in luxury jewelry. I was paid one hundred dollars for forty hours per week. It wasn't much, but the fact that I worked on the twelfth floor of the Empire State Building every day more than made up for it. It was an internship like any internship; I faxed papers, made copies, and tagged along to a few meetings. I tried to act older than I was. I was even sent to Bergdorf Goodman to pick up expensive estate jewelry.

I learned who was who at the company—the motherly figure who ran it, her son, who knew people from *The Sopranos*, and her daughter, who scared all of the interns because she would scream if the smallest task wasn't done properly. I watched the pretty, blond Jersey girl who secretly smoked and was planning her wedding. And I appreciated the young, gay man who always complimented my homemade, open-faced sandwiches (which I only made open-faced to conserve bread). They all went silent at the mention of 9/11. They had known someone who was there that day. These people were real adults. They were really *living* New York City. I felt like a temporary visitor, but I desperately wanted to be just like them.

Beyond the office, the entire city waited to seduce me. I lived in a friend's apartment near Union Square, and I found a waitressing job at a nearby Cosi, a sandwich and salad restaurant, for extra cash. I thought it was a good idea to spend seventy-five dollars of my hard-earned money on a fake North Carolina ID, which was immediately confiscated at a Chelsea nightclub two days later. A friend and I went out with guitar players we met at Caffe Vivaldi on Jones Street. I wore H&M "work" clothes and carried high heels in my purse while I walked through Madison Square Park in flip-flops and learned how to time the lights uptown and crosstown. The finance guys on the subway listened to music through white earbuds on their first-generation iPods, while I hid my portable CD player in my bag, listening to the new Air album I'd discovered through my tall, muscular, tattooed yoga teacher. I was stupidly scammed into buying a fake two-for-one spa package from a woman on Park Avenue because she had complimented my hair.

I found myself alone, for the first time, in the evenings—and in the kitchen. I can't say I really cooked anything interesting. It was simple stuff, like poached eggs on toast and, of course, steamed kale. And on Fridays, as a special treat, I ordered delivery from around the corner, just because I could.

It was all a taste of what could be, a taste of the New York life I could one day live. By the end of July, with the internship over, I'd learned two things: PR was not what I wanted to do, but New York City was definitely where I wanted to be.

I spent my entire senior year figuring out how I was going to get back to the city. After studying the history and culture of New York's big agencies, I knew that's where I wanted to work. So when one of them came to Penn State to recruit students, I submitted my résumé, crossed my fingers, and hoped for the best. After months of interviews and waiting by the phone for good news, right when I thought all hope was lost, I received a job offer as an assistant account executive.

Two weeks later, in August 2006, I flew into LaGuardia with a single suitcase and without an apartment or roommate prospects. Crashing on the couch of the same friend I'd stayed with before, near Union Square, I reported to my first day of work the next morning, walking through the halls of the agency's headquarters, an office with nearly two thousand people. This time it was real. I was there for good. I was a part of the city's rhythm, moving, going somewhere. I belonged to New York. Finally, it was my time.

My new office was located in Hell's Kitchen, a neighborhood west of Times Square, so that was where I looked for apartments. It wasn't the prettiest of neighborhoods. The blocks from Fortieth to Sixtieth Streets between Ninth and Eleventh Avenues couldn't shake the midtown hustle, and they certainly didn't have the frills of upscale uptown or the hipness of chic downtown. Old tenement buildings lined the streets, and Ninth Avenue was a permanent traffic jam as commuters waited to go through the Lincoln Tunnel. The Port Authority bus terminal was an eyesore, and then there was the overcrowded playground of Times Square to avoid. Even so, Hell's Kitchen was nowhere near the same neighborhood that gave it its namesake. By 2006, the prostitutes had been pushed farther west, and drugs were out of plain view. I felt safe. And besides, that was the area of the city where I could afford to live on my entry-level advertising salary.

Eventually, the neighborhood grew on me and became home. I was happy with the proximity to the Hudson River and Central Park, and there were endless options for inexpensive restaurants. And I loved my apartment. My roommate, Sarah, and I rented a tiny two-bedroom on West Forty-Eighth Street. I remembered reading once about New Yorkers being able to touch their ovens from their couches, and living in such close quarters was not a joke. I could touch the refrigerator while sitting on the toilet. The windowsills were permanently caked with soot and grime from the street, and most of the apartment didn't get any natural light, the windows blocked by the brick wall of the building next door. There was only a tiny air shaft between the two, filled with cooing pigeons. But I still loved the place. We had exposed brick in every room, the bathroom was done in black-and-white subway tile, and the fire escape worked well as a makeshift porch for late-afternoon people-watching. We had an accessible rooftop overlooking water tower after water tower to the west, before the piers spilled into the Hudson, and to the east, the midtown skyscrapers loomed.

My New York dream became a reality. Over the next few years, I made new friends, ran the New York City Marathon, and spent weekends exploring the different neighborhoods, my feet throbbing after hours of exploring. With only a few hours to recharge, Sarah and I would head into the night to try new restaurants and dance into the early morning hours. Life was good. It was even better than good—life was grand.

%

I loved my job at the agency. I had smart colleagues and inspiring mentors. I didn't mind working hard, and it paid off with a promotion. It was as if working there was meant to be, because without it, I would never have met Philip, and without Philip, I would never have moved to Paris. It was the end of an August day in 2009 when I saw him for the first time, in an open space with large glass windows overlooking the sun setting into the Hudson. I was having a brainstorming meeting with my colleague and friend Caitlin. I noticed his playful gait, Converse shoes, skinny jeans, and the reading glasses perched on top of his head of messy brown hair. I could feel his presence as he walked back and forth to the kitchen area at least three times to get coffee. I hadn't actually met him yet, and it would be days before I would stare into his brown eyes for the first time, but from afar, I felt *something*.

I gazed at the water below, the sky a mélange of rosé wines, and Caitlin caught me daydreaming. "Kristen. What do you think of the description of this archetype?" she asked, waving her hand in front of my face.

My mind could not have been further from analyzing the type of mom and kid to whom we would be selling sugary cereal. Without thinking, I blurted out, "Who is that guy who keeps walking to the kitchen and pouring coffee? In the Converse?"

Caitlin laughed, closing her computer, acknowledging and accepting that she had lost me for the rest of the meeting. "That's Philip," she said. "He actually runs the other team I work with. He's English, single, and, oh, thirty-seven."

My eyes widened as my curiosity grew. "I've never dated anyone older before." My mind immediately jumped to our potential, übermature, first date. Since he wasn't American, he would show up in skinny jeans and a tailored blazer and lead us to a fancy restaurant, where we would sip expensive wine. The dates I was used to with guys my age—the Sunday-football-and-wing fest for the Giants game—were getting old. Maybe thirty-seven and European was worth exploring.

A few days later, Sarah and I invited our friend Hannah, who lived just ten blocks north, over for an impromptu weeknight dinner. Living so close together, we did this often. After my first sighting of Philip, I was anxious to tell Hannah about this mysterious older man. The front door burst open with its trademark squeak, and Hannah stepped inside. I was already prepping our dinner.

Sarah and I liked to make dinner an event, so cooking never would feel like a chore, and we always tried to plan our meals together. I grew into cooking, slowly, dish by dish, meal by meal. I would call my mom with questions, using my memories of her in the kitchen as constant guidance. Sarah would steam artichokes and roast chicken breasts, leaving the skin on to retain flavor. She prepared *pan con tomate*, rubbing the bread with cloves of garlic and crushed tomatoes. One of my contributions was kale. I introduced Sarah and Hannah to it long before it was on every New York menu. I cooked it as my mother did, lightly steamed, sprinkled with a dash of umeboshi vinegar and toasted sesame seeds.

Hannah set her bag by the couch and took off her suit jacket, which she had to wear to her much more formal finance job. "Hannah!" I greeted her. "I'm washing the kale—can you prepare it your special way?"

She smiled, rolling up her sleeves, and replied, "Of course. You know how easy it is though!" Hannah had developed a special touch with steamed kale. She got to work chopping the greens on the tiny counter space between the sink and stovetop. "Where are your dried onions?" she asked, placing the saucepan on the mini-stove to begin boiling water. "And who is this new guy Sarah told me about on Gchat?"

I looked at Sarah, sitting on the tiny two-person couch a few feet away. She smiled and shrugged. Of course Hannah already knew. There were no secrets between us, and if a new development happened during the day, we would all be sure to update each other in between meetings and emails.

"He's not a new guy," I said. "Just someone I noticed at work. Caitlin knows him and wants to introduce us. But I don't know. I've never done an actual setup like that."

"Well, you know what my mom says," Sarah chimed in as I handed her a glass of Trader Joe's "Two-Buck Chuck" red wine, which we bought by the case to save money. "Men are like jeans. You have to try on a few pairs before you get the perfect fit." We laughed, imagining Sarah's mom delivering the line in her peppy Texas twang.

"I know, but I'm not really looking for the perfect fit right now. If I'm meant to meet him, I will," I said.

If anyone understood this, it was Sarah and Hannah. We were all content with where we were in life. We were twenty-five years old, had good jobs, and enjoyed New York City on our terms. We were not looking for boyfriends. Dates were fun, but none of us wanted to rush into anything serious.

Thinking about this, I added, "Who knows? He's thirty-seven. I've never dated someone older, or English."

"Oh, he'll have an accent!" Hannah said, putting the steamed kale into a bowl. We squeezed together around our tiny table, ready to eat.

"Yeah, I guess he will have an accent," I thought aloud. "And apparently he speaks French."

·· ENTRY-LEVEL VEGETABLE SOUP ··

When I first moved to New York, I had to figure out how to stretch my measly salary when buying groceries, which is how the weekly big pot of soup came into being. This simple vegetable soup got me through many dinners and lunches at my desk, and it always reminds me of the steaming bowl of salty vegetable soup that I ate during my first trip to New York. Fresh green beans and corn are ideal for this recipe, but frozen works well too. Pair the soup with a green salad, baguette, or brown rice, and, if you want, add a healthy sprinkle of parmesan.

INGREDIENTS

- 2 TABLESPOONS OLIVE OIL
- 1 MEDIUM ONION, DICED
- 2 CLOVES GARLIC, DICED
- 3 MEDIUM CARROTS, SLICED
- 2 STALKS CELERY, CHOPPED
- 1 CUP (120 G) FRESH OR FROZEN CORN
- 1 CUP (140 G FROZEN OR 110 G FRESH) GREEN BEANS, TRIMMED AND CUT IN THIRDS
- 1 (15-OUNCE/280-G) CAN KIDNEY BEANS, DRAINED AND WASHED
- 1 (14.5-OUNCE/400-G) CAN WHOLE TOMATOES
- 4 CUPS (960 ML) WATER OR VEGETABLE BROTH
- PARSLEY, FOR GARNISH
- SALT AND FRESHLY GROUND BLACK PEPPER, TO TASTE

PREPARATION

Heat the oil in a large pot on medium heat. Sauté the onion and garlic for 5 minutes, until translucent. Season with a dash of salt and pepper. Add the carrots and celery, cook for 5 to 7 minutes, stirring occasionally. Add the green beans and corn, and cook for 3 minutes, continuing to stir occasionally. Add the beans, tomatoes, and another dash of salt and pepper. Reduce heat, and simmer for 20 to 25 minutes. Add the water or vegetable broth, and bring to a boil. Reduce heat, and simmer for 15 to 20 minutes, or longer if a thicker consistency is preferred. Sprinkle in more salt and pepper as needed. Garnish with the parsley. For a hearty lunch the next day, add cooked brown rice to the leftover soup.

YIELD

· 4 SERVINGS

·· HANNAH'S KALE ··

Even though I introduced Hannah to kale, her twist on steamed kale was a welcome change. We spent many a night in her studio apartment on Fifty-Seventh Street, taxi horns honking outside and Imogen Heap playing in the background, trying to solve all the issues of our New York lives over pots of steaming kale. When Hannah moved out of her apartment eight years later, a few weeks before her wedding, I was lucky enough to be in the city with her for one last kale dinner.

INGREDIENTS

- 2 TABLESPOONS DRIED ONIONS
- 1 BUNCH (12 CUPS/400 G) KALE, WASHED AND ROUGHLY CHOPPED (STEMS INTACT)
- SALT AND FRESHLY GROUND BLACK PEPPER, TO TASTE

PREPARATION

Heat a large pot of water over high heat. Add the dried onions, so that they'll become soft as the water boils. Bring the water to a boil. Add the kale, and stir it with a pair of tongs for about 2 minutes, until it turns a bright green. Turn the heat off, and use the tongs to remove the kale, putting it into a serving bowl. Use a slotted spoon to gather any remaining onions from the pot, and place them on top of the kale as a garnish. Season with salt and pepper.

YIELD

- 3 TO 4 SERVINGS

Chapter 5

The summer of 2009 was when Sarah, Hannah, and I drank tequila. With the economy in midrecession, we spent a lot of time on our rooftop with frozen pizzas, big salads drizzled with tangy cilantro-yogurt dressing, and chilled tequila gimlets. I would meet them at the apartment with a bag of limes from the local grocer on Ninth Avenue. That shop was so disorganized that I could tell it hadn't changed in fifty years. The owner, who was at least seventy years old, would sit outside in his rusted lawn chair in the middle of the sidewalk, his belly hanging out of his shirt and his cigarette nearly dropping out of his mouth as he catcalled women walking by. But his limes were the cheapest, and it took a *lot* of limes to make enough juice for an evening of gimlets. We'd spend the next hour squeezing limes to the rhythm of the ceiling fan, barely moving in the thickness of the summer heat, salivating until our cocktails were chilled enough to take our first sips.

Two weeks after I first saw Philip at the office, Caitlin invited me to a party he was throwing for his one-year anniversary of moving to and working in New York. I already had plans—a fifth date with a tall banker I'd met a few weeks earlier. What had started out as having fun with a guy who seemed thoughtful and interested (we walked on the High Line! He made us a picnic of cheese, roasted red peppers, figs, and a baguette from Chelsea Market! He had a bottle of Lambrusco chilling in the fridge!) was quickly devolving into a one-sided game of me waiting for a text message until Thursday or Friday evening, wondering if we were actually going to do anything. The last thing I wanted was to be *that* girl.

Nevertheless, I forced a fifth date, and then I struggled through an awkward dinner in Nolita. I picked at a boring tuna salad as the banker distanced himself, and the conversation slowly died. I had a habit on dates when I didn't have a lot in common with a person to use travel experiences as a way to connect. Swapping stories about "the time I missed the train in Rome" or "the time I booked a bogus hostel in Budapest" was always guaranteed to get me through a first and maybe even a second date. So by the time the banker and I reached this point, the travel conversation had been more than depleted. Dinner was over. He reluctantly paid. I knew I wouldn't see him again.

I stepped outside and, looking around the corner of Mott and Spring Streets for a taxi, I noticed that I had a few missed calls from Caitlin. Maybe the party had ended, and she was calling to meet up. Her voice mail was insistent: "Come dancing! I'm in the West Village!"

It was nearly midnight, but with the holiday weekend, I only had a half day of work the next day, which meant that all I had to do was show up. I hailed a cab to West Eleventh Street and Seventh Avenue South and got out at the corner of what used to be Saint Vincent's Hospital. I didn't know Greenwich Village very well and was hoping to find the bar without getting lost. As I walked down the quaint, tree-lined street, passing town house after town house, I quickly realized that there was no bar on this block. I wasn't meeting Caitlin at a bar; where was I going?

When I reached the address she'd given me, I approached the

front door, walking over slate steps with bamboo stalks rustling to my left, and buzzed up. This was an apartment, a gorgeous, iconic West Village town house. I gulped. This was Philip's apartment. As I waited at the grand, thick, wooden doors, Caitlin appeared, smiling behind the frosted glass etched with floral designs. She let me in, and I gripped the sturdy black banister as we climbed up the red-carpeted steps, past red-and-white *toile de Jouy* wallpaper, to the fourth floor.

The apartment door was open, and I could hear music coming from inside. And there he was, standing in the door frame, smiling. My heart skipped a beat. The same energy I'd felt the first time I saw him at the office hit me again. Was it possible to feel this connected to a person I hadn't even been introduced to? At first, I was surprised to see him, but deep down, I was excited. I smiled back at him while he ushered me into the entryway.

"We're drinking tequila," he said in a pronounced English accent, walking from the living room into the kitchen. Perfect. I'd been drinking tequila all summer. If anything, I could do tequila.

He picked up a dirty tea towel and grabbed ice from the freezer, saying as he did so, "I'm going to crush some ice for your drink."

I stared at the tea towel and then back at him. "OK, great," I said, slightly hesitating, not wanting to think about the ice for my drink mixing with that tea towel.

He read my reaction. "I'm a single guy," he exclaimed, wrapping the ice in the towel. "I live here alone. One towel is all I need!" He began to make dramatic movements, slamming the ice against the counter.

Caitlin, still standing next to me, whispered into my ear, "So how was your date?"

She wasn't quiet enough, and Philip heard her. He quickly turned, stopping midslam, and asked, "You were on a date?"

"Yes. A fifth date," I said, trying to be coy and nonchalant at the same time. I didn't want Philip to think that I was taken, but I also wanted to appear desired.

"What is it with you American women?" Philip asked. "You are always dating—and sleeping with—multiple men at the same time."

I immediately responded, trying to defend myself, and all American women. "Well, I'm not dating anyone else," I lied, as I remembered the awkward date I'd had a few days prior with an unemployed twenty-three-year-old who lived in his parent's Upper West Side apartment and the pharma sales rep who thought wooing me with coconut popsicles and an apartment balcony would entice me to visit him across the river in Hoboken, New Jersey.

"In England, you meet someone at a pub, drink, snog, most likely shag, and then you're stuck in a relationship that goes on for way too long," Philip said, dropping a few pieces of crushed ice into a glass.

"Well, here, going on a date doesn't mean you're actually dating the person," I explained, then added, "or that you're sleeping with them." There. That should set him straight.

"I don't buy it," Philip said matter-of-factly, handing me my tequila drink, "freshly" made with dirty ice.

The night continued. We danced to Cut Copy songs. We drank more tequila. Before I knew it, it was past three o'clock in the morning, and I was the only person left. I sat in an antique armchair and Philip sat on the floor in front of me. Over jasmine tea, as if I were on an introductory interview with a potential boss, Philip asked the questions. We talked about advertising, our families, and especially our mothers. He told me that he was born in Geneva, raised in England, and had a German passport but didn't actually speak German. He wasn't really sure where to call home. He'd always dreamed of living in Manhattan, and now he was finally here. Maybe New York could be his home.

Then something happened. It was as natural as blinking or breathing—laughter. It was true, genuine laughter: me laughing at him and at myself, and us laughing together at absolutely nothing.

As the hour approached five o'clock in the morning, I rose to leave. Foregoing shoes, wearing just navy blue wool socks, Philip walked me down the red-carpet staircase and asked if I wanted to do something over the weekend. A first date was set for that Sunday. It was during the taxi ride uptown, as the sky began to lighten the slits of emptiness between the streets to the east, that I realized we hadn't talked about travel once.

·· WATER TOWER GIMLET ··

Even though tequila was the drink of choice the evening I met Philip, I wouldn't say that his drink was as well done as the gimlets I made all summer long with Sarah and Hannah. Those were special. An experience. Rooftop gimlet-drinking would become the event of the evening. Tequila gimlets are a different take on traditional gimlets—usually made with gin or vodka—but there is nothing fancy about this drink, just like there was nothing fancy about our roof. Except for the view. So grab a drink, take a seat next to some best friends, picture your favorite New York City water tower, and enjoy the evening.

INGREDIENTS

- ½ BUNCH (7½ OUNCES/250 G) KALE, WASHED
- ½ TO 1 INCH (1¼- TO 2½-CM) PIECE FRESH GINGER, PEELED (MORE GINGER MAKES A SPICIER DRINK)
- 1½ SHOTS* (70 ML) LIME JUICE, FRESHLY SQUEEZED
- 1 SHOT (45 ML) TEQUILA
- ½ SHOT (20 ML) TRIPLE SEC
- AGAVE SYRUP, TO TASTE (OPTIONAL, IF YOU WANT A SWEETER DRINK)
- HANDFUL CILANTRO (½ OUNCE/15 G), LEAVES WASHED AND ROUGHLY CHOPPED

PREPARATION

Juice the kale and ginger in a juicer. Measure out 1 shot of the juice. Pour the kale-ginger juice, lime juice, tequila, triple sec, agave syrup, and cilantro into a shaker with 6 ice cubes. Shake vigorously. Pour and enjoy!

YIELD

- 1 DRINK

*This is based on the American shot glass size, where 1 shot is equal to 1½ ounces or 45 ml.

Chapter 6

On my first date with Philip, we went boating in Central Park. We rowed under bridges as the midafternoon settled into a wash of pink evening, the same color as the now-empty bottle of rosé. After hours of conversation, we were the last boat to pull into the boathouse. But the date continued. We drank martinis at the Palace Hotel and had a late dinner of truffle macaroni and cheese at the Waverly Inn. Walking up and down the tree-lined streets of the West Village, we talked for several more hours. The first date led to a second date, which led to a third date, which led to the fourth date— meeting Philip's mother. Philippa (yes, Philip and Philippa) was seventy-eight years old and flying in from England to stay with him for two weeks. I know, who meets the mother of someone who isn't even officially a boyfriend, after only three dates? That was exactly my first thought; I wasn't sure that meeting his mother so early in our courtship made sense.

Philip didn't seem worried about it at all. "You have to understand," he said. "She means everything to me, and I want her to meet you."

What choice did I have? I was falling in love, and if Philip wanted me to meet his mom, then I would. Half forcing an unsure smile on my face, I agreed. We made plans to have tea on Saturday.

"She will most likely bring the fur hat I bought her last year—even though it's not cold enough yet to wear it," Philip said. I gave him a quizzical look. He began to tell me the story.

The previous Christmas, when Philip had only been living in New York for a few months, Philippa flew over for the winter holidays. Philip was eager to buy her a present and told her upon her arrival that he wanted to give her something fabulous. "Oh no, darling," she said to him, waltzing through the airport in her knee-high, three-inch wedge black boots. "Nothing for little old me. Please don't worry about your old mum. It's just wonderful to be here with you."

That was the song Philippa sang until a few days later, when they were walking along Fifth Avenue, admiring the Christmas windows. Philippa stopped in front of Bergdorf Goodman, whose windows tempted passersby with dreams of Gucci, Balenciaga, and Chanel. Hurried shoppers bustled around them. Gusts of cold air blew south from Central Park, whipping Philippa's long, black velvet coat as she mused, "Well, perhaps you can get me something small. Let's just have a little look inside."

Side by side, they wound through the brass revolving door. Eyeing, touching, and cooing over leather gloves, scarves, and dazzling estate jewelry, Philippa walked through the galleries of fine goods, checking herself in each mirror along the way, making sure her hair was still in place. Stopping in front of a display of hats, her eyes lit up. "Darling, perhaps, just *perhaps* we can look at these hats. I could use a new hat for the cold, damp English winter," she offered, turning and smiling sweetly to her son. "Maybe a fur hat. Just a *little* one. Small, to sit just here on the top of my head," she said as she pointed to the peak of her blond bouffant hairdo.

Philip leaned back from the dinner table where we sat, laughing as he remembered the story. He moved toward me, showing a photo on his phone. There was Philippa at the bottom of his apartment staircase, draped in black, ornately ringed, aged fingers clutching a handbag, red painted lips pursed in a coy smile—with a massive black fur hat perched on her head.

I couldn't wait to meet her.

Saturday arrived, and the elevator at Bergdorf Goodman hummed, ticking past each floor until it reached the store's seventh-floor restaurant. Unsure of what to wear to meet someone who seemed as glamorous as Philippa, I had changed my outfit at least five times, finally settling on a simple, fitted black skirt, a gray, sleeveless sweater, and a long strand of fake pearls, tied in a knot. I wanted to look mature and classic and hoped that the pearls would bring the ensemble together.

I stepped out of the elevator and surveyed the room, searching for a giant black fur hat. Blinded by the bright sunlight shining into the wall-to-ceiling windows, my eyes had to adjust to the elegant room. After a moment, I saw Philip and a stunning view behind him of Central Park, an expansive rectangle of greens outlined by city buildings. And there was Philippa, sitting across from him in an oversized Louis XIV armchair. She turned to greet me. She didn't wear her fur hat, but she did have her signature bouffant, not one hair-sprayed tendril out of place. Her brown eyes were serious but kind, outlined in black liner, lashes long with thick mascara. She wore a long skirt and a sweater and kept her woven Balenciaga handbag in her lap.

"Hello, darling!" she said merrily. "I have heard so much about you. Were your ears burning? Philip was just telling me about your mother and that she, like me, is a very strong woman."

"It's a pleasure to meet you. Thank you for inviting me to tea," I said, kissing both her cheeks and sitting next to Philip, immediately placing the white linen napkin on my lap. I didn't want to do anything wrong or impolite during this meal. A good first impression was imperative.

Sipping her cup of Lapsang souchong, a black tea with smoky, musky flavors, Philippa asked, "Philip tells me that you also work in advertising?"

I nodded, nervously fiddling with the strand of pearls.

"So did my ex-husband, Philip's father," she said, turning up her nose at the mention of him. "Did you know, darling," she continued, "that I flew all the way to Las Vegas with him to get married? We did the ceremony at Caesars Palace and then spent a week in the desert, where he photographed me for his next ad campaign." She bit into a tiny white cake, careful not to drop a crumb onto the table. "I will have to show you the photos someday." Philip squeezed my hand under the table. I must have been doing all right.

We talked about her journey, how she liked New York, and she asked questions about my mother. When tea was over and we parted ways outside of the store, Philippa looked at her son and said, "Well done, darling. What a firecracker!" I had Philippa's seal of approval.

❧

Only a few days later, Philip invited me to join them for a long weekend in the Hamptons. Just as I had been about meeting Philippa so soon, I was hesitant about spending four days with just the two of them, but again, Philip was adamant. Cashing in the two personal days I'd been saving for nothing, I left Thursday afternoon and took the Hampton Jitney bus out east to Amagansett, the second-to-last town before the end of the island.

Philip met me at the bus stop. "You're just in time for dinner!"

he said, greeting me with a passionate kiss. "My mother is ready and waiting for us."

When we arrived at the hotel, Philippa was sitting outside, legs crossed, platform sandals on her feet, a cigarette dangling from her long, elegant fingers. She stood up, her billowing, burnt-orange caftan skimming the ground as she strode toward me gracefully, so unlike most women who are in their late seventies.

"Darling!" she exclaimed, putting out the cigarette and kissing my cheek. "You made it! Now, what are you wearing to dinner tonight?" she asked, eagerly awaiting my response.

It turned out to be the weekend in the Hamptons that I'd always dreamed of: crisp, sun-filled air and never-ending blue skies, dinners at Nick & Toni's, and afternoon naps while waves crashed onto the deserted postseason beaches. Philippa and I sat next to each other in beach chairs, the dunes behind us, and watched Philip fly a beach stunt kite, which ended up ruined in the water. Her sunglasses, a vintage pair from the seventies, were three times bigger than mine, the lenses practically covering her entire face. This woman was unique—a handful, as Philip always said—but I thought she was pretty fabulous, and how could I not? She was the mother of the man with whom I was falling in love.

In the evenings, after Philippa had gone to sleep, Philip and I would sit outside under the stars, with the ocean buzzing in the distance. We listened to the playlist (which he charmingly referred to as a mixtape) that he made for me after our second date. I rested my feet on his legs as one of my favorite songs, by Friendly Fires, played in the background.

One day we're gonna live in Paris
I promise, I'm on it

When I'm bringing in the money
I promise, I'm on it
I'm gonna take you out to the club showcase
We're gonna live it up
I promise
Just hold on a little more...

So go and pack your bags
For the long haul
We're gonna lose ourselves
I promise
This time it's you and me forevermore

When the song ended, Philip placed his hands on my legs, looked into my eyes, and asked me a question that stayed with me during the journey home and for many weeks and months after: "Would you ever live in Paris?"

Chapter 7

The next few months were a whirlwind of dinners out and soul-searching conversations with Philip that stretched late into the evenings and early mornings. We spent the Thanksgiving holiday in Pittsburgh and celebrated Christmas together next to a very overpriced, and very small, tree in his West Eleventh Street apartment. We rang in the New Year dancing in Venice's *acqua alta*, high water, in Piazza San Marco. It felt like I was living in a dream. Back in New York, Philip and I were both working hard and late into the nights—he was working on a pitch to win a major new client, and I had started a new job at an agency downtown. It was time to prove myself again. We had little time during the week to really connect and were both looking forward to the Friday night dinner we had planned.

Leaving my Tribeca office, I walked north on Seventh Avenue South, passing by tiny streets beginning to stir with evening activities. Small businesses were closing down and, even with the sprinkle of snow that was starting to fall, bars were filling up with people out for Friday night after-work happy hour. Carmine, Leroy, Morton, Bleecker, Barrow, Grove, then Christopher—the snowfall grew heavier as I passed each cross street. Finally, I reached West Tenth Street and turned off, leaving the hustle of the avenue. The blanket of snow that covered the road, sidewalks, and stoops had yet to be disturbed, and a pristine forest of white trees stretched to the dark sky overhead. Lights twinkled through parlor windows, illuminating extravagant living rooms inside and the falling flakes outside. If I could have bottled that moment, I would have. Everything was perfect. I was in the best city, in a great new job, and in a loving relationship.

Arriving at the restaurant, I spotted Philip in the back by the bar with two glasses of champagne. We were never a couple that needed a reason to drink champagne, any date night being a good excuse for bubbly, but I had a feeling that these two glasses had a purpose. Good news, I hoped. It must be the big pitch he'd been working on. Did his agency win? It was for a large piece of business and a top global brand, so winning would be a huge accomplishment for both Philip and the agency. With a kiss and a strong hug, he handed me my glass and we toasted.

"Well, we won!" he exclaimed. "What a day. I have to leave for Paris on Sunday night."

Paris? What was he talking about?

Sensing my confusion, he continued, "Yes. We've both been so busy the past two weeks, I didn't get a chance to tell you that winning this means I have to spend two months in Paris for an extended brainstorming session with the client."

Two months in Paris? I was speechless, nearly dropping my still-full glass of celebratory champagne. Quickly downing it, hoping to numb the sudden shock, I tried to remain calm. What would eight weeks do to us? I felt confident in our relationship, but it was still a *new* relationship. Would the time apart stunt it or, even worse, end it?

"Darling, don't worry," Philip said, wrapping his arm around me and squeezing my shoulder. "It will fly by, and you are going to be so busy with your new job you'll hardly notice. Plus, I have a surprise—I already confirmed that you can come over for a few days if you can get away from the office. Imagine! We can walk around Paris together. Drink wine, eat cheese, go for morning runs around the Champ-de-Mars."

That did sound amazing. Who better to gallivant around the most romantic city in the world with than my boyfriend? How could I be upset? I was so proud of Philip. His ambition and success were some of the things I found so attractive about him. I wasn't going to let my needless insecurity get in the way of celebrating. We spent the weekend packing and making plans for my visit, and on Sunday night, we said good-bye.

I put all of my energy into my new job, working endlessly, and a month later, as promised, I flew to Paris. Without a word of French in my vocabulary—except *bonjour*—I handed the taxi driver the name and address of the Hôtel de la Trémoille, which was tucked between the Champs-Élysées and the Seine. I saw Philip sitting in the hotel lobby waiting for me, and the minute our eyes met, I knew we hadn't skipped a beat.

※

This was only my second time in Paris, and I didn't know the city at all. My first trip was five years earlier in 2005, after I'd completed my semester abroad in Barcelona. I had fallen in love with the coastal city of Spain, met amazing people, and traveled throughout Europe. Spain's sunshine, colors, and festive party atmosphere enchanted me. So when I met up with my mom and cousin, Anaïs, at our hotel on the Left Bank, the cool weather and the gray skies and buildings jarred me. Paris could not have been more different than Barcelona. My only memories of the trip were eating a *tarte aux framboises*, raspberry tart, walking around until my feet ached, straining my neck to see the *Mona Lisa*, and eating escargot at dinner. I didn't remember taking the *métro* or even what I saw. How could such an important destination have left such little impression on me?

Our first day began with lunch at Brasserie Lipp and afternoon *café crèmes* at Café de Flore, two iconic cafés in the Saint-Germain-des-Prés neighborhood. Regal waiters bustled about dressed in black and white and carrying silver trays high above their heads, never dropping a thing.

The weather was typical for late winter in Paris. Not warm but not too cold, with gray skies and sparse moments of sunlight splashing in between clouds. We spent the afternoon wandering around the hilly, uneven streets of Montmartre, taking in the view from Sacré-Cœur, and I listened in awe as Philip spoke French with ease. There was no better place to be than walking arm in arm with him along the tiny streets of the Marais or nestling together on the heated terraces underneath the arches of the place des Vosges, sipping red wine and snacking on olives. We strolled through the Jardin du Luxembourg, exploring the Left Bank and, as you do in Paris, walking some more. It was exactly how Paris is supposed to be experienced—with your lover.

As a surprise for my last night, Philip booked a special restaurant. I wasn't sure where we were going as the taxi went farther and farther west, away from the city lights, deep into the Bois de Boulogne, until we reached the restaurant, La Grande Cascade, a circular building that emanated a golden glow. The building was originally one of Napoleon III's hunting lodges but had been redone as if trying to rival Versailles. Considering I had yet to visit Versailles, I had never seen anything so ornate. Light from crystal chandeliers reflected off of mirrored walls, catching the gold-leaf paint that accented the crown molding. It was a warm space with burgundy hues and small, circular tables perfect for a romantic dinner for two. It was also very over the top.

Neither of us had ever been so well attended to. The waiters, as if playing baseball, signaled to each other when we needed more wine, needed to order, needed anything. One furrow of a brow from Philip and someone would rush over to the table, asking what he could do to serve us. It was a well-rehearsed dance as they gracefully moved from table to kitchen and back, serving dishes like *macaroni farcis*—pasta stuffed with celery root, foie gras, and black truffles—or rack of lamb with a side of creamy pureed potatoes.

We dined, drank, and topped off the evening with a cheese plate, which we selected ourselves from a rolling trolley that had three tiers of cheese to choose from, including a creamy chèvre, a soft Camembert, and a hard Comté with a spicy finish. I had no idea that enough varieties of cheese existed to warrant their own mode of transportation on wheels.

Returning to the hotel late in the evening, laughing deep in our bellies as we mimicked the waiters and their baseball signals, we were full, and somewhat inebriated, and fell asleep dreaming of French cheese. I woke up early the next morning, in a haze, for my flight back to New York. Exhausted and sad to be leaving Philip, I slept the entire flight home, only jolting awake when the plane landed at JFK. Already, Paris seemed like a beautiful, distant memory.

❧

I took Spanish in high school and, even after visiting Paris, still didn't know more than a word or two of French. That didn't keep Philip from trying to teach me. When we went grocery shopping, which was one of the first "domestic" activities we did together, Philip would quiz me on colors as we walked through the produce section. He'd point to different vegetables and call out *rouge* (red), *violet* (purple), *vert* (green), and *jaune* (yellow)—which I always confused with *jeune*, so that I'd call a pepper young instead of yellow. He even made me a small notebook titled "French Word of the Day, Volume I," with phrases like *histoire d'amour* (love story), *pour toujours* (forever), *je t'adore* (I adore you), *trop, trop, trop heu-reux* (too, too, too happy), and *un jour on sera à Paris* (one day we will be in Paris). None of these actually prepared me for daily life in France—I never have told anyone at the prefecture about a love story—but the playful game of learning these phrases was romantic.

Almost a year after the day of our first date, Philip and I went on vacation together in Jackson Hole, Wyoming. It wasn't an obvious choice of destination for a less-than-outdoorsy Englishman and his high-heel-wearing girlfriend, but we wanted to get out of the city and into the fresh air. Halfway through the week, Philip brought out a sparkling gold ring with diamonds resembling a *petite fleurette*, tiny flower, and proposed.

"I want you to be my wife," he said, tears forming in his eyes.

"What? Now?! OK!" I agreed, laughing and hugging him.

He had secretly been carrying the ring around with him on all of our hikes. Not sure whether to propose on a mountain, by a waterfall, or while running from a bear, he ended up asking me after midnight in his pajamas. It was late in America, but it was morning in England, so we called Philippa to tell her the good news.

"Well done, darlings!" she said to us both over speakerphone. "Kristen, I told Philip to marry you after the first moment I met you!" she said. "*Félicitations*, congratulations! I always wanted a daughter!"

✻

We set a wedding date for April of the following year. I planned the wedding with my mother and shared details, updates, and secret photos of my dress with Philippa in handwritten letters. Along the way, in between my moving into the apartment on West Eleventh Street and all the wedding planning, Philip found himself going away more fre-quently on work trips, sometimes spending weeks at a time in Europe.

Our lives in New York became more and more individual. While he spent his evenings entertaining clients and sleeping in hotels, I spent my weeknights eating take-out sushi, watching reality TV shows on Bravo, and sleeping alone. Although I enjoyed spending more time with my girlfriends, and Philip had to do what work required, we disliked being apart. We wanted to be together and, over time, we began to realize that being together might mean moving to Paris.

The move was set for August 2011, a few months after our wedding. I planned to quit my job, and Philip assured me that I would have no problem finding advertising work in Paris, as there were plenty of agencies that needed native English speakers.

I struggled with the decision. I wasn't ready to leave New York, my friends, and the life I was very happy with. One night, my emotions overcame me. I shut myself in the back room of our apartment and cried hard, tears running down my face. How could I live in France? I didn't speak French! I would have no one there. No friends, no family. If we stayed for five years, I might become pregnant there. How could I have a baby with no support and no language? What it came to was that I was scared. Scared of the unknown.

As my sobbing slowed down, I realized how silly I was being, how selfish and immature. Maybe it was time for something different, a new challenge. I couldn't hold on to the present. Yes, things in my life were fantastic, but those things could also change. People and situations evolve. I didn't know it at the time, but everyone else would move on as well; I just happened to be the first one to do it. I had to accept that the summer of rooftop gimlets and all that it meant to me couldn't last forever.

I had never imagined leaving New York. Not in a million years. But this *was* Paris, and it was Paris as a newlywed—for many, a dream come true. So I decided to make it my dream too.

Chapter 8

A year before our wedding, Philippa sold her house in England, packed up all of her belongings, and moved to Barcelona. It might have seemed extravagant for someone her age to make such a big life change, but for a woman with her spirit and independence, it was entirely normal. She rented a small apartment, went antiquing on the weekends, joined a gym, and swam every day beneath the Spanish sunshine. Already fluent in French, she thought nothing of enrolling in Spanish classes at a local university, where she was the oldest student by at least forty years. She attended diligently, although she was a bit baffled by the teaching method.

"Philip," she said one day over the phone, "they made me catch a ball to introduce myself. I don't know why I couldn't just sit there and speak, but they kept throwing it at my head!" When not swimming or learning Spanish, she walked mile after mile of the city, taking photos and notes by hand for the book she wanted to write, *Philippa's Guide to Barcelona*.

"You know, darlings," she wrote to us, "I feel like a new woman here. It is my year of living dangerously!"

When I close my eyes and picture Philippa, I see her dancing at our wedding. She is spinning and twirling with Philip on her arm, a smile on her face, her head back as she shimmies to the music, proud to be the mother of the groom. Decked out in vintage black velvet and lace with her trademark platform shoes, she made the dance floor hers for the evening. Everyone commented on how great she looked and how well she danced.

So imagine our surprise when in July, three months after the wedding, on a business trip to Barcelona, Philip discovered his mother was thirty pounds lighter, had given up fifty years of smoking cold turkey, and didn't have an appetite. We knew something was wrong and urged her to go to the doctor. Back in New York, Philip sat on the couch talking with her over the phone, listening as she tried to explain the results. The minute he told me that her white blood cell count was low, a sinking feeling hit my stomach. He could see it in my face. This was bad news. Philip took the next flight out to be with her, and the following day, the doctors confirmed what we dreaded the most. Diagnosed with acute myeloid leukemia, Philippa had two months left to live.

In a mad dash during what we'd thought would be our last few weeks enjoying New York together, Philip stayed with his mother, interpreting blood work in Spanish and trying to find a hospital in Paris where we could move her, to be close to us when we arrived. I felt helpless, left behind in the city to oversee the move and unable to be there for Philip, for the unexpected, upsetting moments when the realization of his mother's impending death would hit. How could I be the wife I wanted to be from so far away?

A week later, after my last day of work, I flew to Spain and went straight to the hospital where Philippa was receiving a blood transfusion. It had only been three months since I'd last seen her, and I tried to hide my shock at how much she had changed.

She slept for hours at a time, sweating through her bedclothes and the white hotel spa robe she insisted on wearing. She could barely eat; food had no taste for her anymore, and even strawberry milkshakes and chicken broth were too much for her to stomach. While Philip made endless phone calls, trying to figure out what to do next, I would read to her or she would show me photographs of her younger years, riding horses, winning competition after competition.

She would fall asleep by early evening, the Spanish heat knocking her out, and Philip and I would eat dinner at a restaurant near her apartment in Plaça Molina, close to the mountainside of the city, in the Sarrià-Sant Gervasi district. We shared plates of fried calamari, dark red tomato slices topped with red onion and salty anchovies, and *pimientos de Padrón*, our favorite small green peppers, grilled and served with flaky sea salt—but we hardly enjoyed them. All our focus was on Philippa. We set aside the excitement of our next step in Paris as we discussed how to move Philippa there before she became more ill.

As soon as possible, the three of us took an overnight train from Barcelona into the Gare d'Austerlitz train station in Paris. Even though Philippa needed a wheelchair to travel, she didn't let her appearance go by the wayside. She wore a flowing dress ("Just a little something I bought for myself at Mango, darling!"), applied a full face of makeup, including sultry, dark eyeliner, and put her best platform-shoed foot forward for the journey.

We didn't pack much for her, only a small suitcase with the essentials—which to Philippa meant her fancy dresses and a gold satin evening bag. "For my first dinner out in Paris with you two," she explained. Philip and I didn't have the heart to tell her that she might not have another dinner out.

We arrived in Paris early the next morning. Philippa had slept soundly through the night, her white robe once again soaked in sweat by the time we woke her to help her get ready to disembark the train. Rain was pouring down and the humidity fogged up the windows of the taxi that took us to the hospital. We were dropped off at the emergency room entrance, Philippa leaning on both of us as we helped her to a wheelchair. Breathing heavily, her mouth dry, she had dark circles under her eyes where her eyeliner had smudged, and strands of hair that had been sprayed perfectly into place stuck to her neck and face, damp from perspiration. The waiting room was small and dimly lit. It was full of people young and old, and we waited as overworked nurses in mint-green uniforms called name after name, Philippa's slowly moving closer to the top of the list. A persistent homeless man, smelling of sweat and warm beer, kept walking in, yelling at the registration clerk at the front desk, and stumbling back out. Babies cried. Old people slept, their heads falling to their sides, jerking as they startled themselves awake.

"*Monsieur*," the clerk said to Philip, "we are not a cancer hospital for senior citizens. We have received nothing from your doctor in Spain. I am not sure why you are actually here." This would be the first of many trying episodes with the French system and bureaucracy; we were getting good practice dealing with it from the start.

Philip, desperate, begged the woman to admit Philippa. "She is ill, she has cancer, and we just arrived this morning from Spain. I don't know what else to do with her. She is dehydrated, has a fever, and needs medical attention. Please, let us keep her here until I do find the correct hospital," he said, his voice strained and tired, nearly giving up.

Philippa waited patiently, doing her best to stay composed and not fall asleep, which is all her body wanted to do. Finally, the hospital agreed, and she was taken back to see a doctor. All we could do was wait.

That evening, Philip and I ate dinner at Les Deux Magots. One of the most famous brasseries in Paris, it was made popular by the writers and artists of the Lost Generation. Hemingway, Picasso, and friends ate, socialized, and drank there. As a student, Philip went there for a blind date that a friend set up, which turned out to be a prank; he waited at a tiny terrace table for hours for a woman who would never show up. For me, Les Deux Magots would always be the place where Philip and I ate our first dinner of our new life in Paris—while Philippa slept in a nearby hospital bed, her prognosis terminal.

Silver ashtrays dotted each table, holding down menus, while waiters dressed in sharp, black uniforms, with aprons long like skirts, walked briskly in and out of the restaurant. They carried out their jobs with ease, maneuvering miniature cups of espresso and shot-sized glasses holding *l'addition*, the check. They opened bottles of wine with one hand and dipped down to deliver plates of food, barely blinking an eye. They shooed away the pigeons that crowded around the corners of tables with their trays as they passed.

The air hung heavy as we huddled together underneath the restaurant's awning. The rain pounded down, splattering onto the uneven pavement. The cobblestones were slick with puddles of water situated between every seam. The bright lights from lampposts and passing taxis reflected along each stone. We sat in silence. Everything about the upcoming move had been carefully planned and seemed predictable. Now, I had no idea what to expect.

The next morning, I flew back to New York, and Philip stayed behind with plans to join me for our last week. It was still raining when I left. I only hoped the sun would be out when I returned. I didn't want rain to be the indicator of our future.

A few days later, Philip found a place for Philippa in Hôpital Charles-Foix, which specialized in cancer treatment for senior citizens. Built in the mid-1800s on land where a seventeenth-century castle once stood, the hospital was inaugurated in 1873 by Empress Eugénie, wife of Napoleon III, with a chestnut tree that still flourishes on the grounds. Resembling a château more than a hospital, it had manicured courtyards, rows of trimmed trees, and arched windows and passageways. Philippa could read during the day and open the windows to let in fresh air and the sound of birds singing. We did not expect her to leave this hospital. The doctors were attempting a medium-level treatment, but we knew not to get our hopes up. It was sinking in for both of us that Philippa was going to die.

Our move came and went. Our departure from New York was without fanfare; the city had shut down because of Hurricane Irene. Our arrival in Paris did not start off with the happiness I expected. We spent most of our first week at the hospital with Philippa. When I wasn't there, I was out trying to navigate the city but inevitably felt like a tourist—and behaved like one too. As the first few days passed, I realized that the uncomfortable sensation of feeling like an outsider was not going to go away. My mother-in-law was dying, we were not going back to New York, and I was a stranger in my new home.

Chapter 9

The agency set us up with a temporary apartment for our first month in Paris, but we needed to find somewhere permanent to live. We told ourselves that we wanted to live in a traditional Parisian apartment, although I wasn't sure what that even meant. I'd never actually been in a Parisian apartment. I had visions of big, wide, open windows with the summer breeze floating in off the Seine. In my mind, the Parisian sky would always be a palette of oranges and pinks streaked with wispy clouds as the late-afternoon sun set into the skyline with, of course, the Eiffel Tower in the distance. Françoise Hardy would play on our record player (we don't even own a record player) while I'd wait, with an aperitif of French 75 cocktails in antique champagne glasses and a tray of *saucisson*, fresh cheese, and olives, for Philip to return home from work. I'm pretty sure I had the perfect little, black dress and a pair of ballet flats on, to top it all off.

In mid-July, as we prepped for the move, Philip gave me the task of working with the relocation agent, Colette, to find "the perfect flat." I emailed her a wish list that was admittedly optimistic, but I didn't think we were asking for *too* much: Haussmannian building, balcony, working fireplace, crown molding, two bedrooms (since we intended to eventually have children), and a kitchen that would actually function as a kitchen, not some sliver off to the side in which it was impossible even to turn around. In my email, I asked for something "very Parisian," two words I later wished I had never uttered. Seconds later, I received an automated response that she was out of the office for her *congé annuel*—France's sacred summer vacation—for the next six weeks. Of course she was.

As for what *quartier* we wanted to live in, we had no idea which neighborhoods would be a good fit. I didn't know Paris from Kansas City, and even though Philip had studied there when he was twenty, he'd lived in concrete, university-owned student housing, nowhere near central Paris. Together, we were clueless. Luckily, we had Emmanuel and Léonie to help us.

Emmanuel is Philip's half brother on his father's side, and he'd been living in Paris for a year. He and Léonie are ten years apart in age and didn't grow up together, but they are quite close. Emmanuel's girlfriend, Léonie, had been in Paris for six years and had lived in a few different neighborhoods. We met up with them at the Marché aux Puces de Saint-Ouen, Paris's famous antique market, for lunch, to talk about arrondissements, and to hunt for a dining room table.

Since both of them work in fashion, they arrived at the market looking like they were ready for Paris Fashion Week. They never overdress but always look just chic enough to turn heads (and make me feel like my outfit is two years too old). Emmanuel, tall and thin with light brown hair, and Léonie, with long, straight, blond hair, both wore skinny gray jeans, black ankle boots, and leather jackets. Emmanuel had a scarf around his neck, not too tightly wrapped, the ends sticking out in an artfully messy way. Léonie wore gold rings and a perfectly situated fedora. Their best accessory was Happy, their long-haired sausage dog, pattering along with his reddish-brown dachshund fur shining in the sun.

"I think you should live somewhere that does not attract a lot of tourists," Léonie told us as we walked along the market, admiring the antique stalls. We passed Louis XIV chairs covered in worn, dark green velvet and tall, frosted mirrors encased in thick, carved, gold-painted wood. Some stalls had plaster statue heads, old photo frames, and delicate glassware.

Léonie continued, "I lived in Saint-Germain-des-Prés, and I speak French, but I still found the shopkeepers to be unfriendly." Léonie was raised in Geneva, but her mother is English, so she speaks both languages perfectly. "They are so used to tourists coming in and only speaking English. You want to live somewhere where you will be forced to practice French and where they will eventually recognize you as a local."

She had a point. I didn't want to be considered just another tourist. And though my vision was to be able to see the Eiffel Tower and be right next to the water, perhaps that was not the most realistic expectation.

"Darling!" Philip called me over. He was standing next to a long table made from distressed wood with industrial metal legs. "This is perfect," he said. Philip has excellent taste, something I had noticed the first time I saw his West Village apartment. If he liked this table, then I knew it would work. It would comfortably fit eight, but I wondered if we'd ever know enough people in Paris to actually fill it.

"What are you doing this week, Kristen?" Léonie asked me, picking Happy up off the ground. "Let's meet for *apéro*," she said, which is France's version of happy hour, "and talk more about the different neighborhoods." Thank goodness I already had someone looking out for me.

✽

Philip and I had arranged to meet with Colette, the relocation agent, later in the week. The day before our scheduled apartment search, she finally replied to my wish-list email.

Bonjour Kristen,

So it seems that you and your husband want an apartment *très Parisien*! We have ten places to visit tomorrow, and you must decide by the end of the day. It will not be possible to look a second day.

We had to decide in one day? That seemed a little aggressive. Already the *ce n'est pas possible*—"it is not possible"—French attitude was coming out.

Now, most Paris apartments do not have balconies. Or fireplaces. And as you may or may not know, most will have only an empty room for a kitchen that you must outfit yourself. Also, it is *très Parisien* to have just a view of your inner courtyard.

I would really miss not having a fireplace, and that became especially true once I'd experienced the damp, misty winter days that Paris is famous for, but I knew that even in New York, the fireplace we'd had was rare. And the kitchen? I'd read about the "Bring Your Own Kitchen" issue, where renters have to buy everything from the stove to the cabinets and sometimes even tiles for the floor. Most apartments only have a hookup for electric and water.

I highly recommend you look in the Sixteenth and Seventeenth arrondissements. They are very family-oriented and close to parks. *Très Parisien*!

Léonie had mentioned those neighborhoods; she wasn't as keen on the Sixteenth as she was on the Seventeenth. Both appeared to be far away from the center of the city. Philip kept talking about some cheesy early nineties song that mentioned Neuilly, a posh neighborhood just outside the Sixteenth, but that seemed even farther outside the city. On the other hand, those areas would be less touristy. It was all going to depend on the apartments.

Early the next morning, while Paris was still waking up, we met Colette. Barely able to see each other in the darkness, we did *la bise*— the customary French double kiss—piled into her Renault Twingo, and started off down the regal boulevard de Courcelles, past the somber Parc Monceau and the mist rising above its stoic iron gates.

I was excited. This would be the first apartment that Philip and I would live in that we'd chosen together. And it would be our home for the next five years, so I knew it was important that we find a place we both loved and felt comfortable with. But were we going to be able to find that place in only one day? Colette had mentioned that if we didn't find something with her, then we would be on our own, and I had no idea how we would navigate the apartment search here. I assumed that it would be as complicated as New York, where people line up for open houses with paperwork in hand, ready to sign on the dotted line.

Colette's Twingo whizzed by gray building after identical gray building, each beginning to show signs of life—lights flipping on, children getting ready for school, and families sitting down together for their *petit-déjeuner* of crusty bread, butter, jam, and big bowls of *café au lait.*

Everything about the buildings was so uniform, orderly, and beautiful. When Napoleon III razed the crooked medieval streets of Paris in 1853 and began building the Paris everyone knows today, his plans included the matching buildings that line the grand boulevards. Napoleon's prefect, Georges-Eugène Haussmann, developed a plan with specific, intentional implications for both city planning and society. To keep people inside the city, instead of fleeing the crime and disease that had plagued Paris, Haussmann's buildings would include both commercial and residential spaces, so that everything Parisians needed would be in one place. The bottom floor would be a storefront with a small apartment behind it, where the storekeeper would live. Above would be apartments and the top floor would house the *chambres de bonne*, individual rooms for maids and other help. Like living in a dormitory, these tiny single rooms would share a bathroom and cooking space. Nowadays, many of these rooms are rented out by students or converted into studio apartments for young professionals. Other than the tight space—from what I'd heard, I had a feeling that just like in my first New York City apartment, you could touch your refrigerator from your toilet in a *chambre de bonne*—these rooms, with slanted windows, afforded some of the best views of Paris.

As we pulled up to our first location, Colette began to explain in her thick French accent, "The thing to remember is that in Parisian apartments, the kitchen is normally all the way in the back." She stepped out of the small car. A shorter woman with wild, shoulder-length black hair, she rearranged her orange-and-gray patched coat, which stopped midcalf and could quite possibly have been made from sofa fabric. "When these apartments were built, the kitchens were placed near the service elevators to keep workers out of sight while the hosts were entertaining guests."

Philip and I took the elevator up to the fourth floor—hoping that a higher floor meant light and views—as Colette ran up the steps, sofa coat flowing behind her, to meet us. "I never take the elevator. This is how I stay fit!" she said when she arrived, huffing and puffing, ringing the bell at the front door. "*Alors*, are you ready?" she asked.

The door opened into a moderately sized entryway with the

salon (living room) and *salle à manger* (dining room) on either side, facing each other and easily creating one large room. This is a traditional setup in old Paris apartments, as these rooms were mostly used for entertaining.

After visiting two or three more apartments, I quickly realized that the front two rooms are a facade. They may look absolutely wonderful and pristine, but the minute you cross the threshold into the rest of the apartment, all bets are off. Once you enter the long hallway to the bedrooms, bathroom, and kitchen, brace yourself—it's a major time warp back to the 1960s era of President de Gaulle.

"It is *très Parisien* to have red carpet covering the walls," Colette purred to us, raising her eyebrows, aiming to convince us that the 360-degree cherry-cola-colored fur was normal and not an eyesore.

"And here in the second bedroom is the hookup for the washing machine," she said, motioning with her arms, Vanna White style, toward an empty space with plumbing. "Or it could work for a dishwasher," she added, smiling at the convenience of having a loud machine used for cleaning dirty dishes in the room where our potential future child would nap.

One apartment seduced Philip with its art-deco stained glass in the living room. I was less seduced by the bathtub that sat openly displayed in a corner of the dining room. No sink. No toilet. Just a bathtub, because apparently there's nothing like enjoying a bubble bath and your Sunday roast at the same time.

After bathtubs in dining rooms, red-carpeted walls, and the realization that none of these apartments were going to have any closets, let alone a view of the Eiffel Tower, I didn't think it could get any weirder. But it did. Off we went in the Twingo, bumping down the streets, heading closer to the river, toward the Marais. Located in the Third and Fourth arrondissements, this *quartier* has historically been one of Paris's Jewish neighborhoods, with scrumptious falafel shops nestled next to high-end fashion stores. Over the years, it has evolved into a shopping and foodie haven popular with both Parisians and tourists. On weekends it's nearly impossible to walk through the thick crowds on the sidewalks.

Mere minutes after stepping out of the car, I could feel the city vibrate—people rushing, brisk and purposeful, all going somewhere. It was a huge difference from the quiet calmness of the Seventeenth. Immediately, my energy increased. While the Marais was buzzing around us, the apartment was on a quiet side street, making this location the best of both worlds.

"I think you will like this apartment," Colette told us. "It has a fully equipped kitchen as well!" After taking the elevator to the top floor, we were greeted by a sunny foyer. The space, shaped like a square, had antique charm, with parquet floors and stained glass doors that opened to balconies on both sides, off of both the living room and the bedrooms.

And the view! Finally, I could see the Eiffel Tower. *This* was my vision. From the balconies, we could see rooftop after rooftop, sunlight beaming down from the patched gray sky in between chimneys and in the distance, illuminating the colorful cylinders of the Centre Pompidou. I could already imagine our mornings, sipping coffee, enjoying flaky, buttery croissants as Paris stirred below. Our excitement was building. This place could be the one—we could feel it. Colette could feel it. Until I went into the kitchen. Or tried to. I wasn't sure if I was actually in the kitchen.

I stood, confused, in a narrow galley space. Philip, sensing my silent hesitation, joined me. I opened a single refrigerated drawer that wasn't even big enough to hold the savoy cabbage we'd purchased a few days before. Philip, just as confused, said to Colette in French,

"There is not a refrigerator here, not even a small one. Well, there is, but it's just a drawer."

"Ah *oui*," Colette replied as we watched her mind calculate how to sell the refrigerator drawer. "*Oui*, it's a small *cuisine* but full of Parisian charm. It is *très Parisien* to just shop for food on a daily basis. So you really wouldn't need a larger refrigerated space." We didn't respond. Colette, trying to revive our excitement about the apartment, continued, "Or you could buy a refrigerator." Her pitch increased as she shared her brilliant idea. "And put it in the foyer! It would be like a work of art!"

A refrigerator in the foyer? She had to be joking. This *très Parisien* kitchen wouldn't do. Perhaps I was being too American about the whole thing, but I spend so much time in the kitchen and I wanted to love the space where I would be cooking. I wasn't expecting a typical American-style kitchen overlooking a living room, but it had to have more than one burner and a refrigerator bigger than a nightstand drawer. I was starting to feel nervous. We only had one more apartment left to see. If that one didn't work out, our next best option would be the place with the dining room bathtub.

Piling into the Twingo again, we trekked back to the Seventeenth, and my dreams of living near the river evaporated into the misty early evening. The Eiffel Tower disappeared. If this day had taught me anything, it was that I would not always have a view of the Eiffel Tower. I could feel the grit of the city waning as we drove across the Seine and back up toward the Arc de Triomphe. Colette drove through the Étoile roundabout, while the twinkle of dusk illuminated the Champs- Élysées and big spotlights highlighted the statues jutting from the Arc, protecting the grand entrance to Paris's heart. We parked next to another old building, with the architect's name and the year of construction, 1910, etched in the wall. Colette entered the code on the front door keypad, and the doors clicked open, revealing a dark cream inner lobby with stone walls keeping the inside cool. We took the antique elevator, its iron door creaking as it slowly closed, to the third floor. Colette climbed up the red-carpeted staircase.

Exhausted and panting from running up yet another flight of stairs, and clearly exasperated by the unsuccessful day we'd been having, she opened the final set of double front doors. The front two rooms, like all the others, were in pristine condition. There was a large entryway and the *salle à manger* had French doors. Would the rest of the apartment live up to the stunning front?

Holding our breath, we crossed the threshold—and, this time, the beauty continued. The hardwood floors were newly redone, the walls were freshly painted a clean white, and the kitchen was mostly outfitted, only needing a few appliances, with space for *at least* a dorm-room-sized fridge. The ceilings were high with detailed crown molding flowering out of every corner. White-and-gray marble mantels anchored each room, with antique mirrors to match. With big windows, it felt open and airy. Even better, there were no tubs in dining rooms or red-carpeted walls.

This apartment felt right. I closed my eyes and could see us here—candles lit, music playing, hosting dinner parties with our new French friends. In my mind, I started to place our furniture along the walls, arranging the couch, the carpets, and our books. This apartment was *très Parisien* to me, and I could tell Philip agreed. We said we'd take it. Colette let out a relieved exhale. "*Bon*," she said. "*Et bienvenue!*"

Chapter 10

I t would be another month before we moved into our new apartment. With Philip back at work, I found myself alone and, to my
surprise, feeling nervous to go out and explore. I didn't know what
was wrong with me. I was always eager to find new things to see and
do. But now, instead of going outside to live my life, I stayed inside
to read about how other people enjoyed the city.

Before leaving New York, I made a special trip to my favorite
bookstore, Three Lives & Company. A small shop with friendly staff,
it was where Philip bought the first present he ever gave me. They
have a perfectly curated selection of books on New York, France, and
food. Never one to read about France, I had a lot of catching up to do.

I bought *Lunch in Paris*, learned more about being *Almost French*,
and laughed my way through David Sedaris's *Me Talk Pretty One Day*.
I studied Inès de La Fressange's book *Parisian Chic* thoroughly and
intended to dress the part and look as French as possible the second I
stepped foot on French soil. I made a mental note to purchase black
Repetto ballerina flats immediately.

I also discovered blogs. Until our move, I'd never read a blog, not
even to plan our wedding, but now these personal accounts by other
expat women were turning out to be a fascinating resource for what
to expect. I learned that the "it" shoes were Isabel Marant brown

suede ankle boots and that I couldn't walk on the streets and feel like a true *Parisienne* unless I was wearing deep red lipstick or Chanel No. 473 nail polish.

Although the books and blogs were interesting and guided me in many ways, they also made me feel self-conscious. These women were enjoying boat rides with champagne on the Seine or meeting up with other expats—their friends. They had places to go and people to see. I couldn't help but think about the scene during the *Sex and the City* finale when Carrie Bradshaw looks longingly into the window of a Parisian tea salon at a group of women laughing together and misses Miranda, Charlotte, and Samantha. I was longing for the lives of the women on my computer screen.

There was one book that did inspire me to eventually go outside: Elaine Sciolino's *La Seduction*, which discussed "how the French play the game of life." Covering things like why the French don't smile and why things are so complicated to accomplish, it was intertwined with excellent interviews and historical anecdotes. Throughout the book, Sciolino made it clear that she was never ashamed to be American, and she made me realize that maybe I didn't need the correct shade of nail polish to begin exploring the city.

One of the first activities I ventured out for was a day for new expats at the American Church. The event featured prominent speakers and breakout groups on things like "Starting a Small Business in France" or "Health Care 101." Filled with practical information and an entire fair with vendors offering different services for newcomers, I hoped it would help ease the transition. And, to my delight, Elaine Sciolino was scheduled to be one of the speakers. How could I miss out on hearing her talk about her book?

The day only proved that forcing myself into situations that appeared scary or uncomfortable was important and would make my adjustment easier. I learned about the *pompiers*, firemen who do so much more than put out fires. They'll do things like take you to the emergency room or assist you if you're in labor and didn't make it to the hospital in time. When in doubt? Call the *pompiers*. I learned the top ten things to do to have a successful visa appointment at the *préfecture*. I learned that starting a business in France is complicated but feasible.

Arriving in Paris friendless was like the first few weeks of college. I was always on the lookout for a potential new friend. One time, I even approached another woman at a wine bar, only after overhearing her conversation about the transition from working full-time to not. We bonded over laundry being our sole purpose (she now has a successful photography business). Who knew? A new friend could be anybody. At the expat day, I finally met one.

I spotted Liz, a cute blond wearing glasses, in one of the breakout sessions. She appeared to be around my age, and I overheard her say that she had also moved to Paris from New York. I thought those two things gave us enough in common for me to strike up a conversation, which I did when I ran into her in the bathroom. I casually started talking while we were washing our hands, awkwardly taking turns pumping soap. Although it felt like I was picking her up, we exchanged numbers, setting up a coffee date for the following week. Perhaps I would be enjoying *macarons* and champagne on the Seine before I knew it.

The highlight, of course, was Elaine Sciolino. She told the audience about her first Thanksgiving in Paris and trying to find a turkey that would actually fit in her tiny oven, knowing that many of us would be in the same position in a few months. I promised myself never to host Thanksgiving. Her speech did leave me feeling excited and hopeful about living in such an interesting country where the citizens are, as she said, quoting from her book, "devoted to the pursuit of pleasure and the need to be artful, exquisite, witty, and sensuous, all skills in the centuries-old game called seduction."

Afterward, she signed books. Proud to already own a copy, I'd brought it with me. As if I were the only person in the room, she looked at and spoke to me directly, asking me how long I had been in France and what I was planning to do with myself. When I told her I had worked in advertising, she gave me her email address, offering to put me in touch with a good friend who she'd interviewed for the book and was, without doubt, one of the most powerful men in the industry. I eagerly accepted, ready to email her in a few weeks when I started my job search. Walking away from the table, I glanced at the inside cover, which read: *To Kristen: A beautiful woman with natural "seductive" power!* Bon courage à Paris, *Elaine*.

If you move to France, are a woman, and like to cook, you will most likely have a Julia Child moment. Not to get all Amy Adams on everyone, but before Paris, Philip bought me the box set of Child's *Mastering the Art of French Cooking*. One day, a few months after moving, I decided to tackle a recipe: *bœuf bourguignon*. I'd never eaten this dish before, let alone cooked it. In fact, in twenty-seven years, I had never cooked beef at all, and making this recipe required going to the butcher. Alone.

Léonie had been right. Moving into a quieter neighborhood was a good idea, and even though I was not friendly with the shopkeepers yet, where we lived was like a little village within the city. Everyone knew everyone.

The dry cleaner was friendly with the woman who owned the Italian *épicerie*, a specialty grocery shop across the street. The *caviste*, the wine merchant, was friendly with the baker who owned the *boulangerie.* And the woman who owned the *magasin de bricolage*, the hardware store, was friendly with everyone. Madame Fix-It, as we called her, was the mother hen of the *rue.* With wiry, black hair cut short to her head, she stood tall, sturdy, and wide outside her shop. Madame Fix-It would take in the hustle and bustle of the street, nonchalantly smoking cigarette after cigarette, waiting for her next customer. If you had a question about the neighborhood, you would go to her, and she always had the answer. She rewired our lamps to work with European outlets, recommended a top-notch handyman and even spent half an hour teaching me the colors of the candles I'd bought. We went through the vocabulary for navy blue, cerulean, olive, and sea green, a subtle but helpful thing to know.

It was also Madame Fix-It who told us which butcher to go to. There were a few within a four-block radius of our apartment, but this *boucherie,* she said, was the best, and the line outside the shop on Sunday mornings only confirmed that Monsieur Chamaret was indeed the gem of the neighborhood.

On the morning of *my* Julia Child moment, while I procrastinated, putting off my trip to the butcher, I remembered a chapter from Elaine's book called "Make Friends with Your Butcher." Grabbing it off the bookshelf, I reread what she had to say. An American smile would not cut it, and I had to go further if I wanted to seduce our butcher. Elaine wrote, "An American accustomed to the direct and forceful appeal of price specials and chirpy exhortations to have a nice day may find a wall of reserve instead. Breaking it requires the right degree of friendliness and a lot of time. But when the wall is breached, a relationship can take root." I was determined to break the wall. It wasn't going to happen during this first visit, but I at least wanted to make a dent.

In Paris my shopping lists had taken on much greater importance, acting as a translation and weight conversion document. I carefully noted how much meat or produce to ask for in grams and kilos instead of pounds. I wrote ingredients down in French, just in case the game of charades or my inability to pronounce the guttural French *R* hindered communication, which happened pretty much all the time.

Grabbing my list of ingredients, I felt brave, like a warrior going into battle. It was just before lunchtime as I walked the few blocks to the butcher, and businesses were shutting down for the next few hours for the all-important midday meal. I had already learned to run all my errands just before lunch, a time when usually no one else was around, so that I could avoid any potential irritation from, or uncomfortable confrontations with, people waiting behind me in line.

Entering the *boucherie*, I exhaled a sigh of relief; my timing was impeccable, and there were no other customers in sight. The glow from the meat cases spilled out onto the street. I blinked a few times, adjusting to the bright light as I surveyed, half with curiosity and half with disgust, the different cuts of meat that glistened in shades of pink and red—*entrecôte* (rib steak), *bavette* (flank steak), *rumsteck* (rump steak), *côte de bœuf* (prime rib), and *veau* (veal), all cut inches thick, along with skinned *lapin* (rabbit) with eyes still intact and *caille* (quail) with tiny feathers stuck to pimpled skin. Signs with harsh, black writing were attached to each item. Behind Monsieur Chamaret was a wall lined with jars of precooked peas, carrots, and white beans and bags of kettle-cooked potato chips.

"*Bonjour, madame. Comment allez-vous?*" he asked me.

While I began to speak, Monsieur Chamaret stood tall with dark, short hair combed to the side, waiting patiently for my order. "*Qu'est-ce que vous désirez?*" What is it that you want, he'd asked me. Let the seduction begin. I smiled slightly, not wanting to be too over the top with enthusiasm.

"Tonight, I am going to make *bœuf bourguignon*," I said slowly, choosing my words carefully, shocked as always to hear French come out of my mouth. Shuffling my feet back and forth over the sawdust covered floor, I thought it might help to add, "It will be my first time!" Perhaps he would find that sweet or cute.

"*Superbe, madame*," he responded. "It is a very good and classic French dish! Perfect for a day like today," he said, continuing in French but kindly speaking slowly enough for me to understand.

Thinking quickly, playing up my role as housewife, I continued in simple French. "Yes! It is cold today. It is for my husband. He will like it." The butcher smiled again at me and I smiled back, batting my eyes ever so slightly, hoping that I would receive extra points for doing something nice for my husband. Practicing the French art of seduction was difficult when I couldn't really say that much!

Pulling the meat from the front of the case, removing the little handwritten sign and sticking it into the next piece, he asked if I would like him to cut it for me. Not sure how to ask for it to be cut in the way that Julia instructed, I declined, immediately regretting my decision. I had no clue how to do it at home. Hopefully Julia had a chapter on cutting meat.

"And what else, *madame?*" he asked cheerily. So far so good. Perhaps my seduction powers were working.

"*Et puis,*" I began, "I would like *lardons.*" He looked back at me quizzically, clearly not sure what I'd just asked for. I tried again, this time emphasizing the *r* more, taking more time to say the "ar" sound: "Lahhr-dons." Still nothing. I tried one last time, to a blank stare. I had three choices. I could mime or act out a pig. I could make a pig sound. Not feeling the first two—they did not seem to fall under the idea of seduction—I opted for the third choice: speak English. Smiling a little more and trying my hardest to not become frustrated, I asked one last time, "Bacon?"

·· BŒUF-LESS BOURGUIGNON ··

Although our butcher recognizes me now and is very friendly, always greeting me with a smile, he also knows that I'm not very adventurous when it comes to meat. The poster hanging behind the cash register outlining the different cuts of beef—essentially making a map of a cow—still intimidates me. And while I love bœuf bourguignon, it takes a long time to prepare, and even when I order it at a restaurant, my favorite part of the delicious dish is always under-represented: the vegetables. I always want more mushrooms, carrots, and tiny pearl onions, their juice bursting in my mouth with each bite. I know Julia Child would never approve, but I went ahead and worked out a vegetarian version with all of my favorite ingredients—red wine included, of course.

INGREDIENTS

- 4 TABLESPOONS (60 G) BUTTER
- 4 TABLESPOONS OLIVE OIL
- 1 POUND (500 G) PEARL ONIONS, PEELED*
- 1 POUND (500 G) BUTTON OR CREMINI MUSHROOMS, QUARTERED
- 1 MEDIUM ONION, SLICED
- 1 HEAD GARLIC, 4 CLOVES MINCED, THE REMAINING CLOVES UNPEELED
- 1 TABLESPOON TOMATO PASTE
- 3 TO 4 MEDIUM CARROTS, CHOPPED IN HALVES
- 2 TO 3 SPRIGS FRESH THYME, LEAVES REMOVED
- 2 CUPS (480 ML) DRY RED WINE,-SUCH AS PINOT NOIR**
- 1 TABLESPOON ALL-PURPOSE FLOUR
- PARSLEY, CHOPPED FOR GARNISH
- SALT AND FRESHLY GROUND BLACK PEPPER, TO TASTE

PREPARATION

Melt 1 tablespoon of the butter and 1 tablespoon of the olive oil in a medium pan. Add the pearl onions, and cook for 10 to 12 minutes, moving them around with a spatula until the sides are lightly golden. Remove the pearl onions, and set aside in a bowl. Melt 1 tablespoon of the butter and 1 tablespoon of the olive oil in the same pan. Add the mushrooms, and stir continuously for 8 to 10 minutes, until they begin to release juices. Set aside in a bowl.

Preheat oven to 400°F (200°C). Continuing at the stove top, or in an oven-safe pan or dutch oven, melt the remaining butter and olive oil. Add the chopped onion and minced garlic, and stir for 3 to 4 minutes, until the onions are translucent. Stir in the tomato paste. Add the carrots, and cook, stirring occasionally, for another 5 to 7 minutes.

While the carrots are cooking, add the thyme. Season with a dash of salt and pepper. Add the cooked pearl onions and mushrooms, and stir for another 2 to 3 minutes. Pour in the red wine, and bring to a boil. Reduce heat, and simmer for 10 minutes, stirring every few minutes. Add the flour, and stir again. Add the remaining garlic cloves to taste, depending on how strong you want the garlic flavor to be. Cover, and place in the oven. Cook for 30 minutes, stirring every 5 to 10 minutes, until the liquid has reduced and thickened. Let the dish cool slightly, and serve.

YIELD

• 4 SERVINGS

*Unless you have an extra 30 to 45 minutes that you're looking to fill with a meditative activity, it is totally acceptable to buy frozen pearl onions instead of fresh, because peeling them is a tedious process. To peel fresh pearl onions, place them in a pot of boiling water for 10 seconds, until the skins begin to crack. Drain them in a colander and run under cold water. Cut the top off each onion, peel, and then cut off the root end.

**Some recipes call for beef or vegetable stock, but I've found that using red wine, without any stock, works just as well. If you're making the dish ahead of time, add an extra ¼ cup (60 ml) of red wine, so that there will be enough juice when you reheat the dish.

Chapter II

I t took me all of one day to realize that I had to start learning French. There was no rest for the weary, and no rest for the language impaired. While it is possible to live life in Paris without speaking the language, I do not recommend it. The game of acting out or pantomiming what you need or want (try telling the plumber that you have a running toilet) is only fun for so long. Aside from melting down when trying to order a coffee and enduring the pure frustration at not being able to properly spell my last name out loud for the dry cleaner (I have a hard time pronouncing *e* so it does not sound like *u*), I also suffered the embarrassment of having the salesperson at the Darty appliance store turn around and walk away from me after I asked her if she spoke English. Perhaps the final straw was when a three-year-old girl toddled up to me and started babbling. I couldn't say anything more to her than "*bonjour.*" I couldn't even communicate with a toddler.

So I registered for an entry-level French class at the Alliance Française. It was morning, and the sky was still dim, a sign of the dark northern European winter mornings to come. Despite the early hour, the streets were busy with people rushing to the *métro* stations and traffic backing up in the roundabouts. Apartment-building concierges rolled out identical green garbage bins to curbs and hosed down sidewalks covered in dog poop, while blue-and-yellow-uniformed La Poste workers proudly pushed their navy blue carts, delivering the mail. Older women sat at corner brasseries, enjoying a quick *café*, espresso, and cigarette, taking solace in the quiet of the morning, their aged hands void of cell phones. A group of ten men, *pompiers*, were out for a morning run toward Parc Monceau; like a collegiate cross-country team, they were wearing matching uniforms of bright red spandex and had identical crew-cut hair. The sweet scent of fresh, buttery croissants filtered through the air, seeping out of the *boulangeries*. My stomach grumbled. I wanted a coffee.

I spotted a corner café. Through the window, I could see baguette sandwiches filled with *jambon*, *beurre*, and *Emmental* cheese lined up next to plastic containers of shredded carrot salads, ready for the midday lunch rush. It looked like a place that would do a to-go coffee. After practicing a few times with Philip, I was ready to try to order by myself. Anxious for the first bitter sip, I was handed the coffee...without a lid. I was sure I'd asked for the coffee *à emporter*, to go. Where was the lid?

Pantomiming with my hands, signaling a cover for the cup, the man behind the counter shrugged his shoulders and shook his head. No lids. I knew France wasn't a country that really did coffee to go, but it was eight o'clock in the morning, I had a forty-five-minute *métro* ride ahead of me before a nine o'clock class. Coffee on the NYC subway was part of my routine. I could throw the coffee away or take it, lidless, onto the train. I bravely decided to take it with me.

Stepping onto the platform, I pushed through the throngs of morning commuters, wedged myself between two people reading *Direct Matin*, the free *métro* newspaper, and waited for the train. It didn't take long for me to realize that there were people staring at me. Not just quick glances either, but full-on stares. Was I dressed strangely? (Jeans, black shirt, and black ballet flats, what's weird about that?) Had I stepped in dog poop? Did my shoes smell? No. They were looking at the cup of coffee in my hand, eyes following every sip I took. How could this simple to-go beverage elicit such curiosity?

The train barreled into the station and I squeezed myself on board. Being rush hour, there wasn't a space to spare, and people stood with arms folded at awkward angles, torsos pressed up against windows, and noses pushed into strangers' armpits. Immediately, I regretted my coffee decision. The moment the car jolted forward, the still-hot liquid sloshed out of the cup, down my hands and legs, and onto the perfectly manicured, sandaled foot of the woman next to me. How could I have been so stupid?

"*Oh là là!*" she exclaimed with a pinched face, exasperated, staring (again) at me. Her disgust was obvious. But I was confused. Hadn't she just said, "*Oh là là*"? Wasn't that expression reserved for exciting things and sexy moments? Like if I wore a tight dress and Philip would say, "*Oh là là*"? It didn't sound appropriate as a reaction to having hot, sticky, milky coffee spilled onto your foot.

Over the next few weeks, I heard *oh là là* more and more and soon learned that it is not a phrase of delight. Instead, it signals annoyance. Packed train? *Oh là là.* Crying baby? *Oh là là.* Someone stole your taxi? Double *Oh là là là là là là.*

Even though I didn't quite yet understand what it meant to be *oh là là*'d, I was covered in coffee and too tongue-tied to even try to explain myself to the angry woman. I did the only thing I could. I got off at the next stop and mouthed *désolé* through the train glass doors as they jerked closed. I turned and ran to the nearest trash can. Dropped your coffee? *Oh là là* is right.

Half an hour later, with a damp coffee stain on my leg, I arrived at the French school. Students of all ages from all different parts of the world mingled outside the main doors in the courtyard. Inhaling their last few puffs of cigarettes and drinking from small plastic cups of cheap vending-machine espresso, they spoke to each other in various languages—mostly broken English and very little French.

A red carpet welcomed new students. Having already registered, I walked into the main office, inquiring where my class was located. Moving up to the desk, I put a big American smile on my face and proceeded to introduce myself: "*Bonjour. Je m'appelle* Kristen Beddard. I am registered here. I took the placement test online. Can you let me know where to go?"

The clerk blinked at me, her eyelids wrinkled around the edges, a result of too much summer sunshine. She coughed, cigarette phlegm caught in her throat, and responded to me in rapid-fire French. Having no idea what she said, I looked back at her with a confused, blank look. This time she responded in barely audible English. "Oh, you do not speak French?"

I shook my head. What kind of question was that? Last time I checked, I was standing in an institution that teaches French to people who do not already speak French. I responded, "Um, no."

She sighed back at me, talking angrily to herself and summoning her colleague to take over. After an oral evaluation, which I was not prepared for, I was told I had a very American accent. I didn't think I needed a placement test to confirm that.

Already feeling defeated, having barely made it past the front office with classroom assignment in hand, I climbed the marble steps, dented from years of previous students trampling up and down them, and arrived on the sixth floor. The classroom was small, with little light and paint peeling off the walls. There was a hodgepodge of desks, chairs, and tables and a big chalkboard.

I surveyed the room, sizing up my classmates: the American exchange students, who were clearly hungover from last night's party, waiting for their next nap; the overeager woman, eyes big and bright like *macarons*, who was spending six weeks in Paris and was determined to be fluent by the time she left; the Asian students, straight backed, who were holding advanced translation gadgets more impressive than smartphones; and the Egyptian heiress to a cigarette company, who was reciting the daily vocabulary in her raspy voice, louder than everyone else's.

A few other women, most of them Anglo, were there too, sitting on their own, interspersed between the other groups. They were "trailing" spouses, like me. Together, we were the women floundering in France after following our husbands' career moves. This was now the box that I checked, the category I belonged to with an identity that wasn't mine—and I wasn't so sure I felt comfortable in it.

With a gust of air, the classroom door opened and a young woman with bushy, dark hair twirled in, a tornado of vibrant colors. Speaking briskly, she tossed her tie-dyed patchwork backpack on the table at the front. "*Bonjour, mes élèves. Je m'appelle Patricia et je suis votre professeur.*" Our teacher had arrived.

Dressed in shades of purple, she stood out against the somber room. She straightened her dark purple suede jumper over her lilac-colored tights and rearranged her lavender scarf, tied into a knot around her neck. As she moved to the chalkboard, I noticed her neon-purple, patent-leather, chunky high heels clicking over the tile floor. Before addressing the class again, she pulled out a pair of plastic-rimmed violet glasses. I didn't know such a variety of purple items existed—or that someone would choose to wear them all together at the same time. It soon became apparent that this was not a one-time thing. The next day Patricia chose shades of red, and green the day after that, always accessorizing with chunky, plastic jewelry to accent the color palette *du jour*.

Patricia wasn't alone in her fashion sense. I started noticing women everywhere dressed in outfits of variations on one color. What I'd thought was a fluke from my eccentric French teacher was actually common Paris street style.

Where was the perfect *Parisenne* that I'd read about? The Frenchwoman I strived to be? American women, myself included, pore over what we can do to be more French, look more French, smell more French, eat like the French, and be thin like the French. I was aspiring every day to be more French, to fit in.

But *la Parisienne*? She is a firefly—a beautiful burst of light, gone in the blink of an eye. You will spot her, rarely and unexpectedly, her tiny, high-heeled feet prancing lightly on the cobblestoned streets (because, of course, the cobblestones in heels are easy for *her*). Demure but confident, she is present—crossing the street, sitting at the corner café, shopping on rue Saint-Honoré—but definitely not ubiquitous.

I soon grew accustomed to Patricia's rainbow of outfits. She was sweet and a good teacher, but a bit odd. It was hard to focus on the lesson at hand because she spent a lot of time spinning around in front of the chalkboard. Clicking her tongue like a dolphin in between her *alors* and *donc*, which are more or less the French equivalents of "so" and "then," she was a constant flash of color before our eyes.

Not wasting any time on the first day, Patricia launched into our lesson, *le marché*. The market! Now this would be helpful.

Working in pairs, I ended up with a nice American woman. Trying our best not to speak in English, we role-played *maraîcher* and shopper.

We practiced phrases, asking for and giving a *boîte*, box, of straw-berries or a *poignée*, handful, of mushrooms. And to make our heads spin even more, Patricia taught us the two words for "piece." To this day, I still don't know if I'm supposed to ask for a *tranche* of cake or a *morceau* of cheese or whether it's the other way around.

During our break, I talked more with my partner about the markets and if she had any favorites. She'd been living in Paris for a few years already, finally enrolling in French classes now that her children were in school, and she said she loved the Marché Bastille in the Eleventh arrondissement on Sundays, because the families that attend it together make it so festive. She also liked the Marché Saxe-Breteuil in the Seventh arrondissement, because of the beauti-ful views of the Eiffel Tower as a backdrop. I immediately asked her if she'd ever seen kale in any of these markets.

"I've been here more than three years, and I've never seen it once," she said matter-of-factly.

After class, I went to the library to complete my homework. In between memorizing fruit and vegetable vocabulary and puzzling over numbers (why does eighty translate to "four twenties"?), my mind kept wandering to kale. Would I ever be able to find it? I must not be looking in the right places. Closing my workbook, I decided to do a little more research of my own.

I typed "where to find kale in Paris" into Google, and a variety of results popped up. There were message boards, food forums, blog posts, and links to Twitter pages all about people trying or hoping to find kale in Paris, but so far, they hadn't had any luck.

Some posts went as far back as 2005, with questions from expats about what kale was called in French. Most of the responses gave incorrect information, recommending *blette* (Swiss chard), *épinard* (spinach), or *chou frisé*, which I already knew was savoy cabbage. No one had the answer I was looking for.

Scrolling through even more search results, I saw blog posts and tweets from prominent food bloggers, including David Lebovitz, an American who has lived in Paris since 2004, and the *Parisienne* Clotilde Dusoulier, author of acclaimed blog *Chocolate & Zucchini*. In 2010, Lebovitz visited Rungis, the largest wholesale food market in the world, located just outside of Paris, and offered one hundred euros to anyone who could bring him kale. He went home with his money. In 2011, Dusoulier hailed kale as the "most elusive ingredient" in France.

I grew excited to see that other people were as frustrated as I was, even people with serious street cred in Paris's food scene. And if Lebovitz and Dusoulier couldn't find it, I knew I wasn't crazy. Maybe someone somewhere in the country was growing it in their garden, but when it came to actually finding kale to buy, it seemed practically impossible.

❧

Taking the *métro* again, without incident this time, I met Philip for drinks and dinner at a newly opened wine bar near the Palais-Royal. Verjus, owned by an American couple, Braden Perkins and Laura Adrian, was garnering a lot of buzz. Their previous endeavor, Hidden Kitchen, a series of pop-up dinners in their apartment, was so popular that guests had to book reservations months in advance. The wine bar, located in an actual *cave à vin*, was dark and cozy, with votive candles illuminating the stone walls. Behind a large, iron gate, like those that line the gardens in the Palais-Royal, were rows and rows of wine bottles, which Laura picked personally for both the wine bar and the tasting menu at the restaurant upstairs.

Making ourselves comfortable at the bar stools, we ordered one of everything on the menu, including the celery-root dumplings with sweet-and-spicy dipping sauce, broccoli with anchovy- and lemon-infused butter vinaigrette, and their now-famous fried chicken.

I was so excited to share the results of my kale research with Philip that I forget to recap my first French class. As I told him what I'd learned, Laura approached with our glasses of wine, and I immediately had another idea: ask a chef. Laura and Braden were already familiar with kale from their American upbringing, and they were sourcing ingredients from the top farmers and distributors in the region. If anyone knew, it would be them.

"So, this may seem like a weird question, but have you ever seen kale here?"

Her eyes sparkled in the candlelight and she laughed. It seemed like she had answered this question before. Her tight, brown curls bounced in the disappointing direction of *no*. "No, I've never seen it—like, ever," she said.

"In fact, when Braden has gone to the markets to try to find it and shown photos, the farmers, *maraîchers*, tell him it's *chou frisé* and that it is the outer leaf of the savoy cabbage that they throw away." We both shook our heads in unison, agreeing that the outer leaves of savoy cabbage were not the same thing. "But you're not the only person looking for it. Apparently there was someone selling kale plants at a cocktail bar in the Marais, but that was a while ago. I wish I could help you."

No kale? *Oh là là.*

Chapter 12

O n weekdays, Philip was busy with work, while I attempted to
   negotiate a new language and a new neighborhood, but we
spent weekends visiting Philippa. We'd bring her little treats whenever
we came to the hospital, but today's visit was special—it was her eighti-
eth birthday. We brought a bouquet of lilies, the Sunday *International
Herald Tribune* ("It's all doom and gloom!" she would say), fresh *beurre
demi-sel*, a strawberry tart, and a mille-feuille, the layers of pastry chock-
full of dollops of vanilla-spiced custard.

After a few weeks in the hospital, one round of cancer treatment,
and a blood transfusion, she seemed stronger and more vibrant, and
her appetite had returned. But she was less than happy with the
hospital food.

Trying to prove that I was a good daughter-in-law, I offered
to buy her a few frozen meals, which is how I found myself at the
frozen food store, Picard, wandering the aisles of bagged frog legs
and premade escargot.

Picard is something of an institution in France, known for its
frozen food that, well, isn't crap. Some Parisian couples will host
dinner parties entirely with Picard food, unbeknownst to their guests.
Restaurants that don't want to hire a full-time pastry chef will serve
Picard desserts. Picard's *moelleux au chocolat,* small chocolate lava

cakes with warmed chocolate sauce in the middle that flows out of the center like a mini-volcano, are practically legendary.

Searching for food ideas for Philippa, I wandered up and down the frigid, sterile aisles, peering through freezer after freezer of cardboard boxes. I stopped in the *pomme de terre* (potato) section and scanned options like potato mille-feuille, *poêlée* (stir-fried potatoes), and *rosaces* (potato rosettes), until my eyes landed on something that I did recognize: *gratin dauphinois*. That's what I would take to Philippa.

I smiled to myself, remembering the day after my first date with Philip. He sent me a text message. Yes, a text message, the day after. I was shocked and perhaps a little confused. When did first dates send a message the day after?! Not used to such immediate communication from a guy, I eagerly read my phone:

Darling KB. Lovely lovely day and night yesterday and already missing you so. Let me do you a Eurotrash dinner next Saturday. X

Darling? How charming! Eurotrash dinner? Sure, why not? I couldn't stop thinking about our date and how easily we could talk about everything. He was engaging and seemed genuinely interested in my life and in me. And there was laughter, over and over, just like on the night we first met. I couldn't wait to see him again.

The next Saturday, it rained all day, leaving an oppressive late-summer thickness in the air. I was nervous climbing the staircase but the moment I entered Philip's apartment, I felt at ease. The surroundings felt calm, cozy, and homelike, with the scent of figs from candles burning on the mantel mixing with Philip's cologne.

"Helloooo, darling!" he greeted me, moving back into the corner kitchen. "Do you want a Bellini?"

A Bellini? How festive! Waiting for him to make the mixture of peach juice and prosecco, I looked around the apartment. Art books lined the built-in bookshelves, and a healthy live tree sat against one end of the living room. He is a painter in his free time, and his easel rested in a corner, holding a half-finished portrait of a Victorian woman. This was a grown-up apartment, a real home.

Philip motioned for me to come into the kitchen. Drinks in hand, we toasted. "*Tchin-tchin!*" he said. "So how are you? How was your week? Tell me everything."

Not accustomed to a date asking me how my week was, I didn't know where to begin. I watched him cook, moving quietly, thin in his navy blue pants—"date-night pants," he later told me. He was graceful in the kitchen, organizing groceries and balancing trays. Pulling out an evergreen-color Le Creuset dutch oven and setting it on the stove, he began to thinly slice potatoes and grate cheese.

Given that I rarely cooked with potatoes or cheese, I asked him what he was making. "*Gratin dauphinois*," he replied. I stared at him blankly. I had no idea what he'd just said to me. It *sounded* like French, but I wasn't really sure.

"Gratin what?" I asked, with more of a Pittsburgh accent than I intended.

Smirking at my pronunciation, he replied, "*Gratin dauphinois*. Potatoes and cheese with cream. My mother used to make it all the time for me when we lived in Geneva, because Switzerland is where you'll find the best gruyère cheese. Just don't say that to a French person."

Trying to be cute, I said, "Oh…so it's just cheesy potatoes." He laughed right as he pulled a tub of sour cream out of the refrigerator.

I stopped him. "Wait a minute," I said. "What are you doing with that?" I asked pointing to the container. Why was he was going to use *sour* cream in a dish that also uses the *best* cheese of Switzerland?

I might not have been able to pronounce the name of the dish, and my American translation was juvenile, but at least I did know not to use sour cream when you needed heavy cream.

"I never can understand these American products!" Philip lamented making his way to the front door to buy the right cream at the nearest corner bodega.

A few hours, and helpings of *gratin dauphinois*, later, Philip and I were sitting on the couch, finishing our wine and talking. At one point, he stared at me, tucked a strand of hair behind my ear. "I really want to paint you," he said. "You smile at me with your right eye. It scrunches up and sparkles." It was at that moment that I knew I was going to marry him.

✾

Philippa was overjoyed by the Picard cheesy potatoes I brought her. "Darling," she said to me. "These are perfect. I can't wait to eat them for dinner tonight!" Setting up her simple birthday celebration, we placed all the pastries on a tray in front of her, waiting as she decided which one to cut into first. Eating away as if she'd never lost her appetite at all, she told us stories about the other patients on her floor, who kept wandering into her room, unannounced. Philippa may have been ill, but her mind was as sharp as ever. As the sun began to set and the outside air grew colder, we bid her good-bye with big kisses, and as we walked out of the room, she called out, "Go on, darlings! Go live your lives!"

The phone call from the hospital the next morning was unexpected. Philippa had taken a turn for the worse, most likely caused by liver failure as a reaction to the treatment. They didn't think she would live through the day. Philip rushed to the hospital to be with her. He sat next to her as her breathing slowed, and she barely moved underneath the foil cover keeping her warm. He held her hands and kissed her forehead over and over, telling her, and convincing himself, that it was time to let go. A few hours later, she did. As the doctors had first predicted, it had been almost two months to the day since her diagnosis.

Barely twelve hours after Philippa passed away, before we'd had time to really process it, Philip and I had to move into the new apartment. It was as if we couldn't have planned the move more poorly. At eight o'clock in the morning, the moving company arrived at the apartment with our entire shipment, which included our things from New York, which had finally cleared customs, in addition to all of Philippa's belongings, which we'd had shipped from Spain. We had no choice but to get through the day, pushing the sadness out of our minds, focusing on the monumental task at hand. The movers shut down our tiny *rue* and used an automated ladder to bring everything up from the street and into the front windows of the apartment. They dropped off box after box, unloading kitchen boxes in the living room and living room boxes in the kitchen. Heaps of clothing and coats piled up into any vacant corner. Seeing that French apartments have zero closets, it would be weeks before our clothes actually were hanging again. Furniture, covered in brown packing paper and taped with bubble wrap, leaned against the walls, creating a maze that I knew would take days to organize. Philip's canvases, including the painting he'd done of me, were leaning again the hallway walls. The movers were paid to get everything out of boxes and onto a flat surface, but nothing more. It was impossible to organize items as quickly as they were being unpacked, and by noon, the house was a disaster.

In the midst of the chaos, we heard a knock at the front door, which was already wide open. A tall, thin man with gray hair and glasses, dressed in suit pants and a sweater vest, called in, "*Allô? Bonjour? Êtes-vous là?*" Are you there? Philip and I, climbing over dresser drawers, half of our bed frame, and a footstool, reached the front door as the man, who had already let himself into the apartment, continued knocking on the door.

"*Oui, monsieur? Bonjour,*" Philip said, hassled.

"Yes, hello. My name is Olivier Sinclair. I am the president of the building. Welcome," he said, nodding to us both, surveying the mess in front of him and peeking around the corner to the dining room, which was as much of a mess as the living room.

"Nice to meet you," Philip replied, extremely aware of Monsieur Sinclair sniffing around. "Excuse the mess, but as you can see, we are moving in today. The movers are working quickly, since we never actually received approval to block the street," Philip added, afraid that Monsieur Sinclair was there to tell us the movers had to halt all work and relocate their truck. It wasn't our fault that the *mairie*, city hall, hadn't gotten back to us in time.

"Of course. No worries. It looks like you have a lot of umm… stuff," he said, continuing his obvious perusal of our belongings.

"Yes, my mother. Well, she passed away yesterday and we have all of her things too," Philip told him quietly, and calmer than you'd expect for someone who had just lost his mother a day ago.

"Oh, yesterday?" Monsieur Sinclair said, uncomfortable. "I am so sorry to hear that. Do you have faith? Well, I have some pamphlets from my church. Please come pray with us if you feel that you need somewhere to be," he said. Stepping even farther into the entryway to inspect a painting, he asked, "What do you do, by the way?"

"Advertising. My wife as well," Philip told him.

"Right. Interesting. What type of clients?"

"Louis Vuitton, IBM, Perrier. Things like that," Philip answered.

"*Très bien*," very good, Sinclair replied, clearly satisfied and impressed with Philip's response. Philip later told me that it was obvious Sinclair was fishing around, to see what type of people were moving into the building. I, of course, had no idea what was going on, trying to make out even a few words that I understood.

"And you, *madame*," he said, pointing to me and then to my stomach. "You must learn French! And you must have a baby soon! The building needs a baby."

Before he could exit the door, we heard another voice. "*Bonjour!*" a woman sang up behind him. Plump, with pale skin and thick, oversized glasses that were perched in the middle of her nose, she carried a tiny, fluffy, white dog and looked to be around seventy years old.

"I'm Amelia. Your building concierge!" she chirped to us both. In Paris, many buildings have a concierge who cleans the lobby and hallways steps, handles the trash collection, delivers mail, and collects packages. They live in small ground-floor apartments, normally right by the main front door. They're also the heart, if not the central line, of communication for all building gossip. Amelia would wear her hair piled in a knot on top of her head, and she'd also wear the same clothes every day. I was never sure if it was that or the fish she cooked every day for lunch (or a combination of the two) that made our building lobby smell so stale.

"If you need anything, I am downstairs, always here to help," she told us. And that turned out to be true—Amelia was kind to me and spoke slowly, always patient with my French.

"Actually," said Philip, "we have a lot of stuff that we would like to donate. My mother passed away, and we can't possibly keep all of her things."

"Oh! I can help," she answered eagerly. "Just leave what you want to donate in the hallway near the courtyard, and I will take care of it." Amelia's dog began to bark. "Don't forget. I am right downstairs!" she said again before taking the elevator down to the first floor.

What we didn't realize was that "taking care of it" meant Amelia would donate it to…herself. By that evening, Philip, being the masterful unpacker that he is, had placed a pile of things that he knew he didn't want exactly where Amelia had instructed. Two days later, one of Philippa's footstools was in our building lobby. Two days after that, I saw Amelia wearing one of Philippa's button-down shirts paired with one of her gold scarves. Amelia had taken everything.

With the visitors gone, Philip and I returned to the mess at hand. I didn't mind our things being disorganized, but I didn't want Philippa's to be. Her entire life's belongings were being deposited— practically dumped—onto any empty surface the movers could find. In between the candlesticks, picture frames, and furniture were miniature Egyptian and African statues, silver trophies and ribbons from her equestrian days, and stack upon stack of books with titles like *You Are Becoming A Galactic Human*, reminding us of her unique spiritual side.

Without blinking an eye, Philip began going through her clothing. As he unfolded and refolded dresses, skirts, and pantsuits she had saved from the seventies, the scent of gardenias, the odor of stale cigarette smoke, and the heaviness of Philip's grief began to permeate the air. Unpacking our way to the last of the suitcases, we found tucked in the bottom her special fur hat, which Philip took out and placed on the mantel. "This is yours now. My mom would have loved knowing that you were going to wear it in Paris."

By the end of the day, our stomachs were grumbling. We hadn't had any food since the *jambon-beurre* baguette sandwiches we'd barely touched earlier that morning. Knowing that we wouldn't be able to find a viable takeout option, I began to rummage through the things on the kitchen floor. Half-hidden in one of the corners, next to a pile of running clothes and lamp shades, I saw the evergreen Le Creuset pot. I knew what we needed: cheesy potatoes. It was the perfect dish to pay homage to Philippa, comfort Philip, and remind us of a sweet memory of our second date, a time when life had seemed much simpler. A time when mothers were still alive, there was order in our apartment, and we lived in a city that actually felt like home.

·· KALE *GRATIN* ··

There is no doubt about it: Philip loves cheese. I once found him in our kitchen, like a little mouse, happily cutting bites off a block of Comté and adding them to pieces of baguette. He told me he was having a "private cheese moment." For his birthday one year, I planned a surprise trip to Gruyères, Switzerland, so he could take in the full experience of where his favorite cheese comes from. Traditional gratin dauphinois *does not use cheese, but since Philip loves it so much, we've created our own version of cheesy potatoes that really goes all out. We use butter, cheese, whole milk, and cream. To balance it all out, kale is a great green to add to the recipe, but you can also substitute swiss chard or spinach. Either way, these cheesy potatoes make the perfect comfort dish for times when you need comforting the most.*

INGREDIENTS

- 4 TABLESPOONS (60 G) BUTTER
- 1 LARGE SHALLOT, FINELY DICED
- 4 CLOVES GARLIC, FINELY CHOPPED
- 2½ CUPS (600 ML) WHOLE MILK
- ⅓ CUP FLOUR (40 G)
- 2 POUNDS (1 KG) POTATOES (YUKON GOLD OR KENNEBEC), PEELED AND THINLY SLICED
- 1 TABLESPOON OLIVE OIL
- 1 TEASPOON FINE SEA SALT
- ½ TEASPOON NUTMEG
- 5 TO 6 CUPS (200 G) KALE, WASHED, DESTEMMED, AND CHOPPED
- 1⅓ CUPS (125 G) GRATED GRUYÈRE CHEESE, TIGHTLY PACKED
- ½ CUP (110 ML) HEAVY CREAM

PREPARATION

Preheat the oven to 400°F (200°C). Grease a 10 x 10-inch (25 x 25 cm) baking dish. Line a baking sheet with aluminum foil, and put the dish on top of it; the baking sheet will catch any drips. Set aside. Melt the butter in a large pot over medium heat. Add shallot and garlic, and cook, stirring frequently, for 2 to 3 minutes, until softened. Slowly add the flour, and whisk until there is a creamy roux. Slowly add 2 cups (460 ml) milk and whisk for 1 to 2 minutes. Stir in potatoes, olive oil, and remainder of milk, and cook, stirring frequently, for about 3 minutes. Add salt and nutmeg, and cook for another 10 to 12 minutes, stirring continuously until potatoes are softened and can be pierced with a fork. Stir in kale until it wilts. Remove from heat. Pour some of the mixture into the baking dish, creating a layer that covers the bottom of the dish. Cover with ⅓ cup (25 g) cheese. Continue this process until the dish is full. Top with ⅔ cup (50 g) of cheese and freshly ground pepper. Add the cream and stir into the mixture. Bake for 35 to 40 minutes, until cheese is bubbling and the potatoes are browned and tender. Let cool slightly, and serve.

YIELD

· 4 TO 6 SERVINGS

Chapter 13

After Philippa passed away, everything went by in a haze as we tried to put some organization and sense into our daily lives. Philip went back to work, navigating a new job in a culture not necessarily known for being very optimistic. His new work environment was a far cry from New York's candid "yes" attitude.

As for me, I was finding that being pushed into the role of housewife was dramatically shifting both the dynamic in my relationship with Philip and my own sense of self. I tried to get our home life in order, but I wasn't very successful, since I couldn't even do simple things like call the electric or cable companies. I felt more and more helpless as I realized how limited I was.

Once an empowered woman with a career and an independent life, I now felt overwhelmed and too intimidated to even leave the apartment. I was afraid of what I might encounter and afraid of having to fake my way through conversation. I was hanging on for dear life (or so it felt) just to meet my basic needs. I felt stripped of my strength and my ability to be a true partner.

And as expected, Philip was sad. He had to make funeral arrangements very quickly after Philippa's death and was slowly coming to terms with the fact that his mother, the woman who had raised him on her own, who was his constant confidante, was now gone. He stayed strong on the outside, but I knew he was hurting on the inside.

I continued taking French classes and attempted new recipes, trying to incorporate more French tradition into my cooking and to practice French phrases with the neighborhood shopkeepers. But things weren't right. Philip and I were fighting a lot. I wasn't really *doing* anything. Cooking only took so much time, so I went back to reading.

Huddled under a café heat lamp in the mid-autumn chill, sipping a cup of *café* or nursing a glass of *vin rouge*, I took myself back in time with F. Scott and Zelda Fitzgerald. Like a lot of expats, I had become fascinated with their lives, especially the time they spent in France. I read his books quickly, which led me to read more about her. It wasn't that I saw myself in Zelda, but I couldn't help noticing the eerie similarity in our situations.

She'd left New York City a media darling, epitomizing the twenties-era flapper, even writing her own account of life as F. Scott Fitzgerald's flapper muse. After moving to France, she didn't write anything for years, and once she finally started writing again, her husband would add his name to it or take sole credit so they'd be paid more money for the piece. They had constant, booze-fueled arguments—nearly ending in separation—many of which stemmed from the fact that both of them were feeling like Zelda lacked purpose and wasn't contributing enough to their partnership. These disputes only added to Zelda's own insecurities that maybe he was right. Was she contributing? What was she doing with her life?

Philip and I were living parallel lives, which did little to help us relate to each other. Many nights we would have screaming fights related to my insecurities and his disappointment that I wasn't working.

"Well, you don't have a job. You don't understand how hard I'm working for us. All the responsibility is on me now," he would argue, lashing out.

I knew he was working, and I knew he was working hard. I didn't need to be reminded that I wasn't pulling my weight. Just like Zelda had to give up her name on the few pieces she did get published, I no longer had my name anywhere—not on a business card or nameplate, not floating midlevel on an organizational chart. I was just Philip's wife now. I was only Madame Heimann.

We'd have this same quarrel late at night, often after midnight, and it would escalate until we'd exhausted ourselves. We'd go to bed angry, only to wake up feeling unsure and unsettled.

When calm enough to talk again, which was always what I *thought* we did best, Philip would try to explain. "I married you because you are ambitious and a strong woman, like our mothers. You're a doer." I was glad my husband had so much faith in me and thought I had potential to succeed, but it had only been three months since we'd moved to France. How could I be expected to be this ambitious, working woman so quickly in a foreign land? And what was the definition of success? I wasn't sure I knew anymore.

❦

One day, after another argument, I was wandering around the apartment, not focused on any task, when Hannah sent me a Skype request. It was early morning for her and midday for me, and I was still in my pajamas, sitting and staring at the computer screen.

"Krissy!" she said cheerily, calling me by the nickname that only a few of the people closest to me use. Even an ocean away, she could tell immediately that things weren't right.

"What's wrong?" she asked, her cheery tone quickly turning to one of concern. I couldn't keep up the happy "I love Paris" face anymore. I told her everything, not holding anything back, realizing that it was the first time I'd actually *really* talked to a friend in six weeks. It was the first time I'd talked to anyone about Philip and me, or how things had been since Philippa passed away.

"Nothing is the same. I'm afraid I've—or we've made a huge mistake," I said to her. "I miss you and Sarah terribly." Aside from Philip and my mother, Hannah and Sarah were the two people who I trusted most, who knew everything about me. They were no longer there by my side, only a subway ride away, and I felt the distance deep in my core.

I needed to get out of the apartment and do something. French lessons were fine, but I never walked out of the school feeling good about myself. That's when I got an idea from Zelda. A ballet dancer as a child, she'd taken it back up again, seriously, at the age of twenty-seven. Perhaps I could start dancing again too. I'd studied ballet until I was sixteen, and although I was nowhere near being a prima ballerina, I'd always enjoyed it. It had been more than ten years since I'd last taken a class, but I'd danced enough to know that the movements would come back to me easily. It seemed like the perfect outlet. I would immerse myself in an all-French ballet class and, who knew, maybe I would even make a new friend. After all, it would be a room full of women.

Ballet wasn't a job, and it didn't solve our fighting, but at least it was *something*. And unlike my everyday life, where I couldn't communicate and every small task was an ordeal, ballet left no room for interpretation. It was black and white. A *jeté* was a *jeté*, just as an *échappé* was an *échappé*, no matter what country I lived in. And as I warmed up at the *barre* during the first class, examining my technique in the mirror and letting the music carry my arms through the air, I felt, for the first time in months, even if for only an hour and a half, like I was doing something right.

※

On my way to dance class one morning, Philip asked me to drop off a spare set of keys with Amelia, in case one of us ever got locked out. Knocking on her glass-paned door, the smell of yesterday's salmon stuck in the stale air, I saw Amelia move the inner curtain aside and give me a big smile. She opened the door, a crumb of her morning *tartine,* bread slice, still on her face.

"*Bonjour* Kreesteen," she said to me. She was wearing the same Philippa button-down, and as I handed her the spare keys, she opened the door wider, revealing an Aladdin's cave of Philippa's possessions. Blue vases, her side table, and another footstool decorated the room, along with three African statues that sat between candlesticks and wooden angels. I stifled my laughter and debated saying something about it, but then her dog started barking, the crumb fell to the ground, and I decided against it. No need to ruffle feathers. We had already been told—to our faces—by our first floor neighbor that she did *not* like Americans. I needed an ally.

※

After a few months of ballet classes, the movement and dancing still felt right, but the finding friends part? Not so much. The problem with making French friends is that most French adults aren't looking for new friends. I completely understand that—I wasn't looking for new friends when I lived in New York either. In between work, Philip, and keeping up with life, I barely had time to see the few friends I did have. As for Parisians, they tend to spend most of their lives in Paris, so their lifelong friends are people they've known since childhood, high school, and university; the last thing they're looking for is a new friend.

Pauline was the ringleader of the ballet girls. Short and pale but with long, flexible legs that extended behind her head, she was by far the best dancer in the class, and she knew it. Wearing her mousy-brown hair slicked back into a tight bun, she would show up to class, still exhaling her last puff of cigarette smoke, and take the same spot at the *barre* toward the front of room. She led the class in warm-ups. She was one of the few girls to practice *en pointe*, on the tips of her toes, in pointe shoes. Our instructor, Daniella, used Pauline's pristine technique as an example for the rest of us. Pauline didn't smile much and didn't seem overly friendly, but she had every other girl in the class fawning over her. In the *vestiaire*, changing room, a gaggle of girls, chatting and giggling, would surround her in a semicircle, gazing up as she laced up her pink satin slippers. I was not one of them.

I was already considered weird because I'd arrived to class on the first day in my dance clothes, instead of changing into them there. From then on, I was too afraid to actually speak to anyone. I kept to myself and was meek when I approached Daniella. A small, stocky woman with thick, brown hair cut short to her chin, she made up for what she lacked in size with her loud personality. She wasn't shy about calling out that I was American.

"I only speak little English," she said to me, as I tried to purchase a ten-class card. I could feel the eyes of the ballet girls staring into the back of my head.

It wouldn't have been much of a problem if I'd stayed quietly in the back of the room, dancing for myself, but Daniella took a liking to me. Soon she was calling me up to demonstrate warm-ups at the *barre* and placing me in the front row next to Pauline during the floor combinations. I wasn't better than Pauline, but I could remember those combinations in my sleep, which meant the other students could follow along with my footsteps.

Still, my comprehension of French couldn't keep up with my feet, and many times I would look confused or do something wrong because I didn't understand Daniella's instructions. I could hear Pauline and the ballet girls snickering behind me, their eyes staring, burning a hole through my back. It happened if I would exit the main floor left instead of right, or do a turn *en dedans*, to the inside, instead of *en dehors*, to the outside. I shook uncontrollably the first time Daniella asked me to do a double pirouette by myself; the ballet girls watched on as my legs trembled and wobbled, and I barely completed the second turn. Somehow I'd found myself in the middle of a *Mean Girls*–meets–*Center Stage* mash-up.

"I don't think I'm going to go back to ballet," I told Philip one evening. "I've been going to class three times a week for months now and haven't broken the ice with anyone. No one even smiles at me," I said to him.

"Well," Philip responded seriously, "do *you* ever smile at them? Or do you have your poo face on?"

I paused. He was right. I was so hung up on my own insecurity over not being able to speak French that I don't think I had ever actually smiled. I probably seemed like the mean girl to them. I was so convinced from the beginning that because I was the outsider, I would be the victim, that I never even attempted to do more than walk into the room with a look of disgust or, as Philip called it, poo.

Next time would be different. I walked into the *vestiaire* and, just as Pauline and her ballet girls do with each other, I greeted the room with a peppy (but not *too* peppy—let's not get carried away here) "*bonjour*," and a big (but not *too* big—let's not get too American either) smile. I walked up to Daniella and gave her a polite double kiss, then sat down to change into my dance clothes, pretending to listen to the conversation. I no longer had a poo face on in front of the large mirrors, and if I didn't understand Daniella, I laughed, smiled again, and replied in broken French. And finally one day, when Daniella called me to the front row and I made sure to smile, out of the corner of my eye, I saw Pauline smile back.

Chapter 14

If you want to get divorced, go to BHV. That's what Philip and I discovered on our first trip to the department store, and it's for that reason that we now avoid it at all costs. Short for *Bazar de l'Hôtel de Ville* and located next to the Hôtel de Ville—Paris's city hall—in the Fourth arrondissement, BHV is five floors of too much stuff with the potential to drive you crazy. It's the place I go to, begrudgingly, with a long shopping list, only to leave hours later, after searching the whole store, with nothing crossed off the list.

Our first trip was to find lamp shades. Being BHV virgins, we didn't know that going on a Saturday afternoon was a huge mistake. It was as if every citizen of Paris had descended upon the store, while (I am convinced of this) the management turns up the heat and tells the staff to take an extended break, because it will always be hot, regardless of the season, and there will never be anyone to help you. There will also never be more than one open checkout counter. The rest will be *fermé*, closed.

Overheated and flustered, we pushed through the throngs of people to the lighting department, where the bright, warm lights only increased the temperature in the already-sweltering store. A jolly, automated sales message played over the intercom every few minutes, announcing the in-store promotions, which after the fifth or sixth time didn't sound as jolly.

As if it were the last day you could ever buy a lamp shade in Paris, people pushed and shoved, blocking the very section of lamp shades that we were trying to inspect. Parisians have a habit of standing directly in front of you and whatever you're looking at. It happens at art exhibitions, at the grocery store, and at BHV.

And we also had questions. After thirty minutes of trying to find a salesperson, another twenty-five minutes of Philip translating back and forth, and several more minutes of disagreeing and then agreeing on colors, we left the store, sweaty but with two new lamp shades—only to return home and discover that they didn't fit our lamps. Madame Fix-It had changed our plugs but had kept the American lightbulb screws intact (who knew there were different sizes?). This meant only one thing: I would have to go back and return them later that week.

BHV didn't become any easier as my language skills improved. Often, they simply didn't have what I was looking for. The mattress department didn't sell air mattresses, and the kitchen department didn't sell pot-lid holders, which are small racks with pegs that sits on a shelf and holds pot lids up, like a row of books. Scanning the kitchen-supply department, I could see hundreds of pot lids for sale, all displayed on metal or wooden pot-lid holders. Naturally, I only assumed that I would be able to buy a pot-lid holder as well.

I waited twenty minutes to talk to a salesperson, and when one finally came to help me, he looked at me in disbelief, "*Madame*, we do not sell anything like that."

"But they're all over the store," I persisted, pointing to the three sitting on the shelves next to me. "Isn't it a bit strange that you sell all these pot lids displayed in pot lid holders, but you don't sell the holder too?"

"*Écoutez, madame,*" he replied, telling me to listen. "You must have a very big kitchen. In fact, you must have the biggest kitchen in Paris! No one has ever asked for a pot-lid holder before!"

Nearly blowing my own pot lid from frustration, I left the store and later ordered a *support pour couvercles* online from IKEA. BHV made me want to buy everything online.

As for the lamp shades, I put off returning them for as long as possible, but the *dernier délai,* the final deadline to return them, was looming. Philip said it would be another good French exercise. I had my doubts. And as I was about to learn, a return in France is never just a simple return.

My mother was in Paris visiting us, so she tagged along, helping me carry the bulky bags on the *métro* ride to the store. Arriving at the lighting department, I could feel the heat from the light-bulbs the minute we stepped off the escalator. Waiting twenty-five minutes in line at the *caisse,* register, I could feel sweat starting to form a puddle in my lower back. When we finally reached the counter, I said, "*Je voudrais un remboursement,*" quietly garbling the pronunciation of "reimbursement."

The woman responded quickly, using her hands to point me in multiple directions, listing a bunch of steps to take. I had no idea what she had said to me. Clearly, this was not going to be a Bed Bath & Beyond return. This was going to be a process, and it was a process I did not understand. I had to go to a special return counter on the floor where I'd purchased the lamp shades, then to a different counter on a different floor to do the actual transaction, and then back to the original counter in the lighting department to physically give the lamp shades back. Or at least it was something like that. After three different salespeople pointing in different directions and telling me different things to do, I still didn't know what to actually do. So I cried.

Apparently this is not just a BHV thing, but a French thing—returning something will take you all afternoon, so you must accept it as a lengthy activity, an event, and never approach it as a quick errand. Block out time in your calendar, and make sure to reward yourself with a stiff drink when finished. Returning things in France is so complicated, convoluted, and annoying that if I think there is even a one percent chance I might return something, I will not buy it.

The first attempt at making a return scarred my mom, and she refused to ever go back to BHV. That proved difficult, since many of her visits coincided with her helping me organize stuff in my apartment, which, by default, meant more trips to BHV. I always promised her the next time would be different. "I have it figured out, Mom. BHV is easier now, I swear." It never was. The pot-lid incident was the final straw. She is now officially on her own personal *grève du BHV*, BHV strike.

I think BHV also reminds her of what she witnessed during her first visit to Paris. She was hoping to find her daughter well settled, confident, and taking the city by storm, but instead she could feel the tension between Philip and me. I was eager to show her around the city and share new things with her, but I wasn't looking forward to the moments when we would argue in front of her. But it was inevitable. We were stressed and our relationship was too. Arguing over lamp shades was just the beginning. We bickered about the password to the bank account and the fact that I was the only one taking out the trash. We never used to fight like this. I didn't know what to do. And my mother could feel it.

Not wanting to be meddlesome, she asked me about it as casually as possible a few days into her visit, while nonchalantly looking through the pistachio-green-colored pears at the weekend market. We talked about everything, so bringing up my marriage wasn't that unexpected.

"I can tell that things aren't normal with you two. Are you all right?" I didn't respond for a few moments, avoiding her question, looking at anything but her eyes. Instead I watched wooden crates of leeks and lettuce roll by.

Keeping my head down, squeezing the same pears, I froze and didn't want to look up. I tried to hide the tears rolling slowly down my cheeks, shining in the cold autumn sunshine. There was no way to avoid it.

"Nothing is the same," I said, trying not to cry even more. "I feel like everything we had in New York has disappeared. I don't have a job. I don't make any money. And I don't feel empowered by just cooking dinner every night." She listened.

"Philip is stressed from work. He's stressed from trying to figure out how to work with the French. And, naturally, he's still dealing with the death of his mom. The dynamic of our relationship is gone. I have no control, and I feel helpless. And that's not how Philip used to make me feel. I don't feel like the woman I used to be."

Leaving the crate of pears, my mother walked over to the crate of onions. She took my hand tenderly. "Come on. There's only one thing that this situation calls for, and while it won't fix anything— only time and talking to each other will do that—it will make you feel better. Just like it always has."

I knew what she was talking about: miso soup. It was what she always made me when I was sick, believing that the broth, brown rice, and kale can make anyone feel better.

Back in the apartment, she started boiling the water. I stared as steam billowed out of the pot. She let me be, cutting onions and carrots, not pressing for any more information. It was such a relief to finally express my loneliness and confusion out loud, instead of constantly thinking about it in my head. She dissolved the miso paste into a small bowl of hot water, while the vegetables simmered in the pot. As she mixed in the paste, one tablespoon at a time until the soup reached the perfect flavor, she asked me, "Still no kale?" I'd told her all about my ongoing obsession with searching for the leafy green, and she was wishing she could have added it to the soup.

Happy to change the subject, I answered, "No luck there. And I actually think it's because it just isn't grown or sold here."

"It just seems so hard to believe that a simple cabbage like kale isn't grown here at all," she said. She had a point. Just because I'd done some research and confirmed that kale wasn't readily available in France didn't mean that I actually knew anything about the vegetable itself.

"Well, you should find out more," she said, placing a steaming bowl of soup in front of me. She gave my shoulders a squeeze and sat down. While the emptiness that I felt didn't disappear, the warm, salty broth, the hearty texture of the tofu, and the sweet bite of green peas were just what I needed to calm my nerves. The medicine my mother had been providing to me since I was a little girl had worked again, at least for the moment.

·· KALE MISO SOUP ··

Miso soup is a simple meal (so much so that I forget how simple it is). I like to make it for a quick weeknight meal—it pairs well with brown rice—and I also make it whenever I feel the first signs of a cold coming on or when I'm already stuck on the couch with the flu. I always have a tub of miso paste in my fridge to add to dressings, sauces, and even pesto, where it makes a great substitute for cheese.

INGREDIENTS

- 4 CUPS (960 ML) WATER
- 1 MEDIUM ONION, SLICED
- 2 MEDIUM CARROTS, SLICED
- 2 TO 4 TABLESPOONS MISO PASTE, TO TASTE
- 1 (14-OUNCE/400-G) PACKAGE TOFU, CUT INTO 1-INCH CUBES
- 3 CUPS (100 G) KALE, WASHED AND CHOPPED
- 1 TO 2 STRIPS DRIED WAKAME SEAWEED, SOAKED IN LUKEWARM WATER FOR 10 TO 15 MINUTES AND CHOPPED*
- ½ CUP (150 G) FROZEN GREEN PEAS

PREPARATION

Bring the water to a boil in a large pot. Add the onions and carrots, and cook for 3 to 5 minutes. Turn the heat down to a simmer. When the water is no longer boiling, ladle out one scoop into a small bowl. Add 1 tablespoon miso paste to the small bowl. Stir until the paste dissolves (note that pushing the paste up toward the sides of the bowl while stirring helps it dissolve faster). Repeat this step 1 to 3 times, until the desired flavor has been reached (more miso paste will produce a saltier soup), and pour the mixture into the pot. Be sure to keep the water from boiling, since boiling water will kill the good nutrients in the miso paste. Keeping the soup on low heat, add the tofu, kale, seaweed, and green peas, and cook for 3 minutes. Ladle the soup into serving bowls, and enjoy.

YIELD

· 4 SERVINGS

*This is not a must-have ingredient. The soup is still hearty and delicious without it!

Chapter 15

When I first started taking French lessons, I would spend a lot of time after class wandering the Left Bank, covering mile upon mile of cobblestone. To me, this side of the river was classic Paris. Exploring the tiny streets, I walked through the Jardin du Luxembourg, sitting on olive-green metal chairs watching nannies push *poussettes*, strollers, and a small group of nuns, dressed in gray and white quietly passed by. The gardens were a peaceful place to pass time. I window-shopped, gazing at the meticulous pastries, the *tarte au citron* filling without a dent and the spiraled *pain aux raisin* speckled with sweet raisins stacked in symmetrical rows. There were wooden toy shops and bookstores with worn encyclopedias piled in dusty windows.

Eating solo lunches, I would sit outside on random café terraces, unable to stop thinking about Philip and our relationship. I was afraid we'd made a mistake. Even more unsettling was that I was afraid *I'd* made a mistake. Did I get married too quickly? Was moving to Paris the wrong decision? Would this move unravel our relationship, which I'd always thought was unbreakable? Why did we leave New York? I'd given up everything, and now here I was with nothing and no one. The one person I thought was my rock wasn't capable of being there for me. And I wasn't doing such a great job of being there for him.

I was embarrassed to admit my doubts, so I kept them to myself. No one else knew what I was thinking or how I was feeling. Phone calls were chipper; I would tell tales of the bike ride we took through the city but not of the argument that ensued. I kept up the facade, posting brag-worthy Facebook status updates with photos of the Eiffel Tower at sunset or a glass of light pink rosé on a café table. After all, I was living in the City of Lights with my one true love. But that didn't mean a lot when the person I loved was unhappy and I didn't know how to comfort him and make things better.

❦

One gray afternoon, just as gray as the afternoon before it, as I was walking down the boulevard Saint-Michel and past the medieval gardens outside the Musée de Cluny, I saw a small restaurant called Le Petit Cluny. The name immediately reminded me of one of our favorite restaurants in New York City, Cafe Cluny, so I went in for that reason only. This café was nowhere near as nice as the corner restaurant in the West Village. It didn't have the history either. At least, not our history.

New York's Cafe Cluny was where everything had happened. It was where Philip made reservations for our third date. Walking into the dimly lit dining room a few minutes late, I found him leaning up against the bar, wearing a navy-blue cardigan and his Converse sneakers, typing away intensely on his Blackberry. He looked up and, seeing me, smiled, staring at me with his serious, brown eyes.

New York's Cafe Cluny had a frisée salad with crisp lettuce, a perfectly poached egg, and lardon that wasn't too fatty or too overdone. It was tossed with a tangy, creamy dressing and finished with a crunch of croutons on top.

New York's Cafe Cluny was where Philip took my mom and

stepdad, sweltering in the city's summer heat, to breakfast and asked their permission to propose. He told them of his plans and dreams, and that France was very likely to be in our future. He told them he loved me and wanted me to be his wife.

New York's Cafe Cluny was where we took my dad for dinner a few months before our wedding. A cheerful evening turned angry when, my lips loose from too much wine, I told him that he wouldn't be walking me down the aisle, but my stepdad would be instead. It ended in a drunken fight; the other patrons stared as my dad left the restaurant screaming and I ran home crying. It would be months before I would speak to him again.

New York's Cafe Cluny was where Philip and I had our last dinner before flying out to Paris. The restaurant was empty, many New Yorkers having fled town during Hurricane Irene and the Labor Day holiday weekend that followed it, but it was filled with our personal moments in time. New York's Cafe Cluny was special.

Paris's Le Petit Cluny mirrored how I felt—lonely, sad, and cold. It felt like a rest-stop diner with walls stained by old cigarette smoke and big-screen televisions broadcasting soccer games. The lighting was dingy, and the seats were made from cheap fabric. Their Salade Saint-Germain had limp frisée lettuce, lacking any bounce or curl, and a sour dressing. And to make it even worse, the poached egg was overcooked.

This was nothing like the frisée salad of Café Cluny. Not even close. After a few unsatisfying bites, I started to realize that I couldn't go on romanticizing a frisée salad. I could feel sorry for myself, or I could be excited about what was ahead. I could make my *own* salad.

Sitting there, watching the city happen in front of me, I thought about Philippa. She left Blackpool, England, for Geneva at age nineteen to embark on an equestrian career. She didn't speak French either, but she'd dreamt of a life with horses in the European country-side. And as she secured her status as a star show jumper, she read French philosophy, was adored by men who invited her to grand soirées, and was even featured in the French society pages of *Vogue*.

She fell in love, married, and had Philip when she was forty years old, only to have it all come crashing down six years later. And in an instant, she found herself back in England, with a young son, feeling lonely, sad, and cold. But she did it. She restarted her life, raised her son, and maintained her dignity. She was vivacious and independent. She was strong. She was always eternally brave and optimistic.

Paris's Le Petit Cluny was where I felt Philippa's presence, pushing me to keep my head up, to keep going. I knew I couldn't let her down. I would be there for Philip, for when he finally did cry. I would learn French and find my place. I would not be weak. Philippa once said to Philip, "France will make a woman out of Kristen." What she didn't realize was just how much of that transformation would be because of her.

·· KALE FRISÉE SOLO SALAD ··

There is a beautiful moment when the frisée salad first arrives. The poached egg sits gently on top, waiting to be punctured open, the yolk running down the valleys of the lettuce leaves. Frisée is a lettuce with curly tendrils that starts in shades of white near the roots and becomes a fresh green toward the tips. A member of the chicory family, it is cousins with radicchio and Belgian endive and has a slightly bitter taste. In traditional French frisée salads, the dressing and egg yolk create a warm creaminess that takes some of the edge off the bitterness. When I make my own version, I like to fry shallots in the grease from the lardons and add a few halved cherry tomatoes if they're in season.

INGREDIENTS

- 1 CUP (30 G) KALE, WASHED, DESTEMMED, AND FINELY CHOPPED
- ¼ HEAD (5 OUNCES/120 G) FRISÉE LETTUCE, WASHED AND BROKEN INTO BITE-SIZE PIECES
- 2 TABLESPOONS OLIVE OIL
- 1 TABLESPOON DIJON MUSTARD (ORIGINAL STYLE, WITHOUT VISIBLE MUSTARD SEEDS)
- 1 TABLESPOON SHERRY VINEGAR
- SALT AND FRESHLY GROUND BLACK PEPPER, TO TASTE
- ⅛ POUND (50 G) LARDONS (OR SUBSTITUTE BACON CUT INTO PIECES)
- 1 SHALLOT, CHOPPED (OPTIONAL)
- 1 TO 2 EGGS, POACHED SO YOLK STAYS RUNNY*

PREPARATION

Put the prepared greens on a plate. To make the dressing, mix 2 tablespoons of the olive oil with the Dijon mustard, sherry vinegar, salt, and pepper in a jar, and shake well.

Add the dressing to the greens, and toss lightly. Heat a small pan on medium heat. Fry the lardons in the pan for 10 to 15 minutes, or until crispy. Remove the lardons, setting them on a plate with a paper towel to drain the excess grease, and cover to keep warm. If using the shallots, add them to the pan, and fry them in the remaining lardon grease for 4 to 5 minutes, or until softened. Fill a small saucepan ¾ of the way with water and cover with a lid. Boil the water. When the water is boiling, crack an egg into the water, being careful not the break the yolk. Boil (poach) the egg for 2 minutes, until the egg white is cooked but the yolk still appears runny. Top the plate of lettuce with the lardons, shallots, cherry tomatoes, and poached egg, being careful not to break the yolk. Sprinkle with freshly cracked pepper, and serve.

YIELD

- 1 SERVING

You can use more than one poached egg if desired. The extra yolk makes the dish even creamier.

Chapter 16

I had turned a corner. My French was coming along, albeit slowly. Philip and I had started to settle into our new normal, talking through things and trying harder to understand how things were different and difficult for both of us. Life wasn't going to be the same as it had been in New York, and I had been foolish to think it would be. I decided that I wouldn't mourn my New York life any longer, and instead, I'd make Paris my own.

I had two tasks to tackle: finding out more about kale and trying to find a job. I attempted the easy one first: kale. Even though I loved kale, I didn't really know anything about the vegetable. And since my kale search was slowly becoming an obsession, it only made sense to learn more.

Now, after years of learning about kale and sharing it with others, I've found that people are always the most surprised to learn that it is actually a cabbage. Like the French (and probably most people), Americans have a negative view of cabbage as a boring, round, green or red vegetable that smells bad when boiled and gives people gas. Who wants cabbage? But in America, kale became a cool cabbage—or, perhaps more accurately, a cabbage disguised as a cool, heartier type of lettuce.

Cabbage and kale are part of the Brassicaceae family of plants, which also includes broccoli, brussels sprouts, cauliflower, collards, mustard greens, turnips, rutabaga, kohlrabi, radishes, and even horse-radish. It's an entire group of superfood vegetables. Kale is one of the oldest varieties of this family (also referred to as cruciferous vegeta-bles), estimated to be around four to six thousand years old years old. It is believed that kale was first grown in Asia Minor, consumed in Ancient Egypt, with Greece and Rome eventually following. In the Middle Ages, as new varieties of headed cabbages were bred, the leafy green fell out of favor (most likely because headed cabbages last longer after being harvested). But kale and all cabbages continued to be grown throughout northern Europe, where the weather is perfect for cabbage cultivation. That also explains why cabbage is prevalent in nineteenth-century paintings and photographs of market scenes. It's rare to see a photo of Paris's iconic central market, Les Halles, without a pile of headed cabbages somewhere in the background.

Different countries have their own relationships with kale. Philip knew the vegetable as "curly kale" from his childhood in England. In Scotland, it's so commonly grown that kitchen gardens are referred to as "kale gardens." A popular Halloween game in eighteenth-century Scotland and Ireland was for young men and women to pull kale stalks out of the ground in order to predict what their future spouses would be like. Kale is grown in the Netherlands, but there, they never harvest *boerenkool* before the first frost, which results in a very subtle and sweeter taste. Northern Germany is home to a winter festival called Kohlfahrt that is based around *grünkohl*, kale and beer. In Japan, powders and strong elixirs are made from the green. In Italy, the deep-green variety with blistered skin (what Americans call lacinato or dinosaur kale) is known as *cavolo nero*, black cabbage, and is commonly sold at markets and used in cuisine.

So what happened in France? Why, in a country where food is so central to the culture, was this particular cabbage not grown or even sold at markets? Unfortunately, I've never found a straight answer, but I have been told a few theories. The first is that cabbage is cheap, and cheap food is eaten a lot during wars, and after two world wars, cabbage became associated with hardship and poverty. No one in France wanted to be reminded of it. Even though some varieties of cabbage were still grown, kale didn't make the cut. The second hypothesis is that the growth of French industrial agriculture after the second World War was based primarily in southern France, a warm region where cabbage, a cold-weather vegetable, doesn't thrive. Since what southern producers grew largely determined what vegetables were available throughout the country, kale was never a common offering. The last theory is that, unlike Italian cuisine, French cuisine simply doesn't use kale and, therefore, there was very little need to grow it for any purpose other than fodder for animals or ornamental uses, which is why you might occasionally see random stalks sprouting up at various parks and gardens.

But, to be fair, America certainly wasn't ahead of the rest of the world when it came to kale. When I was growing up, my mom and I would joke about asking restaurants if they would use their side garnish of kale on our plates. "Maybe I'll go back into the kitchen and ask them to steam a little for us," she would say. Pizza Hut was once the largest consumer of kale in America, but only because they used the leaves as decoration over the ice in the salad bar. Kale was nothing cool—but at least we could always find it.

Then, around 2010, kale started to make it big. Google searches for kale nearly quadrupled between 2011 and 2014. For Americans always searching for the latest quick-fix diet trick, kale was the new health-food darling, at a time when the idea of "superfoods" was becoming part of our daily lexicon. With more calcium in one cup than a glass of milk, more iron per calorie than beef, a lot of fiber, and loads of antioxidants, it's no surprise that kale achieved queen of greens status.

People always ask me, "Why did kale become so popular?" Aside from the fact that it's so healthy, kale was on the rise just as the food world began to explode online. Between food blogs, celebrity influence, and social media activities, like "food porn" photos being posted on Instagram, the Internet gave kale a platform that other foods, like arugula and sun-dried tomatoes, didn't have when they became trendy in the nineties. It was easy for online conversations around kale to grow, and it quickly became an Internet star. Soon it was hard to avoid seeing kale—in salads, chips, juices, cocktails, soups, and, eventually, even in candles, nail polishes, makeup, and face washes. Kale was *everywhere*.

Except France.

※

Next it was time to find a job. When I left New York, I assumed that I would work in advertising again. I kept reminding myself that Philip and his colleagues were sure that plenty of agencies needed people who were native English speakers.

I updated my résumé, wrote a cover letter, and gathered references from previous bosses. I applied to every ad agency in Paris through their online application systems—except where Philip worked. Their Paris office was much smaller than the New York headquarters, and I didn't want to work in such close proximity to my husband. But when I clicked "send," my résumé went into the black hole of job applications. I had no way to follow up or even confirm that someone had received my information. And no one contacted me. Taking Elaine Sciolino up on the offer she'd made when she signed my copy of her book, I sent her an email, hoping that maybe her high-profile connection might lead to something. I never heard back.

Finally, through a headhunter in New York, I was able to secure an interview with a hot agency called BETC. They had an office in London as well, so I went into the interview hopeful that they might have a few English-speaking positions. I walked up to the office wearing a skirt and blazer for the first time in months. It felt good to be in professional clothes again. There were crowds of people outside the main door, drinking espresso in plastic cups, smoking, and talking—like the French version of the water cooler.

The interview went well, and the HR person seemed impressed with my New York experience. The catch? There were jobs for native English speakers, as I assumed, but applicants also needed to be fluent in French. I was out of luck. The HR woman pursed her lips. "Call me in January," she said. "We'll see if anything pops up." Holiday vacations were approaching, which meant I would be out of sight, out of mind, so I knew it was very unlikely that anything was going to "pop up." And I was right. Nothing ever did.

I left the office feeling discouraged. I wanted to work again. I missed interacting with a team, meeting the expectations of a boss, and brainstorming on projects that involved specific deliverables and actual results. There was a huge part of me that really just missed showing up. I was ready to start *doing* something again.

Feeling glum, I boarded the *métro* and was lucky enough to snag a seat by the doors. It was nearing rush hour, and the car was filling up quickly. This train was one of the older models, dirty and tired, with windows that had been sprayed with graffiti, cleaned, and sprayed again. The seats were worn and tattered, the cushion thinning, and I could feel the springs in my back.

Paris's *métro* system, which carries nearly four million people per day, is a well-oiled machine that makes New York City's subway look like amateur hour. It works like clockwork, with trains coming almost every two to three minutes in every direction, and commuters actually *know* when they're coming thanks to the signs at each station. There are rarely delays, and you can trust that you'll get where you need to be without much issue. It's reliable and efficient enough that I don't give it a second thought while I'm riding the trains. Except for this day.

The train halted to a stop mid-tunnel. What was going on? The train never stops mid-tunnel. The lights went out. Passengers sputtered sighs, and I heard a lot of "*Oh là là.*" A dim emergency light, as if from a back-alley tattoo parlor, flickered on, illuminating a quarter of the train. The conductor spoke over the intercom, which produced more static than actual words, making it even more difficult for me to understand what he said. I could hear *patience* and *merci.* I had no idea what was going on, and the people around me seemed restless and worried.

After the announcement, there were more sighs and lip sputters. It didn't sound like good news. I settled deeper into my seat, trying to remain calm. The air immediately grew stale, smelling of soot, cigarettes, and bodies.

I checked my phone and luckily still had service. It was 5:40 p.m. I sent Philip a text message.

> Stuck in the metro. Not sure why we are stopped or what's going on. Might not be able to get to dinner tonight. X

I hadn't eaten since breakfast, having been too nervous about the interview, and by now I was starving. I rummaged through my bag and there, among all the Parisian black, was a bright, shiny orange. I was tempted. My phone rang. It was Philip.

"Darling! What's going on? Are you OK? How was the interview?"

"I'm fine," I whispered, not wanting to draw attention to myself by speaking English. "The interview was OK but now I'm stuck in the *métro.* The train stopped between two stations."

"What's going on? Did anyone say anything?"

"I couldn't understand the intercom. Thank goodness I have a seat."

"Why don't you ask someone?"

"What? No way! I'm not going to speak English out loud on this overcrowded train. Luckily I used the bathroom at the agency. And I'm starving!"

"You're like a little kid. I need to pack you off with biscuits."

"No! I brought an orange...but I'm afraid to eat it."

"Darling, why on earth would you be afraid to eat an orange?"

"Everyone will smell it," I said. It was the delicious scent; I knew the moment I peeled it, the smell of citrus would permeate the car. I wanted to remain anonymous, and the orange wouldn't help.

"Kristen," Philip said, getting serious—he rarely used my first name. "Just eat the orange."

"Nope. I'm too afraid. I won't do it."

"OK, your call. I'm busy. I have to run to a meeting. I'll be home at eight thirty. Keep me posted and be safe. And eat the bloody orange."

After an hour of standing still underground, the train finally lurched forward, the doors opening and clapping closed, and another twenty minutes later, I was at my stop and aboveground. Not having touched the orange, I was famished and cold. I wanted nothing more than something warm and hearty to eat, like French onion soup— which, of course, is just called soupe à l'oignon or soupe à l'oignon gratinée in France. And it was the perfect night for it.

The markets were already closed for the evening, so I did what a lot of Parisians do and went to the nearest supermarché. Many people have a romantic notion about life in France, that every single person is cooking with fresh vegetables harvested from their own gardens earlier that morning. They envision every meal being cooked from scratch three times a day. I challenge this notion, especially as it applies to Paris.

I'm not saying that Parisians don't ever cook fresh from the market, but they generally don't have gardens, and—despite their thirty-five-hour work week and five weeks of vacation—the French work hard and tend to return home late in the evening, which means sometimes food is coming from the grocery store. No one is perfect all the time.

Rushing around the food floor of Monoprix, I grabbed a bag of precut frozen onions, a bag of shallots, and a baguette that had most likely been baked in an industrial factory outside the city. Back at the apartment, I poured the onions into the pot, slowly caramelizing them over low heat, and chopped the shallots. Sipping a glass of red wine, I grated a hunk of cheese and sliced the bread, preparing the gratin dishes for the oven. As I grated in a rhythm, I thought about the day.

Aside from the fact that I was afraid to eat an orange, maybe it wasn't such a bad thing that I was having a hard time finding a job. Maybe I could look into pursuing other interests, or maybe I could take the time to become really good at French. Maybe I could write more, or even start my own blog, although I didn't know what it would be about. I was in a very, very fortunate position where I didn't have to work to make ends meet, so perhaps this *petite pause,* this little break, could give me the opportunity to figure out a new career. I'd enjoyed advertising but I didn't necessarily feel passionate about the actual products I worked on. Maybe I could find a way to get kale to Paris. Hah. At first it felt like a silly, fleeting thought, a nearly impossible endeavor for someone who still had so much to learn about living in France.

Pushing the idea out of my head, I pulled a head of lettuce out of the fridge for a simple salad. Blossoming like a flower, revealing light green leaves on the inside, it was still fresh even though I'd purchased it a few days before. My onions from Monoprix were fine, but it really does pay to buy produce from the outdoor market. And for dessert? I settled on an orange.

·· KALE AND ONION SOUP ··

If we are eating lunch at a brasserie, I love ordering soupe a l'oignon—*especially if it's a cold day. I've noticed that not all onion soups are created equal. Some are really salty, leaving me desperate for a* carafe d'eau, *others have only a few onions and gobs of melted cheese, while some have spoonfuls of soft, caramelized onions and thick crusty bread. This onion soup does not use beef stock, so the sweetness of the onions really shines, and I prefer to keep them as the star of the dish.*

INGREDIENTS

- 3 TABLESPOONS OLIVE OIL
- 8 MEDIUM ONIONS, THINLY SLICED
- 6 SHALLOTS, DICED
- ½ HEAD OF GARLIC, DICED
- 6 CUPS (200 G) KALE, WASHED, DESTEMMED, AND CHOPPED
- 1 TABLESPOON SUGAR
- 2 SPRIGS FRESH THYME, LEAVES ONLY
- 1 BAY LEAF
- 2 CUPS (480 ML) WHITE WINE
- 2 CUPS (480 ML) WATER OR VEGETABLE BROTH
- 1 BAGUETTE, SLICED
- 1 TO 2 CUPS (100 TO 200 G) GRUYÈRE CHEESE, GRATED AND TIGHTLY PACKED, TO TASTE
- SALT AND FRESHLY GROUND BLACK PEPPER, TO TASTE

PREPARATION

Preheat the oven to 250°F (120°C). Heat the olive oil in a large pot over medium heat. Add the onions, shallots, and garlic. Cook, stirring continuously, for 5 to 7 minutes until softened. Add the sugar, thyme, and bay leaf, and mix. Continue to cook, stirring frequently, for another 15 to 20 minutes, until the onions and shallots are caramelized and a buttery brown color. Add the kale, and continue to stir for 3 minutes. The kale will lightly cook. Add the water or vegetable broth, and season with the salt and pepper. Bring to a boil, and then simmer for 20 minutes. Before serving, remove bay leaf. While the soup is simmering, prepare four oven-safe gratin bowls. Put 2 to 3 slices of baguette in the bottom of each bowl, and top with a small handful of cheese. When the soup is ready, ladle it into each bowl, add another slice of baguette, and sprinkle another small handful of cheese on top. Bake in the oven for 5 minutes, or until the cheese on top is melted. Let the bowls cool slightly, and serve.

YIELD

- 4 SERVINGS

Chapter 17

Learning French was confusing for hundreds of reasons. French relies heavily on the subjunctive verb tense, which is used infrequently in English. I never knew where to put articles and pronouns. There can often be multiple words for the same thing, which happened to be the case with kale. To this day, one of the most common questions I'm asked is, "What is kale in French?" Google Translate told me that kale was *chou frisé*, but through my research, I also learned it was also *chou plume*. And *chou frisé vert, chou frisé non-pommé, chou frangé, chou cavalier, chou à lapin*, and *chou à vache*. There were so many names for kale, I didn't know how to ask for it anymore.

I quickly realized that if I was going to survive speaking the French language, I would have to spend a lot of time faking it. As long as I knew a few words and phrases, I could make my way through a simple conversation and try to pretend that I knew what in the world was going on. Doing the same activities repeatedly helped. After a few times I would know what to expect, what questions to anticipate, and what my replies should be. The habitual nature of errands almost became a comfort to me, or at least made me feel like I'd mastered some basic level of the language.

Of course, that tactic didn't work when I was doing an errand for the first time. I was a deer caught in the headlights when the dry cleaner asked me if I wanted Philip's shirts folded or on hangers. Loyalty programs posed a problem too. I was clueless when the cashier at Monoprix told me what discounts I had from the loyalty program. Caught off guard by aggressive salespeople, I'd done things like buy facials for 50 percent off or join a monthly wine club. It was always easier to agree to the offer than it was to admit that I had no idea what the person was saying. So I'd sign up, crossing my fingers each time, hoping I hadn't signed my life away.

I would also routinely show up for appointments and dinner reservations at the wrong time. Sometimes the restaurant wouldn't even have my reservation, even though I knew I'd called earlier that morning to confirm it. Learning military time was hard enough, but adding the complex French number system on top of it was too much for my brain to handle. I'd show up for a haircut at *trois heure*, (three o'clock) instead of *treize heure* (one o'clock). One time I thought I'd made an appointment with a dermatologist only to be told by the doctor that he was an anesthesiologist, *after* I'd showed him the rash on my underarms. He was a cute doctor too.

At least I wasn't the only one who made French faux pas. Philip, although not French, is incredibly fluent, and even he was corrected many times. Perhaps it was because of just how complicated accomplishing things could be.

One of his least favorite activities was dealing with Orange, our Internet and cable provider. The problem was that our Internet, which was set up in the kitchen, didn't work any farther than the kitchen. We'd been trying to fix it for months but kept being told that it was the fault of our apartment, our kitchen, the walls of our building, and even our *quartier*. Apparently the entire Seventeenth arrondissement had crappy Internet service.

Then one day, the future arrived: fiber-optic cables. Surely, we thought, this would solve everything. But not so fast—weeks after the installation, the Internet still didn't work.

Philip had finally managed to schedule a phone appointment, which is done by calling Orange and being told that they would call you back—when they wanted to. And if you missed the call? Well, the process would have to start over again.

They first called while he was at work. Going back and forth with the Orange representative for over an hour, she asked him various questions about the problem.

After going around in circles with the service representative, she said, "I'm going to put you on hold for ten minutes."

"*D'accord*, all right," he said. "I'm going to take the phone with me while I get a coffee," he told the woman, referencing the office coffee machine a few rooms over from his office.

"Well, *monsieur*, I wouldn't mind a coffee right now but I do not get a coffee. Why do you think you should be able to get a coffee right now and not me?" she asked him. Philip wasn't sure how to respond. After being on hold again, she finally told him she would have to call him back when he was at home. Would he be home at 4:45 in the afternoon?

He didn't really have a choice, which is why I found him on the phone, tangling himself in wires from the router, landline, and cable box and cutting through a block of gruyère, stress-eating thick pieces by the slice with an irritated look on his face. I heard him speaking very clear, concise French over the phone, explaining the situation to the service rep, when suddenly he stopped midsentence.

"Well?" I asked him, hoping that the problem had been fixed. "What did she say?"

"She hung up on me," he said, shocked. "She said, 'Well, *monsieur*, we can't all speak French like Molière.'"

Apparently the French even ridicule each other when they speak French. It was no wonder I didn't know what to call kale. I had no hope.

❧

"Philip!" I cried out from the couch when I heard a knock on our front door. He was in the shower and didn't hear me. The person knocked again. I had no choice but to drag my jet-lagged butt off the couch, wearing only my bathrobe, to answer the mysterious knock.

We had just arrived in Paris from our Thanksgiving visit to America that morning, and I was already depressed about my lost, kale-filled suitcases, which had yet to be found. I'd only slept for one hour on the plane, so that wasn't helping my mood. Ten o'clock in the morning felt like four o'clock in the morning, and my head was fuzzy. The realization was setting in that I had to try to speak French again, which I had happily forgotten over the past three weeks. The loud knocking continued.

"*Bonjour. J'habite à côté.*" Hello, I live next door, is what the mystery knocker said to me when I finally opened the door. He was of average height, with short brown hair, and he was wearing a tight, long-sleeved shirt tucked into blue jeans that were pulled up high on his waist.

Unfortunately, what I'd heard was, "*Bonjour. J'habite ecoutez.*" Hello. I live listen! I stood there speechless, staring at him, pleading with my brain to flip on the switch to speak or understand even a tiny bit of the language. I wasn't asking for much, but it wouldn't cooperate.

"*Bonjour,*" I said back. That was all I had. Hello.

The man, who I would learn was our next-door neighbor, continued to speak to me, motioning toward his door.

"Philip!" I screamed, louder this time, putting out my index finger to ask the man to pause.

Philip, convinced that something was wrong given the distress in my voice, came running out, dripping wet, half-wearing a towel. "What? What is it?" he asked, concerned, thinking something much worse had happened than someone at our door. I stood in front of the open door, still speechless, motioning toward our neighbors. What a way to meet them for the first time.

His name was Regis, and he and his wife were hosting a Christmas party the next week; he wanted to know if we could attend. "There will be entertainment," he promised.

If I were Regis, I never would have invited us. I took one look at ourselves when Philip shut the door, and we were a sorry sight. I was exhausted, with bags under my eyes and my hair sticking out in every direction, and Philip was half-naked. I wouldn't have invited us to our *own* party. Then again, it is customary in France to invite your next-door neighbors to your parties, even if it takes you months to actually meet them, as a courtesy. This being our first invite, we decided to attend.

❦

The following Sunday evening, we heard guests begin to arrive next door. We'd stalled for long enough; it was time to go over.

As we waited at the front door, Philip whispered to me, "What are their names again?"

"I have no idea," I answered. "Regis? Rungis? I didn't hear the wife's name."

"Regis and Kelly," Philip whispered to me as the door was about to open, referencing his past fascination with American morning television programs. I muffled my laughter as the door opened.

We were ushered in, the apartment a mirror image of ours, only with modern furniture and abstract paintings on the wall, which Regis had painted himself. Sidling up to us, he handed us each a thimble-sized glass of red wine, saying, "*Bonjour*. Thank you for coming." He quickly turned and walked away, leaving us in the foyer. It would not be the first time I thought to myself, *Regis is one strange guy*.

We hesitantly moved into the dining room, where there was a group of ten people that we spent the next few minutes introducing ourselves to.

"*Bonjour. Je suis* Kristen." Kiss. Kiss.

"*Bonjour. Je suis* Mathilde." Kiss. Kiss.

"*Enchanté*."

"*Enchanté*."

And so it continued until I had met and double kissed every person in the room. It was at this moment that I realized I no longer found *la bise* romantic and missed the informality of a good handshake. No leaning in. No chances of accidentally kissing a stranger on the lips because we both did not start on the correct cheek. Although *la bise* was only on the cheek, there was something that still felt very intimate to me. Not to mention, I always found kissing someone I probably wasn't going to talk to odd. Sometimes I missed a good, old-fashioned, American hug.

By the time the kissing was completed, our wine was gone, but Regis never came around with more. A small bowl of potato chips and a savory German cake (Regis's wife was German) sat on the dining room table next to a bowl of clementines.

Half an hour later, Regis announced that the entertainment was ready. Instructed to move into the living room, where he had set up rows of folding chairs, Philip and I sat, empty thimble cups in hand, and waited. Regis dimmed the lights, and a woman dressed in a leotard, fishnet stockings, boa, and mask slinked from the foyer into the dining room. Prancing and dancing around a sole chair, she shimmied and shook her way across the floor, flinging the boa and rolling down her stockings. Regis's "entertainment" was full-on burlesque. And Philip and I were stuck there, the safety of our apartment literally only a few feet away.

We never did learn Regis's wife's name and now, years later, it would be too embarrassing to ask, so Regis and Kelly stuck. Regis still doesn't say much and always appears in the hallway at inopportune moments, making our conversation even more awkward than it already is. He still invites us to their parties, but we no longer go, instead enjoying the sounds of their entertainment through the walls, from the comfort of our couch.

※

There are two things about Paris that always surprise Americans. The first is that Paris doesn't have good weather. Paris has almost as many cloudy and rainy days as London. The second is that France is much farther north than you might think; in fact, the latitude of Paris is farther north than that of Fargo, North Dakota. Winter mornings are very dark, with the sun not rising until nearly nine o'clock.

Although it wasn't at first, December is now one of my favorite months here. Because the days are so short, the sky never entirely lightens up, and because the sun rarely shines, there is a gray mist enveloping the city. Sometimes the brightest part of the day is the flashing green light from a pharmacy. It's not freezing, but there is a humid chill to the air, which means a cozy sweater and big scarf are a necessity.

And Christmas in Paris is classic. Stores are open on Sundays, and more and more commercialism has crept into the weeks leading up to the holiday, but despite that, it's still easy to experience a simple and traditional Christmas in the city (although, to my dismay, in 2014,

I started to notice a lot more sales and "Black Friday" promotions). Streets are decked out with lights hanging from building to building, spelling out *Joyeux Fêtes* or *Bonne Noël*. The Champs-Élysées is illuminated along the sides, each tree adorned with twinkling lights, leading the way to a Ferris wheel, shining bright at place de la Concorde. There are Christmas markets throughout the city, a popular location being along the Champs-Élysées near the Grand Palais. Stalls selling cheeses, sauerkraut, sausages, potatoes in big vats, cotton candy, hot chestnuts, bonbons, knitted hats and scarves, and small gifts are lined up in rows. During the evenings, Santa and his sleigh appear in the sky, as little children dressed in red and navy wool overcoats look up into the sky with awe. Families and couples walk up and down the streets, drinking *chocolat chaud* and eating sweets.

Philip and I decided to stay in France for our first Christmas. We were excited to decorate a tree together, as we'd done the previous two years in New York. It was the end of the day, and the sky was already dark. Our neighborhood businesses had decorated with vintage-style flashing lights in the shapes of snowflakes and snowmen, illuminating the street corners with red, green, and white lights.

Trees were being sold at the flower shop across the street from Madame Fix-It. Happy to have Philippa's fur hat to keep me warm, I walked up with Philip right as they were unloading a fresh shipment from Russia. This was a lot different than heading to the tree farm and cutting one down, like I did as a child with my parents. Families huddled together, children riding in and out of flowers on their scooters. Madame Fix-It leaned against her shop window smoking a cigarette, looking on as the tree selection chaos ensued.

Personally, I had sticker shock. 120€?! Even the smallest "Charlie Brown" tree that barely reached my knees was 80€. Closing my eyes and pushing the price tag out of my head, we found a tree we liked.

Tall and full, it would stand beautifully in the corner of our living room, framed by the elegant crown molding.

The trunk was supported by another big hunk of pine wood. I wasn't sure how this would fit into our tree stand, and without a tree stand, how would we water the tree?

"*Monsieur, ce n'est pas possible*. And not necessary," the saleswoman said when Philip asked. "These trees do not need to be watered at all. They will easily stay fresh through the month and both holidays," she assured us, referring to both Christmas and New Year's Day. It was only December 5. I was skeptical that a living plant would be able to stay fresh for an entire month *without* water, but what did I know?

Trimming the tree was calming. I played George Winston in the background and talked about every ornament as I took it out of the box. I found the few that Philip and I had bought together at Bloomingdale's during our first Christmas, which already felt so long ago. I laid the ornaments out on the couch and the chair, and we started to string the new lights we'd bought the day before at the department store Galeries Lafayette. Philip strung them around and around, plugged them in and, *voilà*, the entire living room was illumi-nated with an LED light show. Never one for colored Christmas lights, I was also not one for colored LED Christmas lights that pulsated to different rhythms. But they were the only option available at Galeries Lafayette. The store had fluorescent pink, orange, green, yellow, red, and multicolored lights that flashed quickly, slowly, or a combination of the two, the jolting rhythms like a cheap massage chair. It was impossible to find simple, white Christmas lights.

❦

Traditionally in France, the main emphasis of the holiday celebration is placed on Christmas Eve dinner, with feasts of foie gras, oysters, and champagne. Philip and I also decided to celebrate on Christmas Eve, but with a traditional English Sunday roast, just like he had done with his mother year after year.

Even though I no longer had a hang-up about going to the butcher, my task for a Sunday roast is all about cooking the perfect side dish of roasted vegetables. I was becoming more familiar with some of the local producers at the weekend organic market, and I knew that by this time of year, they'd have the root vegetables I needed for our Christmas feast.

That morning at the market, sidewalk corners icy, my breath forming clouds of warm condensation in the air, I walked up to one of my favorite stands and saw the woman who regularly works there, sipping her habitual glass of rosé and chatting with other market-goers. She had dark, wiry hair and teeth stained from many years of smoking cigarettes. She smiled at me, greeting me with a raspy *bonjour*! My heart warmed. It was nice to finally be recognized by someone other than Philip.

My eyes scanned the table as I decided what to choose for the roast. I saw cone-shaped, cream-colored parsnips, yellow-tinted rutabaga, dimpled celery root caked in dirt, carrots of all different sizes, deep red beets with long roots, and turnips that were white on one side and purple on the other, as if they'd been painted with violet watercolors. I wanted everything. I also bought a few heads of garlic, long leeks, and a handful of tiny, crisp endive.

I walked home through the Marché Poncelet and saw families walking together with their large plates of *fruits des mer* piled high with oysters, shrimp, whelk, and the spiky, curly heads of sea urchins. Wine shops encouraged passersby to pick up a last-minute bottle of rosé champagne and the line outside *boulangeries* went down the street, sometimes wrapping around the corner.

We had everything we needed. The roast from our butcher, a cheese plate that was intended for way more than two, red wine, horseradish cream imported from England, and the ingredients for Yorkshire pudding, which Philip always puts in the oven at the last minute, signaling that it's almost time to eat. I set the table, lighting candles and placing the silver cutlery that Philippa had left me. It was old, having come originally from a Swiss château, the knives were dull, and the forks had crooked tines, but it looked pretty on the table. It was nice to have a part of Philippa with us for the evening. I placed branches of holly in a small vase and stepped back and stared, LED lights flashing behind me. Dinner for two. This would be the first time I would spend a holiday away from my family. I wasn't sure if I felt more grown-up or melancholy.

Philip called out, startling me out of my trance; "I put the Yorkshires in the oven! Get ready!" A roast with my husband was always a dramatic affair, like most things he does.

Walking back and forth along the long hallway from the kitchen to the dining room, we brought out all the dishes, ending with the muffin trays that held each individual Yorkshire pudding, popping out and puffed up high.

Mid-meal, I topped up our wine. "So, I've had an idea," I began. "I can't stop thinking about kale. You've seen how it's become this weird obsession. Everywhere I look, I see leafy greens or a near mirage of leafy greens. I'm constantly searching."

"Trust me, I know," Philip said.

"So, I want to bring kale to Paris."

Philip laughed. "What?!"

"I know it sounds crazy," I continued, "and I don't mean trying to bring a few bunches in suitcases. We saw how that worked out. I mean somehow have easier access to it. I have no idea where to begin or how I would do it, but there is no reason why France should not have kale."

"I love it," he said. "What are you thinking? When did you decide this? It's brilliant!" I've always loved my husband's enthusiasm for even the smallest things.

I went on, talking off the top of my head and, for the first time, really thinking about how bringing kale to France could work. "Well, we could import it from Germany or the Netherlands." I paused. "But that would be ridiculous since the vegetable can easily grow here. In fact, France has the perfect climate for growing kale," I said, laying out the first option. "Or," I continued, grabbing another Yorkshire pudding to go with my plate of roasted roots, "we could find some land and grow it ourselves?"

Philip laughed even harder, almost spitting out his food. "Darling, you're the worst. You can't even keep a houseplant alive." He had a point. I was not a farmer. And besides, the red tape we would have to deal with to rent land was a daunting prospect.

"OK. So then what if I found a farmer and somehow convinced the farmer to grow kale? And maybe I could ask a chef at a restaurant to use the kale the farmer grows? An exchange. An experiment." My mind was racing, coming up with ideas faster than I could speak. Perhaps it was the red wine we kept drinking, but for the first time in months, I was feeling energized and inspired by something.

"It's crazy and weird, but if it worked, it could be really cool," Philip said.

"Plus it might fill the big gaping hole on my résumé," I added, very aware that five years of nothing was not going to help me find a job when we one day did move back to America.

We began brainstorming ideas. I pictured working with farmers, harvesting kale, and selling it to people, in the style of community-supported agriculture, or CSA, except this would be a CSA just for kale. I imagined cooking demos and tastings at health-food stores. By the time we finished our meal, a vision had started to come together.

"It will just be a project to work on," I said to Philip. "A project about kale. The Kale Project."

What did I have to lose? If it didn't work, then it didn't work. But it was worth trying.

Our Christmas tree didn't stay alive through December, as the shop-keeper had promised, but we kept it up, even though it was a dried, dehydrated, nearly brown, leaning tower of pine needles by the end of the month.

For New Year's Eve, we had Liz, my new friend from the expat day, and her French husband, Ed, over for New Year's Eve dinner. Lamenting about the tree, Ed said, "Just throw it out your front window. It's easier that way! It's what all the other Parisians do!"

The next morning, knowing we weren't going to throw our tree out the window, taking it out—down the steps—was our first order of business. But that didn't mean that we were going to dress for the occasion. Still in our pajamas, without any underwear, Philip and I started to carry the tree out the front door and tried to shove it into the elevator. The plastic bag meant to make disposing of the tree "easy" ripped the minute it touched the sharp needles, and what pine needles were left started flaking off, covering the hallway carpet. Hearing all of the noise as we wrestled with the tree, Regis poked his head out of his front door.

"*Salut! Ça va?*" He asked if we were all right. *Ça va?* Did we *look* all right? We were covered in sharp, sticky pine needles and struggling to cram a parched tree into a tiny elevator—our pale, nude behinds nearly hanging out of our pajama pants. Definitely not *ça va*. Instead of offering to help, Regis stood at his front door and looked on silently as we continued to maneuver the tree downstairs.

The elevator was not an option, which meant Philip had to carry the tree down the stairs. By the time the tree was outside on the curb, there was barely a pine needle still attached to the dead plant. He spent the next hour vacuuming the stairs, wondering how everyone else in our building managed to get rid of their trees.

Ed was right. We should have thrown it out the window.

·· YORKSHIRE PUDDING ··

Philip has brought a few dishes into my life that have become staples: spaghetti Bolognese, beef stroganoff, and his English Sunday roast with Yorkshire pudding. We bake ours in muffin pans for individual servings, but the traditional method is in a square baking dish, which results in one large, square-shaped pudding that serves as a base for the roast. According to Philip, people actually use the pudding as a plate and then eat it at the end of the meal. I don't know if that's true, but it would make cleaning up a lot easier.

INGREDIENTS

- 3 LARGE EGGS
- 1 CUP (120 G) ALL-PURPOSE FLOUR
- 1 CUP (220 ML) WHOLE MILK
- PINCH OF SALT AND 2 PINCHES OF FRESHLY GROUND BLACK PEPPER

PREPARATION

Preheat the oven to 425°F (225°C). Prepare two 6-cup muffin pans (or one 12-cup pan) by coating each cup with ¼ teaspoon of olive oil. Place the pans in oven for 15 minutes, so oil becomes very hot. Crack the eggs into a large bowl. Lightly break the yolks with fork, and mix. Add the flour and milk, and whisk together. Add the salt and pepper, and whisk until all ingredients are smooth and combined, like the consistency of pancake batter. Remove the trays from the oven, and pour the batter into the muffin pans, until each cup is about ¾ full. Put the pans in the oven, and bake for 12 to 17 minutes, until each pudding rises, and is golden brown on top. Let cool slightly, and serve.

YIELD

- 12 SERVINGS

·· EPIC ROASTED VEGETABLES ··

The title of this recipe sounds much more amazing than it actually is. Don't get me wrong—roasted vegetables are, indeed, one of my favorite things to prepare, but this dish is so simple that there isn't really anything that epic about it. What I do find pretty great is that roasted vegetables can be made year-round, and it's one of the easiest ways to enjoy whatever vegetables are in season. In the winter, chop up leeks, endive, parsnips, onions, garlic cloves, and squash. In the summer, use eggplant, zucchini, yellow squash, and red peppers as a great side dish for grilled fish. Roasting vegetables is the best way to celebrate what's happening at the market. In this recipe, I've provided suggestions for each season. You'll want to use enough vegetables (about 4 pounds or 2 kg) to fill a 13 x 9-inch (34 x 25-cm) roasting pan.

INGREDIENTS

- WINTER: ENDIVE, ONIONS, GARLIC, SUNCHOKES, WINTER SQUASH, SHALLOTS, BEETS
- SPRING: ASPARAGUS, CAULIFLOWER, LEEKS, RADISHES
- SUMMER: EGGPLANT, SUMMER SQUASH, PEPPERS, TOMATOES
- AUTUMN: CELERY ROOT, BRUSSELS SPROUTS, CARROTS, TURNIPS, PARSNIPS, MUSHROOMS, BROCCOLI
- ¼ CUP (60 ML) OLIVE OIL
- FINISHING SALT, TO TASTE

PREPARATION

Preheat the oven to 400°F (200°C). Clean the vegetables, and chop into large cubes or slices. (For example, eggplant can be quartered and then sliced into 1-inch/2½-cm pieces.) Try to chop the vegetables into consistent sizes, so they'll cook evenly. Put the chopped vegetables in an 13 x 9-inch

(34 x 25-cm) roasting pan. Pour the olive oil into the pan, and, using your hands, mix the vegetables together, coating them in the oil. Roast in the oven for 40 to 55 minutes, stirring a few times to make sure the vegetables roast evenly. The vegetables should be tender but still crisp. Season with a sprinkle of finishing salt if desired. I personally find the juices of the vegetables to be flavorful enough!

YIELD

- 4 SERVINGS

Chapter 18

J'en ai marre!, I am fed up!" Daniella bellowed, her tiny body gliding across the wooden floor, smacking legs that were out of place and pinching arms that were bent at awkward angles. We weren't working hard enough for her. "J'en ai marre!" she said again. This time she was really upset at our laziness, yelling her favorite phrase out the condensation-covered window that had been steamed up from our hot breath and sweat. Everyone in the courtyard café below could hear that Daniella's class was not dancing well enough for her standards. I wasn't helping the situation any. At one end of the *barre*, in the back of the room, I hoped to stay out of her sight today. I had a lot more on my mind than following ballet warm-ups, and my performance only confirmed that my head wasn't in it today.

Going through the motions—*tendu, plié, tendu, grand plié*—I was thinking about the Kale Project idea again. I had been excited when Philip and I first spoke about it, but now it was almost spring, months had gone by, and I still hadn't started anything. I repeated the next *barre* combination in my head—*relevé, piqué, grand fondu*. I had been afraid. What if the project didn't work? What if I couldn't find a farmer? Would people think it was stupid? Putting myself out there was half the battle. *Second position, demi-plié, tendu, deusmende*.

The entire idea was based around *one* vegetable that was…a cabbage. Would anyone even care? Did *I* really care enough to do this?

There was still the underlying issue of not having a job. I squeezed my eyes shut, fighting back tears. Things were much better between Philip and I, but I still didn't have a job or a purpose. And again last night, a simple conversation led to overreactions and arguments. I could feel the blood rush to my face and sweat forming around my hairline as my feet miscalculated the timing, and I was offbeat.

Daniella could sense my distraction. She came up to me, and I expected her to scold me, but instead she whispered into my ear in broken English, "We take a coffee after this. You are sad."

After class was over and the *vestiaire* had cleared out, Daniella motioned for us to leave. Bundled up in a puffy black winter coat that went down to her toes, she led me down the narrow wooden staircase, paint chipping away as her coat brushed against each turn of the wall. An avid smoker, she had her long, skinny cigarettes out and ready to light before we'd even reached the last door to the courtyard. I wrapped my black cloak tighter around myself, knowing she would want to take a seat outside for our coffee.

"*Deux café, monsieur.*" She motioned to the waiter, ordering her daily post-class espresso and one for me as well.

"You tell me, what is wrong? I know you now, Kreesteen," she said. "Your cheeks were red, your eyes—you cry. Tell me," she said, reaching out with the hand that wasn't bringing the cigarette to her lips.

Aside from Philip, Daniella had become one of the people I saw most frequently. She was another constant in my life. I immediately felt at ease sitting with her, as if she were my grandmother or the high school teacher who you'd stay with after school for extra help or boyfriend advice.

"I feel lost," I replied. She nodded. "I don't really do anything here. And last night I had an argument with my husband…"

"Ah, *oui*," she said, nodding, taking another cigarette out of the pack. "*Un dispute*." She shook her head. "*Dites-moi*," she said, encouraging me to go on.

"I don't work here. I'm not the same woman I was in New York. I feel like I've lost myself. I miss *that* woman…*that* person," I said.

Our coffees arrived, and Daniella focused her eyes on me, leaning into the table, ignoring the laughter and conversation of the other teachers and students around us who normally sat at her table. "It takes time, Kreesteen. You go home. You talk to him. You say how you feel. Do not stop talking. And you and me. We practice French. You find something soon. Do not give up," she said, squeezing my hand tighter.

Daniella was right—just like my mom was always right. Philip and I had to keep talking. And what about my project? I needed to stop thinking and talking about the Kale Project and actually do something about it.

✻

Apparently it was a trip to Italy that would finally inspire me. At the end of March, my cousin Anaïs, who is like a sister to me, came to visit. I was excited to show her my Paris. I took her to the café with my favorite *croque-monsieur*, made with oval slices of Poilâne's famous bread, longer than the plate, and oozing with sharp cheese and freshly sliced *jambon*. I led her through the Jardin des Tuileries, dirtying our shoes with stark-white dust as we walked around the blossoming tulips. We stumbled upon a flower shop with her namesake and bought a bouquet for the apartment for Philip to enjoy while we were gone.

We were taking a girls' trip to the Cinque Terre region of the Italian Riviera. This would be my first trip in three years without Philip. It would be a week of hiking and exploring the five villages along the coast, drinking Italian wine, and, of course, eating fresh pasta. Channeling our study-abroad days, we were going to travel light, take trains, and leave a lot of things to chance.

We departed Paris early, and a few hours later, right before we reached the French-Italian border, things got prickly. As you would expect at a border, someone was going to check our passports—but for some reason, I hadn't thought about that at all. The police, strong and built like lumberjacks, walked through every train carriage, checking identification. That was when I realized that my passport was at home.

I had nothing but a Pennsylvania driver's license with me, which in Europe is the equivalent of a Victoria's Secret gift card. I don't know why I hadn't thought to bring my passport or my *carte de séjour*, the legal document that allowed me to live in France. It's always mandatory for any travel—or at least air travel. This was the train. But I'd forgotten that we would be crossing borders, and while both France and Italy are part of the Schengen Area (an area of twenty-six countries that allow free travel through their common borders), random passport checks still happen, and I wasn't a citizen of the European Union. Telling border control, "I left my passport at home," was as bad as telling a teacher, "My dog ate my homework."

An Italian policeman, dressed in an evergreen-colored uniform with the Italian flag on one sleeve, approached us and sternly asked for the documents. Anaïs handed hers over. He reached out for mine. Meekly, I told him, in a mixture of English and French, that I had nothing.

"*Madame*, this is not acceptable. You must show your passport and proof that you are in Europe legally. You will not be allowed to cross the border."

Scared, I began to stutter, tears forming in the corners of my eyes, until he barreled down the carriage corridor. "I will be back," he said, looking over his shoulder at me, his eyes burning a hole through mine, making a mental note of where we were sitting.

I began to freak out. My palms started to sweat. Where was he going? To get backup? Handcuffs? A dog to search my luggage for drugs? Anaïs, always practical, remained calm. We'd already spent nearly seven hours on the train, and the Italian border wasn't far away. Perhaps he wouldn't come back. But I couldn't help worrying about what might happen. Our lighthearted girls' trip was quickly turning sour as I was on the brink of being labeled an American trespasser. I didn't know what to do. Should I hide in the bathroom until we were well into Italy? I pictured multiple policemen dragging me out, separating us while Anaïs cried, the two of us torn from each other. She would be left alone, with no working cell phone, and I would be locked away outside of Turin in a small cell, with only a piece of bread and a glass of water, questioned repeatedly in Italian.

Each time the carriage doors opened and closed, emitting a loud hiss, my heart would pound, about to explode out of my chest. I would have to call Philip (do you even get one phone call in Italian jail?) to come get us and somehow negotiate my release.

I started thinking about what I could do to save the situation when I remembered that I had a scanned photo of my passport in my email. I grabbed my phone and scrolled through dozens of emails, the cell service fading in and out as the train rumbled through the Italian Alps. Snowcapped mountain peaks and pine trees, green and tall, towered over us, like the policeman. Finally, I had the document ready to show on my phone, its battery power slowly depleting. We had been in Italy for at least forty-five minutes by now. The carriage doors continued to open and close, but each time the policeman failed to appear. Two hours later, to my enormous relief, we'd arrived in Turin, with no policeman in sight. I was pretty sure we were safe. A drink was in order on the next train.

As luck would have it, the Italian train system was on strike, so the next train wouldn't be coming for another six hours. The only thing to do was find a bar (we had said, after all, that we wanted this trip to be like study abroad). After two canceled trains, three beers, four espressos, two more trains, and no real food, we reached Monterosso al Mare near midnight. And getting to our bed-and-breakfast? It was a twenty-minute walk uphill. Bed never felt so good.

Apart from that bumpy first day (and the fact that we would have to face the exact same train journey to return to Paris), the trip was perfect. We awoke the first morning to a simple breakfast of coffee and sweet, flaky, custard-filled *cornetti* on a terrace overlooking the Ligurian Sea. As we ate, we gazed at rust-colored rooftops standing out against the blue sea and waves calmly rolling in and back out of the pebbly beach. Still starving from the previous day, our first lunch more than made up for it. We started with fresh, white anchovy fillets drizzled with olive oil, followed by fusilli pasta with a light pesto sauce and spinach gnocchi topped with salmon and roasted red peppers, all paired with a local white wine.

In October 2011, nearly six months before our trip, the Cinque Terre region was hit by a flash flood that caused a disastrous mudslide, causing damage all across the region. The area was still recovering and rebuilding, but the five towns that make up Cinque Terre remained beautiful. We jumped in the translucent, teal waves in Monterosso al Mare and wandered the tiny streets of Vernazza, shocked by the flood damage there and the gutted storefronts that gaped open, everything inside having been washed away by water or packed in by mud. One rainy afternoon in Corniglia, we hunkered down in a dimly lit wine bar, drinking too much local wine out of twisted decanters, stumbling as we hiked back through fog and low-lying clouds. In Manarola, we discovered churches and tiny *épiceries* selling local lemons, their green leaves still attached, and garlic and chili peppers hanging to dry. Hungry after our morning hikes, we ate hearty lunches of fresh tagliatelle pasta and homemade pesto, bright green from spring basil with strong garlicky and nutty aftertastes. Late afternoons were for enjoying the sunshine with a glass of prosecco and a square slice of warmed focaccia topped with fennel, sweet onions, and garlic.

On our last day, we took the local train to the town of Riomaggiore, which is the farthest one from Monterosso, planning to hike back. It would be our longest trek by far, but also the most beautiful, overlooking the cliffs and winding coastline, promising some of the best views. At the foot of the town was a small *mercato*. Small and unassuming, it had fruits and vegetables in baskets out front and a small selection of meats and cheeses inside. We hadn't walked more than fifty yards toward the store when my leafy-green radar went off. There before my eyes was the thing I had been so desperately seeking. Kale! Its large, wrinkled, green leaves stood out from the other vegetables, protecting the young zucchini and their delicate yellow flowers and the fava beans that sat underneath it. I shrieked with happiness, running ahead of Anaïs, careful not to slip on the wet mosaic tile under my feet, to see if it was what I thought it was.

"Anaïs! Kale!" I screamed. It wasn't a mirage. I had been explaining my kale woes to her since the beginning. She understood what a big moment this was for me. I eagerly grabbed all of it, afraid that someone else was going to scoop it up right in front of me. I had to buy it. Who cared if we had a good two-hour hike ahead of us? I would carry it, no matter how cumbersome it was.

Anaïs, laughing with me, snapped my photo with the village behind me—tall and narrow houses in shades of pink, yellow, cream, orange, and red with dark green shutters, smushed together and piled on top of one another as if made out of construction paper. The large bunch of leaves fanning out in front of me was like a bride's bouquet. The shopkeeper stood by the front door of the *mercato*, smiled at us, and waved good-bye as we began our hike up a steep hill.

Bags of kale in hand, we climbed, winding through the vineyards. Patches of lush green grew between the vines, stakes, and ropes, fresh from spring rainstorms. Lemon and orange trees peppered the mountainside, their balls of orange and yellow popping against the brown dirt. Up steps and steeps roads, we followed the hiking trail, past tiny homes built into the hillside, connected to the village by a simple path. Every home had a garden, and in almost every single plot, there was kale.

At the top of the mountain, the entire village was below us, small enough to fit into the palm of my hand and fragile enough that it seemed even one gust of wind would blow it off the cliff, into the sea below. We stopped for lunch—more pasta—this time with a light tomato sauce topped with fresh lobster, paired with a bold Barolo. Continuing our hike, we were ten minutes away from the restaurant when I realized I'd left my precious bag of kale under the table. Perhaps the Barolo was a bit too bold for an afternoon. We ran back to the restaurant to retrieve it, hoping that it hadn't been thrown away. Instead, we found it in the kitchen, where the cooks were about to prepare the greens for that evening's dinner menu. They must have been able to sense how desperate I was, because they kindly gave them back.

We made it back to Paris without incident. France let me into the country, kale included. The day after that, on Anaïs's last day of her trip, I made a raw kale salad, my hands relishing the motion of the kale massage, kneading the tougher leaves tender. I sautéed it with young spring garlic that had recently appeared at the markets, and added it to fresh pasta with spring peas and local green asparagus shoots. The rest of the kale made enough morning smoothies to last a week.

Most important, my Italian souvenir gave me something else besides more fiber, iron, and calcium. It gave me the final push I needed to launch the Kale Project. There was no reason that Italy could have kale and France couldn't.

After Anaïs left, I registered thekaleproject.com website domain, set up the Kale Project blog, and launched social media accounts. The mission was simple: bring kale to Paris. I wasn't sure how feasible any of it was, but I thought if I could get just one farmer to grow it, there would be enough people at least from the expat crowd who would buy what was harvested. Even better, if I could convince just one chef to cook a dish that would prove that kale is more than a smelly, boring war vegetable, well, that would be success.

I wrote my first blog post on April 27, 2012. It may have been *slightly* overdramatic, but I wanted to make a statement.

> The time has come. I'm ready to eat kale again. It's been much too long, and I miss the earthy smell and the bitter, yet sweet, taste. And I really miss how great I feel knowing how good kale is for me.
>
> So I've decided that I'm going to bring kale to Paris. And today marks the birth of the Kale Project. The idea has been brewing in my mind for some time now, but I'm ready to make kale in Paris a reality.

It won't be easy and, at times, it might not be fun, but that doesn't matter to me, because I truly believe that kale should be available to everyone, especially in a country where food is so important.

The first step is finding the perfect organic vegetable farmer who is willing to begin growing kale. France is not necessarily known for being extremely open to change or trying new things, so we'll see how my farmer search goes.

I'm looking forward to sharing this journey with you.

And *voilà*. The Kale Project launched. My idea was out in the universe for anyone to find, read, and—if they wanted to—join. There was no turning back now. And things were about to get busy because I had to find a farmer.

·· GARLICKY CAVOLO ··
NERO PASTA

I love garlic. I put it in my salad dressing, in artichokes for roasting, and sometimes, just for the heck of it, I'll roast an entire head of it in olive oil and eat it plain—much to Philip's dismay. Garlic is said to be fantastic for the immune system, among other health benefits, and there are few things better than a creamy clove of garlic melting in your mouth to keep away colds. As luck would have it, garlic also goes very well with cavolo nero, or Tuscan kale. This recipe could be used as a stand-alone sauté, as a side dish for fish or meat, or as a delicious topping for pasta.

INGREDIENTS

- 3 TABLESPOONS OLIVE OIL
- 1 HEAD (8 TO 10 CLOVES) GARLIC, THINLY SLICED
- 1 BUNCH (12 CUPS/400 G) TUSCAN KALE, WASHED AND CHOPPED (CURLY, GREEN KALE WORKS WELL TOO)
- 1 TEASPOON RED CHILI FLAKES
- 1 TO 1⅓ CUP (80 TO 100 G) DRY PASTA PER PERSON (SUCH AS BOW-TIE, PENNE, OR SPIRALS)
- PARMESAN CHEESE, FOR GARNISH
- SALT AND FRESHLY GROUND PEPPER, TO TASTE

PREPARATION

Bring a large pot of water to boil over high heat. When the water is boiling, reduce heat to low to keep warm. Heat 2 tablespoons of the olive oil in a medium saucepan over medium heat. Add the garlic, and cook, stirring occasionally, for 2 minutes. Add the kale, and cook, stirring occasionally, for 3 to 4 minutes. Season with the red chili flakes, salt, and pepper. Continue to stir for 2 to 3 minutes, until the kale leaves turn a darker green but don't lose their vibrant color—do not overcook them. Reduce the heat of the saucepan to the lowest setting, and leave uncovered, as condensation from a lid would overcook the greens. Bring the large pot of water back up to a boil. Add the pasta, and cook as indicated on the package, until al dente. Drain the pasta, and put it back in the pot. Add the remaining olive oil, and season with salt and pepper. Add the kale and garlic from the saucepan, and stir. Serve with a sprinkle of grated Parmesan on top.

YIELD

- 4 SERVINGS

Chapter 19

I wasn't sure how I was going to find a farmer, but I knew that one possibility was to find one at the markets, which had become part of our weekend routine. We spent Saturday or Sunday mornings going for a run, ending at a market. This meant that we did our market shopping in exercise clothes.

In France, exercise clothes are worn *only* when you are actually going to *faire du sport*, or do sport, which encompasses pretty much every physical activity. If someone sees you in exercise clothes outside of a gym, there is a good chance they will ask if you are going to "do sport" or say that you are *très sportif*, very sporty.

The problem that Philip and I had was that we could very easily spend our entire Saturday in *très sportif* clothes, wearing them for more than just "doing sport." In New York, this wasn't an issue. The streets on Saturday mornings are like a runway for the latest Lululemon and Nike fashions, and no one thinks twice.

I once asked a French acquaintance why walking around in exercise clothes—post workout—is so frowned upon. She told me it's considered unhygienic. I lived in a city where you practically have to play hopscotch around dog poop on the sidewalks and where, according to city officials, 350 tons of cigarette butts are collected off the streets every year; yet, somehow, my black yoga pants were considered unhygienic.

We learned pretty quickly that our weekend wardrobe choices were not acceptable in France—everyone we passed on the street stared at us unapprovingly. The staring took some getting used to. For a while, I was convinced that I had toilet paper stuck to my shoe or food on my face for how often people seemed to be staring at me. It's not that I personally was garnering that much attention—everyone stares at everyone. It was more that I was not accustomed to always being blatantly looked at. Even now, if I spend a few weeks in America, I'm taken aback by the staring when I return to Paris.

One day, fed up with a woman that had stared at me for my entire *métro* ride to French class, I asked Patricia what the French verb is for "staring."

"*Regarder*," she responded to me, with the same verb that is used for "to look." I was confused. How could staring and looking be the same word in a language that often has multiple phrases for only one word? There was no way that staring and looking were the same word.

Asking again, trying to articulate my question, I said, "No. Like when someone really looks at you, deep in the eyes, up and down your body, investigating every detail," I elaborated.

"*Oui*," she said. "*Regarder*."

It had only been a week or so since I'd published the first blog post for the Kale Project, and I woke to a Saturday bursting with welcome sunshine. Like every Saturday, I threw on my running clothes and headed out for a pre-market jog. "See you at Monoprix in two hours?" I confirmed with Philip, planning to meet up to finish our errands together (and so that he could carry the bags).

The morning was glorious. Paris felt different. Did I even see a few people smiling as they walked down the street? Blossoms peeked out behind the statues in Parc Monceau, children were running toward the *manége*, the merry-go-round, anxious for the first ride of the spring season. Birds chirped in the trees lining the cobblestoned boulevard de Courcelles. Café chairs even seemed more inviting as sunlight shone through the wicker, their shadows crisscross patterns on the sidewalks. As I finished my run, arriving at the market, the Sacré-Cœur even shimmered more brightly on the hillside behind place de Clichy.

I wandered through the market stands taking in the vibrant signs of the new season. Thin, green asparagus or thicker *asperges blanches* with white stalks and specks of violet throughout the skin. One producer had a pile of green peas still in their shells. After months of dark root vegetables, the sprouts of green were welcome. I reached one of my favorite stands, which sold juice shots of wheatgrass, apple, ginger, and curcuma.

And that's when I saw them: mustard greens. Young and tender, with green and violet leaves. I looked to my right and then to my left. No one else seemed to notice, but I felt like yelling to the entire market, "Don't you realize? These are so difficult to find! So rare! What a treat for us to be able to purchase these local greens on such a perfect spring day!" I could barely contain my excitement. When it was my turn, the stand's farmer, a fierce, weathered, tiny woman with a long, gray braid looked at me. I stuttered my way through my excitement and nerves, asking for four bunches of her gorgeous greens.

"*Quatre?*" she asked, looking at me quizzically.

"*Oui, quatre, s'il vous plaît,*" I responded confidently, confirming that I wanted four bunches and adding a polite "please" at the end.

She continued to stare. Quietly, without a tone of judgment, she asked, "Well, what are you going to *do* with four bunches of these?"

I did my best to reply, since I knew this woman didn't speak any English. "I am going to make a raw salad with olive oil and lemon juice."

Her gaze was not interrupted, curious at my response. "Oh, but as a mixture with lettuce, of course?" she asked.

I smiled back, thinking about how happy I was to have a leafy green that *wasn't* lettuce, chard, or spinach. "No. Alone."

Her gray braid flipped to the other side of her back as she did a double take and looked back at me, filling a bag with the greens. "Alone? Where are you from?" I wasn't sure if it was my American accent or the fact that I was planning to eat her mustard greens on their own and raw that made her ask. She finally showed me a small but reserved smile. "Most people would not eat these greens alone."

I'm not sure where I found the courage Saturday—perhaps it was the newfound spring light, the novelty of having some semblance of a conversation in French, or the fact that I was now on the hook to find a farmer—but I decided to ask her if she had ever grown *chou frisé non-pommé*. After I described it to her, she pondered my question for a moment, then answered, "No, not at all. But I do not grow cabbage." It was true; there wasn't a cruciferous vegetable in sight at her stand.

The line behind me was growing with loyal customers waiting for her young lettuces, wheatgrass, herbs, and potted plants. Sensing that it was time to move on, I quickly said, "Next week, I will bring you a photo of the cabbage." She still did not react much, so I added, "My name is Kristen."

Nodding, she replied, "Hermione," which she pronounced *air-mee-own*, "like in 'arry Potter."

"*Enchanté et à bientôt*," I said, skipping away from the stand, saying I would see her soon. Already I had an update for the Kale Project. I couldn't wait to tell Philip.

✻

"It was amazing! I formed a sentence! She understood me!" I said to him, recounting my morning and meeting Hermione. "And look at the mustard greens," I exclaimed, opening the plastic bag with my market treasure.

We walked into the Monoprix together, toward the escalator. "That is so exciting, darling!" Philip said. "See? I told you that your French is getting better." Although Philip and I rarely spoke French with each other, we had been dabbling more and more, trying out few ten-minute conversations every once in a while, but speaking with a stranger is entirely different.

We stepped off the escalator, and our running shoes had barely hit the floor when an older woman, with her white hair tied back and a red-and-green-plaid caddy dragging behind her, approached us and hunched over her cane, blocking everyone's way.

"You do not wear clothes like that," she spit out, her mouth turned down and eyes narrowed. "*Pas de tout.*" Not at all. "You go back home in those!" We stopped, unsure what to do. Do we respond? Do we apologize? Frozen in place, we resembled two mannequins from an athletic store. Having said her piece, calling attention to our spandex, she continued on her way.

✻

In my opinion, I have an excuse for wearing workout clothes to run errands. In Paris, *faire des courses* can easily take up to three hours. It requires planning, and I return home exhausted, my back and arm muscles burning from the heavy bags and market caddy, sweat dripping down my lower back. It's a workout. But a fun one.

There are two ways to shop here. It is completely possible, like in America, to buy everything you need at a large retail store like Monoprix or Carrefour. But I don't recommend it. The experience isn't the same. Instead, I prefer to go to the butcher, the baker, the candlestick maker. Well, not really the candlestick maker, but I do enjoy purchasing a lot of our food from specialty stores where the proprietors and employees are passionate about their meats, cheeses, and wines. They want to share their *savoir-faire*, their know-how, which I don't have. I always learn something new. They want to ensure that I'm cooking the meat the right way and pairing the best wine with my dinner.

Plus, I like to support their businesses, which is where the workout begins. First, Philip and I go to our favorite *fromagerie* on rue Poncelet, and then, if we want a dessert, to the *pâtisserie* right next door, which has our favorite chocolate éclairs. We prefer the bread at a different *boulangerie* that is closer to the best butcher in the neighborhood, Monsieur Chamaret, who is also by far the friendliest. There is a shop for foie gras and terrine, another shop for horse meat (and whoever actually buys it), and a stand that only sells smoked fish. One place is better for *huîtres* (oysters), and the other for *crevettes crues* (raw shrimp). Flowers will take at least twenty minutes, as the florist kindly arranges your selections into delightful bouquets, whether they're a gift or not. The *caviste* is always the last stop, since the bottles of wine are heavy.

Then there's the game of trying to find ingredients beyond basic staples. Often I go out with a shopping list and only manage to retrieve about half the items. It's a guessing game to remember who sells what, when they sell it, and where they display it. I can't imagine the money Monoprix must spend to pay their employees to rearrange shelves that don't need to be rearranged; it seems like I can never find anything in the same place twice. One week the organic store would sell large bottles of grape-seed oil, and the next they would not. Just as one week, the corner *vendeur* would have walnuts—the next week, he would not.

And every single place would have a line.

Just thinking about the shopping extravaganza can make me break into a sweat, which is why, stares or no stares, I will not budge on the exercise clothes. I will *faire des courses* and *faire du sport* in the same outfit.

The following weekend, Philip and I went to the market together, in our running clothes, of course, to show Hermione a photo of kale. She inspected it with the curiosity of a baby, as Philip said, "Kale is one of the most popular vegetables in America. People love it and are buying it more and more. It has amazing health benefits. If you grew it, we know people would buy it."

Hermione looked up at us cautiously. She didn't flinch or show any reaction at all. Philip continued, "Can we take you to coffee next weekend after the market to talk more? My wife has an idea, and we would like to talk with you more about it." Hermione agreed.

As soon as we got home, I wrote a new blog post telling the (few) followers I had about the exciting exchange we'd had with Hermione. Not sure if she would want her real name on the Internet, I decided to call her "Madame Mustard," since I first discovered her through her mustard greens.

The next week went by quickly. I went into high gear working on the Kale Project. I diligently put together a document to show Hermione during our *rendez-vous*. I worked for days on a PowerPoint deck outlining my vision for the project. What was kale? Why was it good for you? How do you grow kale? How was I planning to promote it? And, most important, who the heck were we to even attempt this project? I highlighted the already-existing demand from expats, who would be the first group of people to buy it, and the potential for how the project could grow from there. And the hardest part? I tried to do it all in French.

When the day of the meeting arrived, we settled into a small café next to Hermione's stand. The weather had turned chilly again and wearing oversized blue-jean overalls, work boots, and a wool scarf that she had wrapped around her neck, practically up to her eyes, Hermione seemed pleased to take a moment and get out of the cold. Her hands, grasping a cup of *chocolat chaud*, were leathered, with days of dirt lodged underneath her fingernails. Looking back now at this very first "meeting," I feel silly that I even put together such a formal document to share with her. What was compelling in a New York conference room meant nothing to someone whose office was nature. I still had a lot to learn about how to interact with farmers.

Even if Hermione thought the document was out of place, her face didn't show it. She was stoic and kind. Her gray eyes followed along with interest as she listened to Philip speak about my idea and why we thought growing kale could be successful. And without much additional conversation or fanfare, she said, "If you bring me the seeds—and they must be organic—I will grow it." We didn't talk about money or about working together in a business capacity; it was to be a simple collaboration. She would try to grow the kale and I would find the people to buy it.

As we walked away from the market, I leaned into Philip, wrapping my arm around his back. He looked down at me and smiled. "Darling, I think you just found your first farmer."

·· HERMIONE'S MARKET JUICE ··

Long before Hermione's mustard greens connected us, I was attracted to her stand for her wheatgrass juice shots. In 2011, juice bars were unheard of in Paris. Most restaurants only made the typical fresh-pressed orange juice, and finding someone doing a green juice was like trying to find kale—nearly impossible. Hermione once told me that other vendors at the market were convinced that she was selling something alcoholic, because they couldn't fathom the idea of a small paper cup of green juice selling so well. Juice recipes are really all about trying new combinations to see what flavors you like best. This recipe is a simple base that is written with experimentation in mind. Try adding cucumber, spinach, or lime juice. Play around with fennel or celery. My only recommendation is to keep it green!

INGREDIENTS

- 3 TO 4 CUPS (125 G) KALE, WASHED (STEMS INTACT)*
- 1 LARGE HANDFUL SPINACH (4 OUNCES/100 G)
- 1 APPLE, STEM REMOVED
- 1 (2 TO 3-INCH/5 TO 7½-CM) PIECE FRESH GINGER
- JUICE FROM ½ LEMON

PREPARATION

Add all ingredients to a juicer, juice, and serve chilled.

YIELD

- 1 CUP (240 ML)

Kale stems juice really well. If you are an avid juicer, save any stems you are not cooking with for juicing later.

·· DIY SPROUTS AT HOME ··

Contributed by Emily Dilling, writer

One of my favorite things about Hermione's stand is her variety of sprouted beans. She has lentils, chickpeas, and green peas on a regular basis. They are fabulous on sandwiches and add a great crunch to any salad. Sprouting beans at home is really easy—all you need are dried beans and a glass jar. You can buy a jar made specifically for sprouting, or you can use a regular jar covered with a piece of cheesecloth or muslin. You do need to be diligent about changing the water, but it's like watering the plants or brushing your teeth—once it becomes a habit, it's easy.

INGREDIENTS

- ½ CUP (90 G) DRIED BEANS, SUCH AS LENTILS, GREEN PEAS, OR CHICKPEAS
- 1 CUP (240 ML) WATER

PREPARATION

Put the beans and water in a 1-quart (½-liter) glass jar. Cover the jar with a piece of cheesecloth or muslin, and secure it with a rubber band. Put the jar by a window to ensure green sprouts, and let sit for 12 to 24 hours, until the water is absorbed. Rinse the beans twice daily by adding water to the jar and then pouring it out, leaving the cheesecloth on. Make sure to drain as much water as possible. Within 3 to 5 days, the jar should be full of sprouts.

YIELD

- 1 JAR OF SPROUTS

Chapter 20

R iding the excitement that I'd potentially found my first farmer, I knew the next step was to find a few restaurants that would actually use kale. I cold-emailed a few veggie-friendly places. Perhaps it was too bold, but I was feeling confident after my farmer find. The email didn't hide my passion for the vegetable or that I was determined about my mission. In fact, looking back on the email now, I laugh at how serious I seemed. I'm not even sure that I would've written myself back.

And only one person did write me back: Laura from Verjus. We had only met once, months earlier at her restaurant, when she told me that she and Braden had never seen kale in France. Her email reply was short, sweet, and positive:

> This sounds awesome! Of course we would love to have kale.
> Come to the wine bar and we can talk more.

When we did meet a week later, she gave me the contact information for their distributors. One was Terroirs d'Avenir, a small distribution company founded in 2008 by Alexandre Drouard and Samuel Nahon, two young Frenchmen who only worked with local producers and only sold seasonal produce. I was hesitant to call them. If I was certain about one thing about this project, it was that I wanted to work with farmers directly. The Post-it note with their phone number sat on my desk, untouched.

❧

One category of French vocabulary that I never thought I would need was anything to do with *voleur*, thief. Philip was working late, and I returned home from Verjus just as it was getting dark. Unlocking our door, I walked inside and flipped the light switch. Nothing happened. I tried again and again. I used my phone flashlight to guide myself to the fuse box. Every fuse was on, but still there was no light. I panicked, convinced that I'd forgotten to pay the electric bill. I went to my computer to look up our account, only to remember that the Internet wouldn't work without electricity. I knew one thing for certain: I didn't want to call the electric company myself. I had two choices. I could bother Philip or sit in the dark. I chose to bother Philip.

He was not pleased. After his unsuccessful phone call with Orange, he had no interest in battling with EDF. Hopefully it was only a missed payment. He called them and then called me back. "You've paid the bill," he said. "They don't know what the problem is. Surprisingly, they're sending someone to the building right now. Go tell Amelia as well, in case it's a building issue."

I went downstairs and knocked on Amelia's door. Her dog yapped, jumping at the door, and ran into the lobby as soon as she opened it. By this point, I was no longer shocked to see Amelia wearing Philippa's clothes. This time it was a long, safari-green dress. As I was explaining the situation, another building resident walked in. A handsome, older man wearing corduroys and a sweater, I had seen him before going in and out of the building, walking his dog. He began to speak to me in English.

"You are the American woman who moved in. Right?" I nodded, thankful to have someone to help me explain my blackout predicament to Amelia. "I'm Jean-Luc," he introduced himself, leaning in for the double kiss. Quickly telling him the story, he translated for Amelia, who ran into her apartment and came back out with an extension cord.

"There are outlets in the hallway," she said. "Take this and you can at least put on a lamp inside the foyer."

Jean-Luc accompanied me to our apartment. "You do not have to wait here," he said. "Come have a tea. You can meet my wife, Chloé. She does not speak English, but she understands. I can show you pictures of my grandchildren!"

It wasn't exactly the most convenient time to go chitchat with the neighbors, but it was either meet Chloé or sit outside our front door. I chose Chloé.

Jean-Luc lives in the top-floor apartment and has a big balcony filled with flowers. He gets the late-afternoon sun for the longest amount of time and uses orange shades to keep the apartment cool in the summertime. I immediately had balcony envy.

In fact, anytime I saw a balcony, I was filled with envy. During one of the first warm spring days, I was so excited about the idea of sitting outside our windows, I convinced myself throughout the day that we had a window ledge large enough to fit two chairs. I made a special trip after French class to buy two small, metal patio chairs, never doubting that they would fit. Returning home, I opened our wide windows and excitedly placed the first chair—well, half of the first chair onto our ledge. It most definitely was *not* going to fit.

When I walked in with Jean-Luc, Chloé greeted me, and Jean-Luc immediately began to tell me about his apartment, the remodeling they did, and his family.

"I've had six wives!" he told me, very pleased with himself. "But I am an inventor, you see, and it was a lifestyle that not all of them understood. Chloé understands," he said, nodding toward her. Right as she started to pour the tea, my phone rang. It was Philip. He was downstairs, and the electricity repairman had arrived.

Saying thank you and good-bye, I ran down the three flights of steps. Even if I couldn't actually help out in this situation, I could at least be there for moral support.

Philip and the man, dressed in a shiny silver jumpsuit, were outside our front door, staring at a different fuse box in the hallway. Philip said, "Apparently someone got into the building and stole the fuse that controls the electricity for the entire apartment."

I didn't understand. Why would someone want to steal the fuse? Do they sell for a lot of money on the street?

The electricity repairman, who said that the fuse looks like a large, brass bullet, explained that the fuse thief was most likely trying to get into our apartment. "He saw that your door had an electric alarm. If he took the fuse, then the alarm would be disabled and he could break in."

I was frightened. We chose this boring *quartier* because it was supposed to be safe, and now someone was trying to break in? As soon as the fuse had been replaced and we had our power back, I immediately emailed Colette, our relocation agent.

She called me the next day. "Kreesteen," she said, "it is totally normal to be broken into. Almost every Parisian apartment has been broken into. It is *très*—" I cut her off. This is where I was going to draw the line. I was not going to accept her telling me that it was *très Parisien* to be robbed.

Chapter 21

Philip and I decided to have our first dinner party only a few weeks after we moved into the apartment. "They'll be here in ten minutes," I called to him in the living room. While I prepped the food for *apéro*, he was busy creating ambience by lighting candles and rearranging the Roman statue heads on the mantle (sometimes I do feel like I live in a museum). Since our kitchen was at the other end of the apartment, down a long narrow hallway, I knew he probably hadn't heard me. Walking quickly from one end to the other, my high heels clacking on the wooden floor and cocktail dress fluttering behind me, I asked him, "Did you hear me? They'll be here in ten minutes."

"That's fine. We're ready. Aren't we?" Philip responded, fluffing the couch pillows and refolding the blankets that I'd tried to fold a few hours earlier. Philip is always tidying up after my tidying up.

"The room looks nice," I said, setting the tray of hors d'oeuvres down on the coffee table. I rearranged the champagne glasses, added the chilled bottle of champagne to the sterling silver bucket we'd been given as a wedding present, removed my apron, and waited.

This was my first time entertaining in Paris, and to make it more stressful, we were hosting a couple that wasn't just French but Parisian. I'd spent the entire day preparing, cleaning the house, and running the marathon of errands to find the best food and drink for the evening. I was still shaky on converting measurements and accurately ordering the right amount of food in kilos and grams, and hoped I had enough food.

Keeping to French custom, our guests arrived thirty minutes after we suggested. We welcomed Juliette, who worked with Philip and whom I had met once before, and her husband, Bertrand. *"Bonsoir,"* Philip and I said in unison.

"Salut," Juliette chirped back, giving me a double kiss and handing me her coat. I carefully placed it on our brasserie-style, six-prong black coat rack and simultaneously checked out her outfit. *Parisienne* perfection. This woman was the firefly you rarely see—here, in my home—which meant I would be comparing myself to her for the rest of the night. She wore skinny jeans, boots, and a chunky sweater; her lips were a deep red, and her hair was perfectly messy from her scooter helmet. She exuded casual yet chic poise. I immediately felt like a little girl who had gotten into the dress-up box. My outfit was entirely wrong. I looked like I was going out for drinks with girlfriends in a Manhattan cocktail bar, not hosting dinner for four. She was French chic, and I was a toy doll. All I needed was a big bow on the top of my head.

Taking a pack of Marlboro Lights out of her Givenchy handbag, Juliette pointed toward the window and said, "It's been *such* a busy day. I only had time for a few breaks today." She walked over to the window, opened it, and lit up. Bertrand followed.

Philip finished pouring the champagne as they returned from the window, a ring of smoke around them. When they saw the food on the coffee table, their eyes bulged and their mouths dropped as if I had served a dead animal. Juliette stopped speaking midsentence.

"My," she said. "What a display. So much…err…choice!"

The tray was laden with sun-dried tomatoes drenched in olive oil, marinated artichokes, fillets of white anchovies, and salty roasted red peppers with blistered skin. And to top it off, a sliced baguette and a mound of sweet and sour onion chutney. Perhaps it was too much.

Since no one was taking any food, I nervously rearranged the Eiffel Tower napkins and paper plates, Juliette finally took a napkin and one sun-dried tomato and one anchovy, and, not sure what to do with the rest of the food, eventually retreated back to the window for another cigarette.

The main course wasn't much better. After the Mount Kilimanjaro of appetizers, I brought out a Mount Everest of pasta, because there is nothing more French than pounds of family-style pasta.

"So sorry. It's so much pasta!" I said, secretly scolding myself for apologizing. Julia Child said *never* to apologize for what you cook. "I swear I told the woman at the pasta shop that we were only four people, not fourteen," I explained, shouting out to the window, where Juliette and Bertrand looked at me through another cloud of smoke.

Finally sitting down at the dining room table, Juliette, with her nicotine-stained hands, held out her plate and took *three* noodles, cutting them slowly with a knife and fork. Not wanting to come across as too hungry, I took four.

I did, at least, know enough to serve the cheese plate at the end of the meal. Aside from the fact that we cut the cheese the wrong way, Philip, who considers cheese his favorite food and would eat an entire block of it like an apple if I let him, cut a larger than average (but normal for him) slice of Comté.

"You really want a slice that big?" Bertrand questioned. "You know cheese will kill you."

By spring, it was time for another dinner party. Although I was still recovering from the disastrous dinner with Juliette and Bertrand, this time I had no choice. Philip had clients coming in from America, Brazil, England, and Singapore, plus a few important colleagues from Paris, and he wanted to host everyone, *chez nous*, our house. There would be ten of us, and it would take a lot more planning. I felt a bit more prepared this time around. My French had improved from that of a one-year-old to that of a two-year-old, and I was slowly learning the metric system. Plus, Liz offered to help me. She was always entertaining her husband's French friends and trying to impress her French mother-in-law. While we organized everything, she taught me a few French dinner party rules.

"You were right not to have cheese before the meal," Liz said after I told her about the pile of food I had served for *apéro*, "but you never need that much food. Just have breadsticks and cherry tomatoes. The French love cherry tomatoes." She was right. Anytime we went to anyone's house for dinner, there were always cherry tomatoes, no matter the season. Regis and Kelly had cherry tomatoes for their burlesque party.

"The cheese comes after the main dish, with the green salad," she continued. "Never serve the green salad before the meal. And it's only that: a green salad. No need for lots of toppings. It's not an ice cream sundae."

As we set the table together, she asked, "Are you having asparagus?" I shook my head no. "Just checking, because your French guests *will* eat those with their hands." As I placed the dishes and glassware on the table, she continued, "Always set the forks so they are face down." I gave her a puzzled look. "I know. Another rule from my mother-in-law," she said.

My mother had learned how to entertain from her mother, who loved having guests over. And I had learned from my mother. Everyone has their own style, of course, but now I realized that I would have to relearn everything I *thought* I knew about dinner parties.

Exhausted before the evening had even begun, Liz and I took a breather on the couch as we admired the elegant table. She sighed. "I just remembered. For the seating arrangement, your most important female guest sits to the right of Philip, and your most important male guest sits to the right of you. And if a couple has been married for more than a year, you don't sit them together." Realizing I'd been holding my breath, I let out a huge exhale, gathered more energy, jumped up, and ran off to make place cards to make sure that nobody sat in the wrong seat.

❧

It was with that rule that I, the hostess, found myself sitting next to our most important guest, Marc-Antoine. One of Philip's closest colleagues and head of the strategic planning department, Marc-Antoine was extremely intelligent and also very French. A thin, Gallic-looking man with long hair and a pointed nose, Marc-Antoine politely used his knife and fork in a way that would amaze any American. He could peel an entire orange using *only* a knife and fork.

Aside from asparagus, the French don't necessarily use their hands for eating like Americans do. For starters, Americans are always eating something, whether they're walking down the street, driving a car, or taking a train or plane. It's something I really notice when I am visiting the States. People have food or drinks near them all the time. The French find this habit strange.

Philip and I once attended a French-American wedding where the American bride included savory appetizers at the cocktail hour, which started at four o'clock in the afternoon. That time of day also happens to be the golden hour when the French have their *goûter*, the sweet afternoon snack that children are given after school, in between their rigidly scheduled lunch and dinner hours. As French kids become adults, the temptation for the *goûter* never really disappears, so they often eat something sweet at that time. The idea of eating something savory at that time of day baffled most of the French wedding guests, while the Americans happily chowed down.

It wasn't only the savory snacks that were confusing to the French guests but also *how* to eat the appetizers as finger food. A young girl about ten years old had chosen a bite-size piece of marinated chicken in a pastry cup, which Americans would pop into their mouths without thinking twice—and the Americans at the wedding were doing just that. For this little girl? She was at a loss for what to do—not only was this snack not sweet, but how was she supposed to get it out of the cup? I watched her as she quizzically looked at the cup, looked around in hopes of discovering a clue from someone else, looked back at the cup again, and sighed. Eventually, she found a way to maneuver the chicken onto a cocktail napkin and nibble away at the tiny piece of meat, keeping her fingers perfectly clean.

I watched Marc-Antoine with awe as he carefully spooned out the *chou-fleur*, cauliflower soup, that I served for the first course. "*Comment ça va ton projet du chou?*" he asked me nicely, inquiring about the Kale Project.

"Oh! Philip told you about my project," I exclaimed. I was nervous to explain what I was doing to a French person, but I would have to talk to French people about kale eventually. This was a good opportunity to practice with a tough audience since Marc-Antoine is *so* French and *so* intelligent. I had to start somewhere. I began to talk.

Not even thirty seconds in, Marc-Antoine interrupted me, abruptly setting down his cutlery. "*Non, non, non*. Kale. It's a horrible word for the French to say," he declared, saying it how the French might say it: *Kah-leh.*

After what felt like a long pause, I nervously stuttered, "I know. I'm not wed to the name. I'm happy for it to be anything, as long as there is one name that almost everyone uses." He pursed his lips, pondering my response. Not sure what he was thinking, I continued. "It's really the health benefits that I would want to talk about the most. Kale is a superfood. It's full of fiber, iron, calcium, and cancer-fighting properties!"

He shook his head again, "*Non. Pas de tout.* Not at all," he said quickly. "That will not matter to the French."

How could I not tout the healthy virtues of kale? That's what made it so great. That's why it was America's favorite superfood.

He explained, "We do not look at any food in a superior way. For us, all vegetables are created equal."

As I thought more about what he'd said, it started to make sense. France has a very strong food culture, deeply rooted in history and ingrained in their society. Culinary tradition is taught in their schools and supported by their government. Babies eat leek puree, and toddlers at the *crèches*, public day care centers, eat three-course meals with lentil salad, sole, foie gras, and Roquefort cheese. Unlike Americans, the French way of eating means that they don't need to latch on to food trends that claim to be the secret for weight loss or glowing skin. Their philosophy is that if they eat with moderation, as they were raised to do, superfoods and other diet solutions aren't necessary.

Our conversation was put on hold while I collected the empty soup bowls. Walking to the kitchen, I wondered if my idea was pointless. Would the French even care about kale if the health benefits were irrelevant? I headed back into the dining room, and Marc-Antoine was smoking out the window, his napkin left in a pile on the table, about to fall off, so I grabbed it and started to put it back when he yelped, "*Non!*"

I was startled, not sure what I could have done wrong. He rolled his eyes. "Sorry," he said. "But each time I am in America for work and eat out, the waiter always refolds my napkin when I get up from the table. I can't *stand* it." I laughed, quickly removing my hand from the table and his napkin. "*Oui.* Every time. It is like touching someone's underwear," he added, exhaling a puff of smoke into the outside air. I made a mental note to tell Liz to add this latest rule to her list: do *not* touch your guests' napkins.

When everyone settled again at the table and was eating the main course, Marc-Antoine continued our cabbage conversation. "The idea is lovely," he said. "Did you know that this type of *chou* is a *légume oublié*? A lost and forgotten vegetable?"

I shook my head no. "I've never heard that term," I said, thinking back to all the markets I went to, showing photos of kale, without one person knowing what it was. Lost and forgotten? Marc-Antoine wasn't kidding.

"That is what will matter to the French. There is an entire category of vegetables that fell out of fashion after the war. It's a part of our history and our heritage. Go to the King's Kitchen Garden at Versailles. That is what they grow there," he said.

I loved it. The idea of a lost and forgotten vegetable would be perfect. Besides, I did not want to change French food culture or French cuisine, and I wasn't trying to educate the French on eating healthy. Tapping into their history made the most sense. Kale was the forgotten cabbage of France, and the Kale Project would not bring kale to Paris but *reintroduce* it.

·· ALLY'S SALAD DRESSING ··

A few weeks before Philip and I left New York, Hannah fell in love. She met a man named Jonny who swept her off her feet. Jonny's parents have lived in the south of France, in the Languedoc region, for more than thirty years. His mother, Ally, moved to the country from Ireland when she was only twenty-six, and, like me, she was often left to figure stuff out on her own because her husband had a busy job. Sympathizing with me and remembering how lonely she was at times, Ally invited me to stay with them for a few days in the quaint village of Pézenas, not far from Montpellier. We hiked through the vast vineyards, while Ally pointed out the almond trees and native flowers. I looked forward to her simple lunches of boiled potatoes, cheese, a baguette, and green salad with her special dressing. This dressing beats any creamy sauce you're likely to find on a typical brasserie salad in Paris, so memorize the recipe, make a jar, and keep it handy for whenever you want to spice up a salad. It also pairs well with blue cheese, summer tomatoes, and cucumbers.

INGREDIENTS

- 1 HEAPING TABLESPOON DIJON MUSTARD (ORIGINAL STYLE, WITHOUT VISIBLE MUSTARD SEEDS)
- 1 TABLESPOON WALNUT VINEGAR*
- 8 TABLESPOONS CANOLA OR SUNFLOWER OIL, DIVIDED
- SALT AND FRESHLY GROUND BLACK PEPPER, TO TASTE

PREPARATION

Mix the mustard and vinegar in a jar (7.3 ounces/203 g), and shake vigorously. Add 3 tablespoons (45 ml) of the oil and shake. Keep adding oil by the tablespoon and continue to shake until the dressing has emulsified into a thick consistency. The dressing will keep in the refrigerator for up to a week.

YIELD

- ½ JAR

*Vinaigre aux noix, *walnut vinegar, is not easy to find in the United States. If you can't find it, substitute with 1 tablespoon of white wine vinegar and 1 tablespoon of walnut oil and only use 4 tablespoons of canola or sunflower oil. You can find a few varieties of the vinegar online, or, if you ever find yourself in France or the UK, bring a bottle back with you.*

·· ROASTED *CHOU-FLEUR* SOUP ··

I always feel a little overwhelmed with first courses. Growing up, my mom didn't always have an official first course. We would have a beautiful spread of cheese, fruits, and vegetables for hors d'oeuvres, so a proper first course wasn't necessary. But the French wouldn't dare eat cheese before the main meal. I like this custom because it saves the best for the end. Now, for first courses, I've learned to lean on light soups, like this cauliflower one. You can add milk or cream, but the cauliflower makes it creamy on its own, and the sautéed mushrooms and kale add a nice heartiness.

INGREDIENTS

- 1 HEAD CAULIFLOWER, CHOPPED
- 1 MEDIUM ONION, SLICED
- 6 TO 7 TABLESPOONS (90 ML) OLIVE OIL
- 4 CUPS (960 ML) WATER OR VEGETABLE STOCK
- ¼ TEASPOON RED CHILI FLAKES
- 15 MUSHROOMS, SLICED
- 6 CUPS (200 G) KALE, WASHED AND CHOPPED
- TRUFFLE OIL, TO TASTE
- SALT AND FRESHLY GROUND PEPPER, TO TASTE

PREPARATION

Preheat the oven to 400°F (200°C). Put the cauliflower and onions in a roasting dish. Add 3 to 4 tablespoons of the olive oil, and mix with your hands, coating every piece. Roast for 25 to 30 minutes. Continue to check and stir the vegetables so each piece roasts evenly, until the edges of the cauliflower are golden brown. Put the roasted cauliflower and onions in a blender or large pot (if using an immersion blender). Add 1 tablespoon of the olive oil and the chili flakes. Pour in 3 cups (720 ml) of the water or stock. Using the blender, puree the soup until the texture is fine and creamy. Add salt and pepper while blending. Add the remaining water or stock. Cover to keep warm. To make the sauté*, heat the remaining olive oil in a medium pan over medium heat. Add the mushrooms, and stir for 2 minutes. Add the kale, and continue to stir for 3 to 4 minutes, until the kale is soft but retains a vibrant green color. Ladle the soup into 4 serving bowls, and place a spoonful or two of the sauté on top of each bowl. Drizzle a few circles of the truffle oil over the soup. Add salt and pepper, and serve.

YIELD

- 4 SERVINGS

*You can make the soup ahead of time and reheat it, but the mushroom and kale sauté should be made right before serving.

Chapter 22

Aside from making me second-guess all of my table manners, Marc-Antoine had given me a lot to think about. My intention for the project had never been to change the way the French eat. I wanted to reintroduce kale for its health benefits, but now I knew that I couldn't expect its superfood status to be a selling point—or at least not the primary selling point. The more I thought about it, I doubted that an American talking about health to the French would work, since the French think very little of the diet and health habits of Americans. But this idea of a *légume oublié* was intriguing, so I decided to go visit the King's Kitchen Garden at Versailles, just as Marc-Antoine had suggested.

Philip and I had another reason to go to Versailles. Since October, Philippa's ashes had been sitting in a velvet bag on our mantle. Philip felt ready to take them to a final resting place. Philippa had a strong belief in some form of afterlife but she never specified what she wanted. She'd loved roses, statues, and gardens, so we thought, where better than Versailles?

Although it was spring, the day was cold, with rain clouds sitting low in the sky and a thick fog covering the head of the Louis XIV statue at the front of the palace. With Philippa's ashes secure in Philip's backpack, we walked around the side of the château, pushing our way through the mist, past manicured gardens, cone-shaped pine trees, and stoic statues, through the tidy paths all part of a large garden maze, and toward the Grand Canal, a large body of water shaped like a cross, where we planned to say our final good-bye.

Philip was quiet but not sad. I held his hand, and we walked in silence, listening to our footsteps crunch the gravel. It was the only sound, along with the occasional calls from the swans and ducks that waddled on the grassy knolls. We walked under an archway of trees, with forest on one side and tiny bushes trimmed into circular bulbs on the other, forming a barrier between us and the water. The light became even dimmer from the darkening clouds overhead.

"There," Philip said, pointing to the center of the canal, the spot where the cross breaks into left and right arms. "That's where I want to do it."

He let go of my hand and walked ahead, kneeling in the grass right beside the water's edge. Giving him space, I watched as he pulled out the blue velvet bag and let Philippa go. As he spread her ashes into the earth below, I joined him and handed him a small bouquet of white peonies, which we both laid into the dark water, watching as the flowers floated off. Neither of us said much. Philippa was with the kings and queens now.

We reached the *Potager du Roi*, the King's Kitchen Garden, just in time for the afternoon tour. Strolling through the grounds, up and down the worn steps, we noticed the signs of new life everywhere. Despite the dismal weather, it was still spring, and the frequent rain showers interspersed with strong bouts of sunshine encouraged the flowers and vegetables to sprout, dotting the land with shades of green. Cats wandered in between rows of vegetables, slinking up against stone pillars and resting below apple trees that grew against crumbling stone walls.

The garden was started by Louis XIV in 1678 and run by his gardener, Jean-Baptiste de La Quintinie, a horticulturist who made a name for himself by growing vegetables *hors saison*, out of season. It is now one of the top suppliers of fresh organic produce to the town of Versailles. As we followed the tour guide, she told us about the apple and pear trees lining the garden's quadrants (Louis XIV enjoyed eating soft fruit compotes, since he lost all of his teeth). Each quadrant featured different vegetables favored by the Sun King, such as asparagus (which he forbade women from eating because they were too phallic) and green peas (which he was known to eat too much of at once, making him sick). I kept hoping and waiting for the mention of the lost vegetable, *chou frisé non-pommé*.

As for *légumes oubliés*? In 1890, there were more than a thousand varieties of vegetables grown in the garden, but today there are only around thirty. As agriculture evolved to feed more people, it became important to implement techniques that would cultivate and harvest more produce faster—especially produce that had a longer shelf life. This led to more industrial practices, which meant growing fewer varieties as producers focused on increasing the quantity of one type of vegetable, rather than offering many varieties of high-quality vegetables. This in turn influenced taste and cuisine, and over the course of generations, older *légumes* like kale were completely forgotten.

The King's Garden was slowly working to reintroduce many of the forgotten vegetables, valuing their importance to French cuisine and the biodiversity of the garden, and believing in the need to preserve these species for future generations. And, as our tour guide told us, "What if Marie Antoinette ever comes back for a visit? We must have the garden as she remembers it!"

At the end of the tour, after most of the guests had meandered off, dropping their *pourboire* (tip) into the guide's hand, Philip and I approached her. We had become accustomed by now to how ridiculous our question about kale was and became a lot better at asking it—now using the appropriate name, which hopefully this horticulture student would know.

Beginning in French, Philip said, "*Bonjour, madame*, thank you for the wonderful tour," making sure to compliment her on the job well done first. "Does the garden ever plant *chou frisé non-pommé?*"

"What?" she replied, confused. Philip repeated himself, looking over at me to help him out. I attempted to tell her more.

"*Je ne comprends pas*," she said, telling us that she didn't understand. "Perhaps you should ask one of the gardeners. Unfortunately, there is no one here at the moment, but you can always call or send an email."

Later that evening, I sent an email to the head gardener, asking if we could meet to talk about kale and the history of the vegetable in France. A few days later, I received a response.

Dear Kristen,

Thank you for your note. Unfortunately, the gardeners are not particularly inspired. In Europe it is much more a northern or central European tradition. You are welcome at the gardens anytime. Perhaps I would learn more from you on the subject!

Best Regards,
Pierre

It wasn't the response I'd hoped for, but it didn't mean that the door to Versailles was closed. As with everything else with this project, I knew I had to wait for *bon moment*, the right moment. Besides, Philippa was there now. Perhaps she could pull a few strings.

Chapter 23

I distinctly remember four things from my French classes. First, the curriculum sorely needed an update concerning how it presented other nationalities. The worksheets we were given—with 1980s-style cartoons of Mexican people in sombreros, Chinese people in rice paddies, and Americans in big cowboy hats sitting on horses next to cacti—were not exactly the best way to teach nationalities in the twenty-first century.

Second, I learned an excessive amount of vocabulary for *le camping*. I found this to be an odd category to study when terms related to doctor or pharmacy visits or to successful residence card appointments would have proven much more practical. But if I ever find myself camping in southern France (which is actually a very popular activity for the French during summer *vacances*), I'll be prepared. I'll know how to discuss *randonner* (hiking), I'll be able to read signs to find my *gîte* (cottage), and I can easily locate landmarks on a *carte* (map).

The third thing I remember is learning about a special day at the end of May in which the French celebrate their neighbors. Appropriately called *Fête des voisins*, Neighbor's Day, is when apartment buildings often hold official parties for residents. It's like a block party but just for the building. Considering that I didn't find our residents to be that neighborly, aside from the occasional grunt from Regis, I assumed our building would not participate.

And the fourth thing? I couldn't wait to quit my French classes. I enjoyed learning French, but the attitude I first received from the "welcome" office never improved; they made it painfully difficult to register for new classes, and they changed our instructors every four weeks. The biggest issue was that I never really learned to *speak* French. Rather, I never gained the confidence to speak French. My knowledge of French grammar and vocabulary was improving, but I did not find the classroom setting to be the best place to actually practice talking and form more than a few sentences. I wanted to be able to have a real conversation.

Here's the thing: when you've only heard yourself speak English for twenty-seven years, hearing yourself speak a new language is bizarre. I didn't sound the same, my intonation was different, and my English facial expressions were out of sync with the toddler-level French phrases that I spoke. My mind, which knew what I *wanted* to say, worked faster than my mouth, which didn't seem capable of actually *saying* it. Philip would joke that he preferred my French because I had no capacity to be mean or angry when speaking it. Whether I liked the sound of French coming out of my mouth or not, improving my conversation and comprehension skills was important, so I was on the hunt for a private tutor.

Marion happened to be my last professor at Alliance Française and agreed to meet with me twice a week. Young and pretty— another firefly—she wore her perfectly messy, dirty-blond hair up in a tortoise-shell claw clip, with pieces falling down in all the right places, framing her face. She rocked skinny jeans, brown suede ankle boots, and the *Parisienne* trend of glasses with oversized, black plastic frames. She engaged the class with her bright eyes, and she was easier to talk to than any of my other professors—and I'd had a lot of them by then. Most important, she seemed to understand our perspectives as students—that learning a foreign language is difficult and that many of us were learning out of necessity, rather than passion.

I soon discovered, through our very basic conversations, that Marion had spent a year teaching French at Bucknell University in Lewisburg, Pennsylvania, the same year that I was a freshman at Penn State. We had only been an hour apart on Interstate 80, experiencing the same February blizzard. She had witnessed what a Saturday night looks like for a nineteen-year-old American in the middle of nowhere, so she understood how rural and desolate central Pennsylvania is, and most importantly, she understood that America is more than New York and Los Angeles. And although it still puzzled her, she no longer questioned why students wear pajamas to their 8:00 a.m. classes. It was as if we were meant to be. With Marion, I didn't feel like I had to constantly apologize for being American, and that immediately made trying to speak French easier for me.

※

One day during the last week of May, I was rushing to a lesson with Marion, already feeling more confident in my French after only a few sessions, when I noticed a new sign posted in our lobby by Monsieur Sinclair: *Mesdames et Messieurs, Fête des voisins, Thursday! To prepare: Women to your ovens, Men to your vines!* Since my role was to "go to my oven," I knew I would pick something up when I went to the market the next day. But it wasn't going to be just *any* market; the next day, I was scheduled to meet Joël.

Joël Thiébault is one of the most well-known vegetable producers in Paris; his family's farm has grown vegetables for the Paris area since 1873. He is a rock star farmer, and his produce is in very high demand;

chefs from all over the city arrive at his stand early in the morning to handpick their ingredients. Joël is one of the few producers in Paris who grows a vast array of vegetables, experimenting with new seeds and varieties season after season. He loves growing *légumes oubliés*, giving them life again, showcasing their beautiful colors, shapes, flavors, and quirks. His stand at the market jumps out from the rest with his purple, yellow, and green cauliflower heads; his rainbow Swiss chard, with stems and veins the color of blood running through the dark green leaves; and his multicolored carrots tied in bunches, with red, orange, and purple cones poking out from their green frond tops.

It was thanks to a woman named Rachel, an early follower of the Kale Project on Facebook, that I first heard of Joël. "He is the best producer," she wrote to me. "I'm sure he would be interested in growing kale."

I arrived at the corner of rue Gros, deep in the Sixteenth arrondissement, early in the morning and waited for Rachel, the market not far from view. The streets were mostly empty except for a few miniature, fluorescent-green street-cleaning trucks driving by, washing and sweeping the sides of the street, cleaning up old cigarette butts and pigeon feathers. Men in green suits with long, green brooms followed the trucks, sweeping away anything the machinery missed. Fathers dressed in perfectly tailored suits rushed their children to *crèche* (day care), pulling them along on their *trottinettes* (scooters).

The plan, which was perfect, was to be introduced by Rachel's husband, who owned a restaurant and sourced produce from Joël's stand. Her husband was French, he appreciated and understood his wife's desire for kale, and he offered to help with the translation.

Fifteen minutes later, as more and more people made their way to the market, their caddies rolling behind them, I saw a pretty brunette rushing over to meet me. "Kristen?" she asked out of breath. "I'm

Rachel! So nice to meet you. I'm sorry I'm so late. Unfortunately, my husband won't be able to make it. I hope that's all right."

I stopped in my tracks. "Umm, well, I guess so?" I replied, trying to hide my disappointment. "My French is not very good, but I'm happy to give it a go."

"Oh good," said Rachel. "My French is not very good either, so I won't be able to help much."

Hmm. This was not how it was supposed to happen. Did I still want to go through with this? Stalling at the corner like two schoolgirls afraid to approach a boy we had a crush on, we each waited for the other to make a move. Finally, I took the first step, and we walked over to Joël's stand.

Seven or eight tables were lined up, filled with a myriad of colors. There were salads with green and red leaves, purple potatoes, white radishes, and acorn squash with thick, almost black end-of-winter skin. Behind the table, stacked in crates, were gold and red beets, their green tops jutting out, and a mound of brassica vegetables, including small broccoli florets, cauliflower, and red and green cabbages. The last table was filled with piles of fragrant herbs. Ready-to-go bundles of bouquet garni, mixed herbs, were placed prominently in the front, for those needing the ideal combination of herbs to make homemade soup stock.

A team worked the stand, moving along the already-growing line of customers. They all wore jean aprons and the ladies kept their necks warm with decorative cotton scarves. It was all business. They were cutting off quarter pieces of pumpkin; chopping off the leafy tops of carrots, turnips, and beets; letting the greens fall to the ground; wrapping the remains in brown, crinkly tissue paper. Behind them was a wall of red crates, each marked with only one word: THIÉBAULT.

Behind the crates sat boxes, prepacked for restaurants and ready for pickup. Chefs arrived, parking their scooters next to Joël's white truck, VIP style, to retrieve their produce for the day. Pulling off their helmets, they walked to the back of the truck, and there he was: Joël. He was the main attraction and chefs buzzed around him, doing *la bise* and quickly taking *un café* with him. The coffee was brought on a round, mirrored tray in small cups, as if Joël's stand were part of Istanbul's Grand Bazaar. Once caffeinated, Joël would personally lead each chef around his truck behind the main tables, so they could inspect and choose any extra produce that might inspire a menu for that evening.

I watched this from afar, waiting for a quiet minute to approach him—the last thing I wanted to do was interrupt the well-choreographed dance between Joël and the chefs. When there was a pause and Joël was alone, Rachel and I walked around the side of his stand, toward the back of his truck, where he was sipping another *café*. Rachel greeted him, "*Bonjour*, Joël." He looked up from his computer and, recognizing her, smiled. Dressed in navy-blue overalls over a thin, long-sleeved shirt the color of oatmeal and knee-high olive-colored rain boots caked with mud, he reached out his red, weathered hand and took mine as Rachel introduced us.

And then she stopped talking. All eyes were on me. The bustle of the market slowed down, or at least it did in my head, as if a dream sequence had commenced. Marion, who never thought she would learn so much about a leafy green, had been prepping me for this very moment. She'd coached me on how to tell him that I believed that if he grew kale, I could gather enough interest and people for him to be able to sell it. I thought to myself, "Just pretend that Joël is Marion. Joël is Marion." I began to talk…slowly. I could tell by the look on his face that he understood me. Nervous, shifting from foot to foot, playing with the buttons on my jacket, I continued. I told him how I wanted to inform more people about kale and that I could bring him seeds.

Joël grinned and quickly responded, "*Oui*, I've grown this *chou* once before, many years ago, but not many people bought it. They didn't know what it was. But all right. I will grow it again. Around September. And I do not need your seeds. I have a guy." At least, that's what I *think* he said.

The market bustle picked up again, the hazy dream sequence over. Could it really have been that easy? Did I imagine it? Did he really say he would grow kale? Had he actually understood what I was proposing? Only time would tell.

Thanking him and completely unsure of the next time I would see him or check in with him (confirming "next steps" has never been a strength of mine when working with farmers), I joined the end of the line for his produce.

With so many options, it was hard to choose, but I needed something, since I had to "go to my oven" later that day for the *Fête des voisins* party. In the middle of a table, I noticed the long, reddish-green branches of rhubarb poking out. Another one of the first signs of warmer days to come. I immediately thought to make a crumble. It seemed like the perfect idea—rhubarb, which is used a lot in French cooking, prepared as an American-style dessert (the French use the word "crumble" for the dessert, as an Anglicism, pronouncing it like *croom-bell*). The tart rhubarb would be a welcome combination with the sugary crunch of the rolled oats. Like every other customer, I was ushered along, adding a few mustard greens, yellow turnips, and a bright purple cauliflower to my red basket, along with the rhubarb stalks. I paid, caught Joël's eye again, and smiled as I said *au revoir*. I couldn't wait to tell Marion how our conversation had gone. Better yet, I couldn't wait to *thank* Marion.

Later that afternoon, Amelia and Monsieur Sinclair were busy setting up for the party. It must have been the most exciting day of
the year for them, because they even put up a balloon by the door
that opened on the courtyard. Murmuring a quick *bonjour*, I bolted
upstairs to get started in the kitchen. After all, my oven was waiting! Setting out the ingredients, I prepared the rhubarb, scrubbing
it, dicing it into one-inch pieces, and adding granulated sugar. I'd
forgotten how easy it was to make a crumble. I quickly mixed the
flour together with bits of unsalted butter and then the oats and
brown sugar.

While the crumble was baking, the hour approached seven
o'clock, and Philip arrived home from work with a bottle of rosé (why
was "going to the vine" so much easier than going to the oven?).
Joining me in the kitchen, he peered out the window, where we
had a direct view of the party getting started in the courtyard below.
Amelia was setting out plates of packaged food on a table toward
the back. Monsieur Sinclair was escorting the older residents, all
widowed women, to their seats. Dressed in elegant skirt suits with
panty hose, and their gray hair pinned up into chignons, they were
the first to arrive.

Philip and I kept staring down, watching as more and more of
our neighbors filtered in, dropping off their food and taking a glass
of champagne from Monsieur Sinclair. Regis and Kelly showed
up, dragging their two teenage sons. My oven timer went off. The
crumble was ready, which meant it was time to join the fun.

I wasn't sure why we were so hesitant to show up. Maybe it was
the fact that we would finally be matching our neighbors' faces to the
sounds of the building. Although we didn't live with each other, we

did live with each other's noise: the early-morning phone calls, the toddler's cries at night, and the constant scolding of teenage stupidity. We lived with the clinking of plates at dinner, the crashing of a blender at breakfast, the droning of a vacuum as the woman above us cleaned her floor every day at 5:30 a.m. and again at 5:30 p.m., and the routine nose blowing every day at 7:45 a.m., like clockwork, of a man on the fifth floor. I knew how the woman on the fourth floor answered her phone—always chirping, *"Oui? Allo?"*—but I didn't know what she looked like. All our neighbors were about to become a lot more real.

"Bonsoir, Madame et Monsieur Heimann!" Monsieur Sinclair greeted us, handing over two thimble-sized plastic glasses of champagne. I was starting to notice a trend in the size of drinking glasses at parties. He turned around to the courtyard and, as if we were arriving at a seventeenth-century ball, announced us to the group. *"C'est la Américaine!"* Gulping down my shot of champagne, I whispered *bonsoir* and rushed to the table to set down my crumble. Surveying the table, I was not impressed. Where were all of the wonderful dishes, freshly prepared and cooked from everyone else's ovens? I saw a bag of potato chips, packets of cold-cut lunch meat, miniature hors d'oeuvre rolls of cold dough and ham, and a plastic container of olives. I was the only person who had actually cooked something.

Jean-Luc's dog, with its wiry, brown-and-gray hair, jumped up onto my legs. "Excuse me," Jean-Luc said, grabbing and calming his dog. His friendly smile deepened the tan creases by his eyes. "How are you doing? I hope you have had electricity since we last saw each other! What is that you have there?" he asked, his eyebrows raising as he gestured toward the crumble.

"Rhubarb crumble," I said, proudly holding the dish out in front of me.

"An American thing?" he asked. "It looks…interesting," he said hesitantly, inspecting the dish of glistening fruit and crispy rolled oats. His dog jumped again. "So what are you doing these days?" he asked me, making a plate of food, leaving my crumble to the side. I began to explain.

"*Génial!*" he exclaimed, complimenting the idea, showing his approval. "Such spirit! So American of you," he said as his dog ran off, and he went to follow.

I could see that Philip was cornered by Regis and Kelly. I went to join him, dodging Amelia, who was wearing one of my old shirts from Forever 21 and wandering around offering supermarket foie gras on Philippa's serving tray. Seeing Amelia with our old belongings didn't even phase me anymore. "Foie gras?" she sang out to me, pushing the dust-colored duck liver into my face.

"Darling!" Philip greeted me, handing me a glass of rosé in a slightly bigger cup. "We are talking about New York!" Ah, New York. This I could handle, even in French, as I had talked with Marion ad nauseam about how much I missed my old home.

"I loved living in New York City," Kelly told us in English. "We went dancing to all the clubs. The Tunnel! Danceteria! It was the eighties, you know; everybody was *wogue-ing!*" Philip and I quickly looked at each other, not sure if we'd heard her correctly. Kelly could sense our confusion. "Yes! *Wogue-ing!* Did you *wogue?*" she asked, looking at Philip, who looked at me. Did she mean "vogue-ing"? Not wanting to be rude, we stifled our laughter at her stereotypical German pronunciation of V's as W's (the joke was on us, of course, since neither of us speak German, even though Philip technically *is* German).

The ever-silent Regis spoke up. "*Oui,*" he said, swaying quickly from side to side and moving his hands around his face in the well-known Madonna dance move. "Madonna. *Elle est incroyable.* Madonna is incredible."

An hour or so later, the courtyard had grown darker, the rosé supply had diminished, and Philip and I were restless. We'd spoken with a lot of our neighbors, introducing ourselves and making small talk. We met the oldest woman in the building, who was actually the daughter of the original architect. We met Florence from the fifth floor and talked more with Jean-Luc, who was eager to tell us about the inventions he had been working on. Amelia came around with the tray of foie gras ten more times, and Monsieur Sinclair, after too much of his own champagne, pointed at and touched my stomach, whispering and reminding me again, "The building needs a baby."

When we finally said our good-byes, double kissing everyone at least twice, I walked over to the table to retrieve my crumble, which not one person had touched. I was disappointed. I wasn't sure if it was my crumble, the rhubarb, or the fact that the average age in our building was eighty years old, but if no one here wanted even one bite of a sweet dessert, what would the French think of kale?

·· RHUBARB CRUMBLE ··

During the early days of my kale searching, I was so obsessed with finding leafy greens that I once eagerly grabbed rhubarb leaves at the market, without the knowledge that they are actually not supposed to be eaten. Luckily, the kind maraîcher quickly informed me that they are poisonous! Rhubarb stalks however, are best bought in the spring and early summer months. This crumble recipe can be adapted with other fruits, like peaches, apples, or berries.

INGREDIENTS

- 6 STALKS RHUBARB, WASHED AND CUT INTO 1-INCH (2½-CM) PIECES
- ¾ CUP (112½ G) SUGAR, MORE OR LESS TO TASTE
- ¾ CUP (90 G) ALL-PURPOSE FLOUR
- 7 TABLESPOONS (105 G) UNSALTED, ROOM-TEMPERATURE BUTTER
- ¾ CUP (75 G) OLD-FASHIONED OATS

PREPARATION

Preheat the oven to 400°F (200°C). Add the rhubarb and a little over half of the sugar into a bowl. Mix, and let sit for 30 minutes, and set aside. In a separate bowl, mix the flour and butter together, rubbing the mixture with your fingertips until it starts to bind together. Add the remaining sugar and the oats, and mix together with your hands. In an 8 x 8-inch (21 x 21-cm) baking dish, add the rhubarb mixture, and then add the crumble mixture on top. Bake for 30 to 45 minutes, or until the crumble is golden brown.

YIELD

- 4 TO 6 SERVINGS

Chapter 24

To my delight, word of the Kale Project was actually spreading. Not like wildfire, but a few people were reading the blog and sharing it with their friends. It was encouraging.

My next blog post was my wish list of restaurants that I hoped might be interested in cooking with kale, once the first few farmers had grown it. I thought some restaurants with Anglo chefs or French chefs who had worked abroad might be interested. I was aiming high, for places like Frenchie, whose well-known chef, Gregory Marchand, had spent time working in London in one of Jamie Oliver's kitchens, and Le Bal Café, whose two British chefs, Alice Quillet and Anna Trattles, do a lovely dinner service, having gotten their start at the original Rose Bakery, one of Paris's first English cafés.

Another place on my wish list was Coutume Café, a coffee shop and café in the Seventh arrondissement. When it opened in 2011, it was the first place in the city to roast ethically sourced coffee beans, and one of the first to break the monopoly that Cafés Richard, an industrial coffee supplier, has over the majority of cafés and brasseries in the city. Coutume, which also features a hip, New York look and feel, with white subway tiles, was paving the way for the coffee revolution that was about to happen in Paris.

Coutume was a pioneer not only in craft coffee but also in food, and that was largely thanks to Emperor Norton. Run by husband-and-wife team Omid Tavallai and Alannah McPherson Tavallai, Emperor Norton is an artisanal baking and catering business that cooked Coutume's weekend brunch.

Omid and Alannah moved to Paris in 2008 for Omid's job. They soon started pining for foods and ingredients that were common in their West Coast upbringing, like tomatillos or even just plain-old American doughnuts. So they began to cook comfort foods and nostalgic flavors from their childhoods for themselves, for fun. Then they started inviting a few friends, and as time went on, their dinners became bigger. Friends brought their friends, and before Omid and Alannah knew it, they could no longer host dinners at their apartment. The dinners became pop-up brunches at small restaurants, and word spread that Emperor Norton was serving hard-to-find breakfast burritos chock-full of market veggies, doughy apple-cinnamon doughnuts, and chocolate-chip cookies with the perfect mix of crunchiness and gooey bits of chocolate. They took over Coutume's brunch service, and within a few weeks, it had become a huge success with a line down the street of hungry Parisians waiting for a table.

Turns out tomatillos weren't the only thing that Omid and Alannah had been missing. They had also been searching for kale, and Omid had read my restaurant wish list blog post, which mentioned Coutume. We decided to meet up and talk more at a wine bar in the Second arrondissement, off rue Montorgueil.

Greeted by their friendly dog, Fergus, I felt self-conscious and geeky to have come to the bar so overly organized, with a typed list of interview questions. Alannah, whose long, dirty-blond hair was in a thick braid, said to me in her sweet-as-cherry-compote voice, "Oh, I was a project manager in California. I appreciate how organized you are!" I immediately relaxed, feeling at ease with her warmth.

"We will absolutely use kale in our brunch if you're able to bring it to Paris," Omid said.

"My husband and I went to your brunch last weekend. It was fantastic," I said, gushing about the breakfast burrito. "I saw that you put *chou frisé* in the scrambled eggs," I added.

"Oh, yes," said Alannah. "Clearly we had to use the savoy cabbage, as we've never been able to find kale in Paris, although we have been known to bring it back with us from the Netherlands. For one brunch we made colcannon, the popular Irish dish, with kale, mashed potatoes, and sausage. It was a hit and there wasn't one leaf left!"

"The issue here," Omid said calmly and very matter of factly, "is that there isn't just one name for kale, making it even more difficult to find because you don't really know what to ask for. If one farmer knows it by a certain name, that doesn't mean every farmer does."

I, of course, completely agreed. "Well, what have you found out? What do you call it?"

"We've done extensive research on this," Omid said. "*Chou vert demi-nain.*" He set his beer down firmly as he said it, adding authority to the name. "Which literally translates to 'semi-dwarf green cabbage,'" he finished.

Kale is not a small plant. Could this name be any less intuitive? I promised to let them know when Hermione's or Joël's kale was ready.

A few days later, I found myself on another RER train, this time heading to Vincennes, a town right outside of eastern Paris. I had a big day ahead. I was meeting another potential farmer and then flying to Berlin for a blogger conference.

Similar to the way I'd met Joël through Rachel, I was headed to meet a new farmer through a woman named Marie, who contacted me after seeing a post on Facebook. A young, petite Frenchwoman, she had recently returned to Paris after years of living in New York City, working as a private raw-food chef for the Upper East Side's elite. She'd only been back for a few weeks, and already she was missing one of her key ingredients. Kale.

"I want to build a business here," she told me, pushing aside the standard tea bag she'd been given at the café where we'd met up, pulling out her own homemade, organic tea bag and placing it into a cup of hot water. "But how can I coach people on raw food and healthy living and eating if I do not have kale?" she asked me, nowhere near desperate but certainly concerned. "That is why I contacted you. I love your idea and totally agree that kale needs to be reintroduced."

Leading me to the Marché Vincennes, she said "Sebastien is a great guy." Sebastien was her favorite producer, who we were on our way to meet. This market, which occurs on Fridays and Sundays, is a neighborhood market, much less of a tourist destination than some other markets in Paris. The majority of people who shop here live around the corner, and the stands, in addition to selling produce, cheese, and meat, also sell housewares, clothing, hardware, and kitchen supplies. Winding our way in between the stalls, we reached a corner stand, and Marie waved to a young man. Sebastien saw her and waved back. Dressed in a plaid flannel shirt, with floppy brown hair and soft-brown eyes, Sebastien more than made up for what Marie lacked in size.

"*Bonjour*, Sebastien," she began. "*C'est la femme qui fait le projet du chou—comme je t'ai dit.*" This is the woman doing the project on cabbage—like I told you, she said to him. He smiled again, his face round and red like one of the tomatoes he grew, and nodded, signaling to us that he'd be with us in a few minutes, after he finished serving his current customer.

Sebastien, whose farm is about twenty-five miles south of Paris in a commune called Vert-le-Grand, sells his own produce, and to round out his stand, he'll also bring other items from surrounding farms and producers.

"Look at these green cabbages." Marie gasped, slowly feeling the large leaves of the *chou pointu* between her fingers, as if touching expensive velvet. "The leaves," she continued. "They are perfect for veggie wraps." She was right. We toured the stand, in awe of the quality of his cabbages, peas, spinach, and carrots. Sebastien's produce was beautiful, and he already grew cabbages, which made him a good fit for kale cultivation. He had a much larger variety on offer than Hermione *and* his stand was on the other side of Paris, which meant it would reach an entirely different group of people. Luckily Marie had already done a lot of convincing a few days earlier, so it didn't take long to get him to agree to grow kale. Just like Hermione, Sebastien said, "Just bring me the seeds." I now had three farmers.

❧

Berlin turned out to be a worthwhile trip. As the last few weeks had shown, the Kale Project was becoming more serious and real by the day, with farmers signing on, more content being posted on the blog, and people—other kale lovers out there—reaching out, sharing things online, and helping spread the word. And the blogger conference would be a good test because for the first time I would be talking about and explaining my project to people I didn't know, many of whom had very successful blogs. I had my elevator pitch and business cards ready.

On the last day, I was introduced to two bloggers from Paris who also happened to be journalists for various online publications. It didn't take me long to realize that Bryan and Lindsey were actually two of the bloggers I'd been following and reading since before we'd moved. They were the people living the Paris dream while I was figuring things out those first few months, and I'd often looked to their blogs for advice. Now I had a story to tell too, a new *raison d'être* for my life in Paris.

Once I finished my quick explanation of the project, Bryan's eyes lit up. "This story would be perfect for my column on *SmartPlanet*," he said.

"And I want to interview you for 'Franco File Fridays,'" said Lindsey, referencing the series on her *Lost in Cheeseland* blog that features interviews with people doing interesting things in France. "It's so interesting that there is no kale," she said. "I never noticed. We'll talk more."

I knew right then that the moment these two posts were published would mean *everything* would be real. There would be no turning back.

When I returned home from Berlin, I had a package waiting for me. Eagerly, I shook it and heard a sound like maracas—my kale seeds had finally arrived. I'd searched and searched (in English, since my Google-searching skills in French were less than stellar) for a company in the UK that would ship to France. Since both countries are in the European Union, there are no laws against buying and shipping kale seeds from England, and I found a small company, Tamar Organics, that sold multiple varieties of kale seeds in bulk. I ordered Winterbor, a curly, green variety; Tuscan, the Italian *cavolo nero* dark-green variety with longer, thinner leaves; and even a red Russian variety, with bigger leaves that are less curly and a deeper bluish-green.

When I dropped the seeds off with Hermione and Sebastien, I could tell they were both excited to start. As I told Bryan when he interviewed me for his article, which was published a week later, "I'm just trying to get the seeds in the ground." That was Hermione and Sebastien's job. Now, all I had to do was wait.

·· IRISH KALE-CANNON ··
Contributed by Emperor Norton

By the time kale was available in Paris, Emperor Norton had moved on from doing the brunch service at Coutume Café. Omid and Alannah eventually started doing brunch pop-ups at other locations, and, true to their promise, kale almost always made an appearance on the menu. They put it in farm vegetable breakfast burritos and eggs, and sometimes made the traditional dish of Irish colcannon with kale, which they cleverly renamed "kale-cannon." Omid wrote to me when he sent me their recipe: "While the male half of our crew would probably die without rice a few times a week, the female side is of Irish descent and must have potatoes with every other meal. We first had colcannon together during our first Saint Patrick's day in Paris, and it has since become a go-to when we're flush with potatoes and kale. We were previously substituting cabbage. Can you even imagine? It would be easy to say, 'Just make whatever recipe for mashed potatoes, and add sautéed kale,' but this is exactly how we do it."

INGREDIENTS
For the Mashed Potatoes:
- 6 LARGE OR 10 MEDIUM POTATOES, PEELED AND DICED
- 4 TABLESPOONS (50 G) UNSALTED BUTTER
- 1 CUP (240 ML) MILK
- SALT AND FRESHLY GROUND BLACK PEPPER, TO TASTE

For the Sautéed Kale:
- 2 TABLESPOONS (30 ML) VEGETABLE OIL
- ½ WHITE ONION, FINELY SLICED END-TO-END
- 1 BUNCH KALE, (12 CUPS/400 G) WASHED, CHOPPED

- ¼ CUP (60 ML) WATER

- SALT AND FRESHLY GROUND BLACK PEPPER, TO TASTE

PREPARATION

Cover the potatoes in water and bring to a boil, cooking for about 20 minutes, until tender. Once cooked, drain the potatoes, return them to the pot, and mash with a potato masher. Gradually mix in butter and milk, then add salt. Place a separate pan over medium-low heat and add oil to pan. Add the onions, and cook for about 10 minutes, or until soft. Raise heat to medium-high and add kale, making sure to stir around to warm through evenly. Add water and cover pan with lid to allow kale to wilt, 3 to 5 minutes. Add a pinch of salt to taste. Mix sautéed kale into mashed potatoes, top with freshly ground black pepper and you have basic but delicious and satisfying colcannon...*

YIELD

- 4 SERVINGS

*For some worldly variations, top the colcannon with smoked sausage, and you're magically transported to the Netherlands, and what you have now is boerenkool stamppot (mashed pot of kale). Or allow the colcannon to cool. Heat a frying pan over medium heat and add vegetable oil. Form the colcannon into hamburger-sized patties, and fry until golden brown—around 5 minutes per side. You now have what's often referred to in England and New Zealand as "bubble and squeak."

Chapter 25

By June, Hermione's kale seeds had sprouted, and soon after, she invited me to visit her farm, Terre d'Émeraude, "Land of Emerald." There was a catch: because Hermione came into the city each weekend for the market, I had to visit her farm during the week *without* Philip, who up to this point had been my main source of coherent communication. Luckily, my kale networking had introduced me to Emily.

I first contacted Emily to interview her about her experience with leafy greens in Paris (and to find out her favorite kale recipe). Having lived in France since 2006, she started a blog, *Paris Paysanne*, in 2010 to chronicle her experiences with living a more sustainable and local lifestyle in an urban environment. I knew she would be a good resource for insight into the city's markets and maybe even for some kale intel.

"Let's meet by the Anvers *métro* stop," she said in her email. "That's also the same place where I found kale—the one and only time—at Marché Anvers. But it was years ago."

Climbing up out of the *métro*, I paused outside the entrance, adjusting to the dirty buzz of boulevard de Clichy, the uphill walk to Montmartre to my right and the downhill slope to Pigalle to my left. Straight ahead, I spotted a tall, thin woman with long, dirty-blond hair that she wore

straight, with bangs. Headphones in place, she also seemed to be searching for someone. She looked like Emily based on the photo I'd seen of
her online, but I wasn't sure. Dressed in a knee-length, black cotton
dress, black flats, and an army-green jacket, this woman had apparently
lived in Paris for quite some time, as she easily blended in with the other
Parisiennes walking in and out of the *métro* gate.

Making awkward first-time eye contact, both of us unsure if the
other was the person we were looking for, we smiled and burst into
laughter. Emily's outfit may have been *Parisienne*, but she grinned and
laughed like an American.

We immediately fell into nonstop chatter about her time living
in the French countryside, how she ended up in Paris, and why she
became more interested in healthy food. We bonded over memories
of studying abroad: taking overnight train rides, drinking cheap beer,
and eating Nutella by the jar.

Our biggest common interest, of course, was vegetables, but Emily's
true passion (which has come to greatly influence me) was searching for
and supporting local producers from the Île-de-France region. "I chose
to use the word *Paysanne* because I think Parisians often feel separated
from both the land and the people who cultivate the land and give us
food to eat," she told me when I asked about her blog's name.

"I believe that you can have close relationships with producers and
the *terroir*, the land, even if you live in a city like Paris, or anywhere,"
she continued. "It just means you have to try a little harder to find
them. There is a common misconception about Paris's outdoor markets
that every stand is run by a farmer and that all the produce is grown in
this region. The majority of the stands are actually operated by middlemen who source their offerings from Rungis. They act like selling green
beans from Morocco or red peppers from Spain in the middle of winter
is completely normal, when it shouldn't be normal at all."

She was right. Most of the stands at outdoor markets did have a lot of produce that wouldn't be in season in the region or that wasn't native to the region at all. It was normal to see strawberries front and center, whether it was July or January. And even when local French cherries were available, it was common to also see cherries from as far as Washington or Chile.

"Only about one-third of the vendors at the markets are selling their own produce nowadays, and that number decreases every year," she explained. "Always look for signs that say *notre production* to ensure that the produce is their own."

Our conversation turned from farmers and markets and, of course, kale to more about her life in France, the man she was in love with, and their dreams to one day start their own vineyard in the Loire Valley to produce natural wine. But for now, she was still in Paris, and we became fast friends. It's amazing how one minute you don't even know someone and the next you're gushing about your love of vegetables, having girlfriend dates over wine and cheese, talking about everything in life *but* vegetables.

Emily, unintentionally, became an unpaid volunteer assistant for the Kale Project. We made early morning market dates together, meeting up at different locations all over the city. And because she was fluent in French, she was often there to assist me when I needed help speaking to someone about the project. Everyone needs a fairy godmother, and Emily was mine. So when I wanted someone to come with me to Hermione's farm, Emily was the first person I thought of.

The day was hot; the heat wrapped around us like a sweaty hug. We were two city girls dressed in old sneakers, cutoff jeans, and big sun hats, ready for a day in Madame Mustard's fields. Emily drove us out of Paris, merging onto the A4 toward Coulommiers, a small town forty miles east of the city.

We left the windows down, letting the warm summer wind blow our hair in every direction as the smell of the air changed from city smoke to country sweetness. The landscape became field after field of rhubarb leaves the size of elephant ears and fennel fronds swaying in the breeze. The highways quickly turned to country roads, lined on either side with tall, uniformly planted trees, their leaves creating a canopy overhead. We rounded a bend and saw a one-room stone church with flying buttresses and a skinny steeple piercing the sky. Hermione had told me that this was a sign we were close to her farm.

Emily turned off the main road, down an unassuming, steep gravel road until there were only small fields in sight. We stopped in front of a tall fence with a handwritten sign that read: Terre d'Émaraude.

Hermione began to unwrap the chain around the lock, quieting the dogs who were barking nonstop at our arrival, "*Tranquille*, Tiloup *et* Reglisse," she said. She opened one door slightly, peering out from under a large sun hat that shaded her eyes, and greeted us.

I had only known Hermione for a few months, seeing her every weekend at the market. But aside from that, I knew very little about her. I felt honored she had invited us to her farm and was welcoming us into her world.

Opening the gate the rest of the way, hanging on to the dogs' collars, Hermione welcomed us to her farm. "*Bienvenue*," she said quietly. She closed the gate, the dogs jumping behind her. "Don't worry, they are sweet," she said.

Dressed in a long skirt, tank top, and work boots with thick socks, she looked small compared to the vast land behind her. She walked ahead of us, pushing a wheelbarrow, clearly a woman of few words. Her property was not big—only about five acres—but had one working greenhouse and another that had been destroyed in a fire in 2008 (along with almost everything she owned).

Hermione, born in the fifties in Paris, grew up with parents who instilled in her the idea that nature is something to embrace and encouraged her to be one with the earth. But, like most of us, she went on to work in various office jobs, and the lifestyle that comes with living and working in a city made her feel unhappy and unhealthy. She dreamed of starting a small farm to grow herbs, flowers, lettuces, and sprouts. Taking early retirement, she used the money to buy the land she now farms and lives on, in a 130-square-foot, one-room structure with no electricity, running water, or heat.

Walking past the ruined greenhouse, we reached a long row of baby kale plants. "*Voici*," said Hermione, smiling, "Here is the *chou*." The plants were tiny, but they were there, small, green sprigs shooting up and starting to sprout small, green leaves. As I took photos, Hermione picked up a hoe and started shaking up the dirt around the plants.

"On days like today, where it is hot," she said, slowly warming up to us, "I will get up early and work and then take a nap in the afternoon to avoid the heat. On days before the market, I will wear a light around my head and work in the dark. That's the best because it is the coolest," she said, pulling tiny weeds that grew around the plants.

"This is the first thing I've done with my life where I feel truly happy," she continued. "I eat when I want to eat, and I sleep when I want to sleep. It's a life I completely dictate."

We walked around the entire farm, reaching a border of *cassis*, black currant, bushes that bulged with tiny, red and dark-purple berries. "Pick some!" Hermione told us. "I have so much to share. Take some home and make a syrup!"

We spent the rest of the morning picking berries and plopping them into our hats. We sat on the grass outside her house, and she started to slice zucchini and add a homemade paste of chickpeas and sunflower sprouts, which she made into small courgette rolls. While we ate the rolls and fresh berries, Hermione brought out an old book. Titled *Culture Potagère*, it was a gardening book written in 1913 by a professor of horticulture.

"Kreesteen," Hermione said, her small hands grasping the leather-bound book. A black-and-white illustration of peasant women wearing long skirts and cloths covering their heads, standing in a garden surrounded by different cabbages, graced the front inside cover. Opening to a page in the *chou* section, Hermione pointed to another illustration. "*Regarde*. Look. There is kale!" In block print, next to a tiny drawing of a kale plant, the book discussed the growing and harvesting technique for *chou frisé vert grand* (another name to add to the list), saying that it was best eaten as a soup. As I continued to read, I saw the last sentence: "Today, this vegetable is very rarely grown."

KALE AND CHICKPEA
·· COURGETTE ROLLS ··

Contributed by Hermione Boehrer

Not only did Hermione make these zucchini rolls for Emily and me, but she also makes them during the summer to sell at the market. During the warmer months, when summer squash is in season, you'll find Hermione behind her stand, rolling her "courgette sushi," as she calls them. When she shared this recipe, she made sure to point out that her special touch is adding in the mint leaves, which give a freshness to the mixture. Just as some people at the market think that her green wheatgrass juices are strange, they also find her courgette sushi unusual. "My trick," Hermione told me, "is to add a touch of tamari. The savory flavor gives people the idea that it tastes meaty, which will encourage more people to try vegetable-based or raw foods. This recipe also adds in a few leaves of baby kale.

INGREDIENTS

- 2 TABLESPOONS ROASTED SUNFLOWER SEEDS (OR SPROUTS)
- 1 (15-OUNCE/425-G) CAN CHICKPEAS (OR CHICKPEA SPROUTS)
- 1 CUP (30 G) KALE, WASHED AND DESTEMMED
- 5 TO 6 LEAVES MINT
- LEMON JUICE, FRESHLY SQUEEZED FROM ½ LEMON
- ½ TABLESPOON TAMARI
- 1 MEDIUM ZUCCHINI, SLICED VERTICALLY ON A MANDOLIN SLICER*

PREPARATION

Heat a small pan over medium-high heat, and roast the sunflower seeds for 4 to 5 minutes, until golden brown. Be sure to roast evenly by constantly stirring. Put the roasted sunflower seeds, chickpeas, kale, mint, and lemon juice in a food processor, and mix. The mixture will never be smooth like hummus, and it should be thicker to keep the rolls together. If more liquid is needed, add warm water by the teaspoon until a smoother consistency is reached. Add the tamari, and mix again. On one end of each slice of zucchini, spread 1 tablespoon of the chickpea mixture. Roll the zucchini slices up, and secure with a toothpick.

YIELD
8 to 10 rolls

If zucchini are not in season, you can use thin slices of large carrots. It helps to lightly steam them first so they roll more easily.

Chapter 26

I once thought about trademarking the kale massage. Not because I needed to own the rights to it, but because it is an idea that I truly believe in. A kale salad is not a kale salad without a good massage.

After almost ten months of not having kale and three months of living, breathing, and blogging about kale, I was more than ready for a properly massaged kale salad. Luckily, the French five-week summer *vacances* was upon us, and I was heading back to the Big Apple, where I knew I could easily find one.

Les vacances in Paris is like the last day of school. Everyone kisses good-bye, their cheeks receiving well-deserved pecks, filled with the anticipation and excitement of what the next five blissful weeks might hold. Who knows what adventures they'll have and stories they'll be able to tell come September's *la rentrée*—the grand return.

When I was a preteen, my hope on the last day of school was that during my summer vacation, I would finally grow boobs and return to school a new person. I'd read stories about girls waking up one morning with a chest that grew overnight. Now, as I prepared for this summer break, my dream was to return to Paris fluent in French. I'm still waiting for both.

It was obvious that the city was shutting down. Amelia fled to Spain for six weeks, leaving piles of mail that wouldn't be distributed until her return. Monsieur Sinclair was spending four weeks in the countryside and, upon his departure, reliable as ever, reached out to touch my stomach, whispering questions in my ear about when the building's baby was coming.

The Saturday market was nearly empty, with very few vendors and shoppers. Even Hermione was away; her spot was an empty square of pavement. The neighborhood shops started to close one by one, posting notices in plastic sheet protectors on their locked front doors that they were on their *congé annuel*, paid vacation period, many of them planning to be gone from July 25 through September 1. Even the local public pool was closed, just when people want a pool the most.

The French do not mess around with their *vacances*.

As luck would have it, Philip was the one person in France who did not get a five-week *vacances* and would be staying behind in Paris. With global clients who don't have August off, being away from the office for five weeks in a row wasn't feasible. Plus, it seemed like there were always issues cropping up—even if we were on vacation. His experiences so far with the French office had been *comme si comme ça*. Things weren't bad per se, but they weren't always easy. Just because someone speaks French does not mean they will easily understand the culture.

A few months earlier, in May (which is a month when practically every week contains a bank holiday, and the French *faire le pont*, do the bridge—take off an extra day when a holiday falls on a Tuesday or Thursday, resulting in an extra-long, four-day weekend), one junior account executive refused to organize a call with the global CEO based in New York, protesting to Philip, "But it is a holiday, and we are closed." Philip repeatedly told her that he couldn't reschedule a meeting with the busiest man at the agency because France was closed. So she called up the CEO's assistant and canceled the meeting herself.

In June, in the days leading up to an important business pitch, the office's high-end printer broke, and the repairman wasn't available to fix it. Instead of finding another way to print the materials, Philip's team chose not to print anything. He came into the office on Monday morning without any pitch materials ready. In America, someone would have been fired or at least reprimanded. In France, it wasn't a big deal; the attitude was simply, "Everyone was closed or busy." No one scrambled to make sure everything was done correctly and on time. There was no Plan B.

Frequently, employees would go see a doctor when they were having a hard time with a client or struggling with a campaign, claiming to be too stressed. In France, it's not uncommon to see the *medecin de travail*, the work doctor, and be granted two months off, paid, because work is too emotionally draining.

One of the most frustrating things for Philip in his new role was trying to improve his office in the face of French employment laws that made it nearly impossible to fire staff members who needed to be dismissed. And even when it was legally possible to let someone go, the probability of the office being sued was very high.

As I prepared to head to New York, that was the problem *du jour*. Someone was trying to sue the agency…again. "This time," he told me over our last dinner together before I flew out, "it's someone who actually left the agency more than a year ago. He is suing us because he claims the job stressed him out so much that he still can't get an erection." I can't imagine how *that* meeting with HR went.

✻

As for me, my heart was full as the jet to New York landed with a thud, slowing to a stop. "*Mesdames et messieurs, bienvenue à* John F. Kennedy Airport. Local time is one thirty-five p.m. The current temperature is ninety degrees Fahrenheit." Already I could feel the electricity running through me, just from landing on American soil.

New York was as hot, balmy, and dirty as it had been when we left. Putrid-smelling steam rose out of the sewers, blacktop sizzled in the heat, and the sidewalks reeked of garbage. But people were smiling. Laughing. The energy was electric. Uncontrollable. And it was busy—there was no summer *vacances* happening here.

I had left New York when the kale craze was just beginning. After only one year away, it seemed like I was seeing more juice bars than Starbucks, which was saying a lot, since there seemed to be one on every corner. Kale was popping up on nearly every restaurant's menu—even at cocktail bars. I decided to organize my own *Tour de Kale*, so I could meet and talk with people who were knee deep in it: growing kale, cooking kale, and doing business with kale. My first stops were Northern Spy and Back Forty, two restaurants that were leading the kale salad trend.

Walking down East Twelfth Street through the East Village to Northern Spy, I passed places that were once a part of my life but were now only New York memories: a friend's old apartment building, where she kissed the man who was now her husband for the first time; the wine bar where I went on a date with a college student; the tiny boutique where I had my wedding veil made by hand; the ramen noodle shop that Sarah, Hannah, and I would trek to on snowy, windy nights to enjoy steaming bowls of salty broth with hand-pulled noodles, topped with pork, bamboo, seaweed, and poached eggs.

Approaching Northern Spy, I remembered the first time I ate there, in early 2010. Hannah was the one who'd suggested it. "They do kale, Kristen," she said, excited to tell me about her new restaurant find. "But they do it raw, like a salad." Raw? I had never heard of that.

"And get this," she continued. "They massage it first! When I took my first bite the leaves were so tender, I had to know what they did. They add a simple dressing and use their hands to knead it for a few minutes. How amazing is that?" she asked. It was an interesting way to prepare it. Kale leaves are a lot tougher than lettuce, so it certainly seemed like a little rubdown wouldn't hurt. Hannah went on and on about the salad for weeks, until we finally went to the restaurant together, and I could try the raw kale salad for myself.

Chris Ronis and Christophe Hille opened Northern Spy Food Co. in 2009. They were among the first in the New York City restaurant scene to popularize the kale salad, which is the one dish they have never taken off the menu in their regular rotation of selections.

"Kale is the cornerstone of my restaurant right now," Chris told me. "It's so versatile and fun to play with. We put out more kale salads than any other dish. The only time we don't serve it is if we've run out of the vegetable. We make sure to reserve kale now."

Chris invited me into the kitchen to watch the chef prepare a salad. "What do you think is the best way to reintroduce a vegetable like this?" I asked.

"Pair it with something that people already know," Chris advised. "Or just sauté it—with olive oil, thinly sliced garlic, fresh orange juice, and salt and pepper. That's one of my favorite ways."

Chris was kind enough to pack a salad for me to go and I took it to a bench in Tompkins Square Park. The air had cooled down, and the sun was sparkling through the leaves of the trees, creating shapes and shadows on the paved footpaths, as pigeons and squirrels jumped around and kids played in the fountains. The leaves were massaged with olive oil, lemon juice, and salt, and there were chopped almonds, pecorino cheese, and roasted squash mixed in. It was kale bliss. This was what I had been craving for so long. Every bite melted in my mouth like the finest chocolate.

My second restaurant interview was at Back Forty West. The Soho location brought more memories flooding back to me, from back when it was occupied by a different restaurant called Savoy. The space was unique because it was an old, brick, nineteenth-century town house, narrow and tall, that stood alone between larger, more modern loft spaces. Inside, the dining room felt cozy, with beamed ceilings, wooden floors, a staircase, and a fireplace.

I brought my mom here during one of our girls' weekends. She would come to the city on Thursdays, and we would go out for a long dinner, talking for hours, lingering over wine, updating each other on everything that never made it into our hurried cell-phone conversations. During this particular Thursday night dinner, I had news to share.

"I think I'm going to marry Philip," I told her, my eyes rising over the candlelight to see her reaction. She smiled. Good. She was happy to hear this news.

"We also might move to Paris," I added. She was silent, processing the thought that her only child might be living an ocean away. It would take time for my mother to warm to the idea.

At Back Forty West, I introduced myself to the chef, Shanna Pacifico, who began to explain more about their kale salad. "We started our salad in 2009, when I was looking for a heartier twist on our original Caesar," she told me as she added grilled kale to fresh escarole and mixed in creamy parmesan dressing. "People went crazy for it. In fact, they would call us beforehand to check and see if it was on the menu." Adding the finishing touches of anchovies and baked chickpeas, she said, "You know, I think kale is more than just a trend. It's cool to have it on your menu now, but it's so much more than just cool."

My meetings with restaurants, juice bars, and even a popular kale-chip company based outside Philadelphia were informative, but the best part of being back in New York was visiting my favorite places and seeing friends. We ate french fries with melted Gorgonzola cheese at a coveted outdoor table at Extra Virgin, a West Village café. I ran every morning through Central Park. I drank drip coffee and ate bagel-and-cream-cheese sandwiches from corner bodegas. For my birthday, Sarah and I spent the morning buying ingredients at the Union Square Greenmarket for a dinner party that she and her fiancé hosted. We had kale salad, of course, and a Momofuku Milk Bar confetti cake lit with twenty-eight candles.

The view from Sarah's twenty-eighth floor apartment, to me, was one of the best in the city. Looking down at the grid of buildings, traffic lights, and taxis below, and skyscraper after skyscraper in the distance, I'd always felt invincible. I may have been just another person in a city of eight million people, but the vista invigorated me, with promises that anything could happen. But this time, while it was great to be back, after a few days, something wasn't entirely right. My instinct for the city—the kind where you can shut your eyes and do anything blind—had still been intact when we'd visited last Thanksgiving, but now it wasn't as strong. My steps faltered while I crossed the street. I found myself pining for the Paris *métro* as I took the subway uptown instead of downtown. I could not for the life of me figure out why there were so many options for "enhanced" water. The aisles of candy, cookies, and chips in the drugstores and pharmacies overwhelmed me. I was confused to feel so out of sorts in a place that had once felt so comfortable. And even at the Greenmarket, which was big and filled with variety, including plenty of kale, I missed my favorite Parisian vendors, who knew me and greeted me every Saturday morning. New York was moving on, and I started to realize that I was moving on too.

·· NEW YORK'S BEST KALE SALAD ··

Contributed by Chris Ronis, Northen Spy Food Co.

These days, New York City has a lot of kale salads. It's hard to go out to eat without seeing a kale salad on the menu. That does not mean that all kale salads are created equally. Yet one of the first is still the very best.

INGREDIENTS*

- 4 CUPS (200 G) KALE (LACINATO OR DINOSAUR), RIBS REMOVED AND CUT CROSS WAYS INTO ½-INCH WIDE STRIPS

For the Delicata Squash

- 2 SMALL TO MEDIUM DELICATA SQUASH, CUT LENGTH WISE, REMOVE SEEDS, CUT AGAIN LENGTHWISE THEN INTO ½ PIECES, DO NOT PEEL
- 1 TO 2 GARLIC CLOVES, CRUSHED
- ½ CUP (160 GRAMS) HONEY
- ½ CUP (180 ML) OLIVE OIL
- 1 TEASPOON RED CHILI FLAKES
- ½ TEASPOON PEPPER

For the Almonds

- ½ CUP (65 G) RAW ALMONDS
- 2 TABLESPOONS OLIVE OIL
- SALT AND FRESHLY GROUND BLACK PEPPER, TO TASTE

For the Dressing

- ½ CUP (180 ML) OLIVE OIL
- 3 TABLESPOONS LEMON JUICE
- 1 TEASPOON SALT
- ½ CUP (60 G) CHEDDAR CHEESE, AGED AND CRUMBLED
- PECORINO (OR OTHER HARD CHEESE), FOR SHAVING
- FRESHLY GROUND BLACK PEPPER, TO TASTE

PREPARATION

Preheat the oven to 350°F (180°C). Toss the squash with the garlic, honey, olive oil, chili flakes, salt, and pepper in a bowl, place in shallow roasting pan, and cook in oven for 25 minutes. In a separate bowl, toss the almonds in olive oil, salt, and pepper. Roast on a baking sheet with the oven at the same temperature for 7 to 10 minutes, or until the almonds have turned a golden brown. Let cool, and roughly chop the almonds. While squash and almonds are roasting, put the kale in a mixing bowl and mix well before adding squash, almonds, and cheddar cheese. Toss ingredients gently. Divide salad into bowls and shave pecorino on top of salads.

YIELD

- 2 SERVINGS

Instead of using squash, you can substitute sweet potatoes or carrots if desired. Add two poached or over easy eggs for a perfect brunch or lunch dish.

Chapter 27

I had one last thing to take care of before heading back to Paris. Google Translate. As the top search engine and service for quick-and-easy translations, the way Google rendered the word "kale" in French was important. And as I learned during my first search for kale, Google's translation for the vegetable was *chou frisé*. This wasn't incorrect, but *chou frisé* was also savoy cabbage, which could also be *chou de Milan*. Calling both savoy cabbage and kale the same thing would be confusing and only make my mission more difficult, and I certainly did not want people confusing the two in France. I wanted to find a consistent translation for kale.

Luckily, Philip and I were friends with someone working at Google, and he was able to arrange a meeting with a coworker to talk more about the translation issue. And this person also happened to be French.

Thomas looked as you would stereotypically expect a Frenchman to look: thin, with round, tortoise-shell glasses that rested on a long nose. After a week away from Paris, I found his French accent surprisingly comforting. With a carefree smile, he led me to one of Google's cool cafés (which, of course, was serving kale that day), turned to me, and said, "I love your project! And I love kale!"

"Oh, you know what kale is?" I asked, anxious to hear his opinion.

"Yes!" he exclaimed. "I discovered it when we moved here. My wife and I and our French friends just can't get enough. Salads! Juices! Smoothies! Oh, and the chips!" he cheered, as if auditioning to be kale's first French mascot. "We are complete converts, and I can't believe I never ate it as a child. So I think what you are doing is great!"

Humbled and relieved to hear his reaction, I responded, "Wow, thank you. I'm so glad you like kale and the idea." I decided to talk translation right away. "Here is my issue: the name. The Google translation says *chou frisé*, which is misleading." I told Thomas about the numerous instances I'd seen on social media of excited but misinformed people who were sharing photos of the kale chips they'd made, unknowingly, from savoy cabbage leaves.

"*Non*," Thomas replied. "I understand completely. *Chou frisé* is not the same thing as kale. So let's figure it out. What do you think it should be called?"

Ah, the loaded question.

The French are extremely protective of their language. The Académie française, a council that regulates the French language, makes a concerted effort to ensure that there is a French equivalent for every English word, to prevent Anglicisms from creeping into the French vernacular. "Sexting" is *textopornographie*, Wi-Fi is *acces sans fil a l'internet*. The list goes on. I respected the Académie, and the last thing I wanted to do was offend the people preserving a language I'd been trying so hard to learn. It would scream American ignorance if I asked farmers or chefs to use the English word "kale." I had decided not to decide. Let the farmers decide. Let the chefs decide. Let the people decide. I wanted the project to evolve and see what happened.

"I like *chou kale*," he said. "At least it would only be one name, versus all of the other names you have discovered. Do you think it would be masculine or feminine?" he asked.

I paused, thinking about how I constantly struggle with the gender of nouns in French. "You tell me. I am the worst at gender in your language, and there are no rules. Either you learn it from birth or you're stuck misrepresenting everything each time you open your mouth." Thomas laughed, clearly agreeing with me.

Take, for example, the *boulangerie*. It is the one shop in France where you do *not* want to mix up your genders. A baguette is feminine, *une baguette*. A croissant is masculine, *un croissant*. I learned that distinction the hard way, and even now I still have to build up my courage every time I go to a bakery.

The whole *boulangerie* experience can be a bit militant. Enter through one door, get in line, have exact change ready, quickly survey the glass case to see whether they have any *croissants au beurre*, clearly place your order, pay immediately, using the exact change, and exit through the opposite door. Some bakeries actually have automatic change machines to keep lines moving during the Sunday morning rush. They are that serious. I often think that the *boulangerie* is the French version of *Seinfeld*'s Soup Nazi. You can't mess around. I cringe when I hear American tourists in front of me, speaking loudly, taking their time to decide what kind of tart they want. They're totally unaware that the stern woman (it's almost always a woman behind the counter at the bakery) is ready to kick them out for not following protocol.

On one memorable visit to a *boulangerie*, I learned the hard way to never mistake the gender of a baguette again. I thought I was prepared. Patiently waiting in line, I could see that they had plenty of baguettes (yes, bakeries sell out of baguettes). I had my one euro and twenty *centimes* in my sweaty palm, ready to go.

When it was my turn to order, I stepped up to the counter and politely asked, "*Un baguette, s'il vous plaît.*"

"*Excusez-moi, madame?*" she barked back, staring at me with her beady eyes. I repeated myself, again using the masculine article.

"*Je ne comprends pas,*" she shot back, telling me she did not understand. I started to panic. How could she not understand? I had asked for a *baguette*. Even if all baguettes aren't created equal, the word "baguette" is practically universal! What could I have possibly said wrong? The line behind me was growing, and I heard sighs of impatience. I had to resort to the one thing that makes every nonnative speaker feel even worse in a situation like this: I pointed. You only point when all else fails, and at that moment, after two tries, all else had failed.

"*Ah, ben oui*, une *baguette, madame*. Une *baguette*," she taunted me, sliding the bread into a long paper sleeve. I could feel all eyes on me. The younger women placing hot, fresh *croissants au beurre* and *pains au chocolat* into the glass case shook their heads. The little boy behind me, who waited impatiently with his mother, stared at me too. He knew better than to call a baguette a man. Anxious to escape the small shop, I kept my eyes down, quickly handed over my coins, muttered a quiet *merci*, and ran out.

❦

Now here I was, trying to decide whether kale should be masculine or feminine. I was definitely not the right person. I shrugged, letting out a long sigh. "See? You have already become French!" Thomas said to me, laughing. "Let's see. *Chou* is masculine, and since kale is a cabbage, it should probably be *le chou kale*," he said.

It did have a nice ring to it as he said the phrase aloud. Now I would have to see what the farmers thought.

·· MARKET BAG SAVORY SPREAD ··

Contributed by Anna Brones, writer

A French person once told me that while it is true that Americans are stuck with being stereotyped as only eating big hamburgers, big hot dogs, and big ice cream sundaes, the French have to deal with being stereotyped as walking around Paris (always with the Eiffel Tower in the background), wearing berets and carrying baguettes. I can assure you that Americans eat more than just big ice cream sundaes and that French people do more than just walk around the Eiffel Tower wearing berets.

But the baguette? That part might be true. Walk down any street during the evening rush hour, and you'll see most people walking home with a baguette tucked under their arm. And, most likely, they will have already torn off the top and eaten it. It's hard to resist a warm, freshly baked baguette, with its crunchy crust and fluffy inside. Eating the top off of a baguette as soon as you buy it is practically a national sport in France. **Bonne-mamans do it.** *Dads do it, moms do it, and even babies are given the crunchy top to gnaw on.*

Another thing that you'll frequently see popping out of market bags and caddies are leeks. Even for me, a market bag is not complete without a baguette and a few leeks poking out. This confiture is an easy combination of caramelized leeks and onions with kale, to be spread on sliced baguette anytime of day, with or without the top.

INGREDIENTS

- 3 TABLESPOONS OLIVE OIL
- 2 LEEKS, THINLY SLICED
- 1 CUP (30 G) KALE, WASHED, DESTEMMED, AND FINELY CHOPPED
- 1 MEDIUM ONION, CHOPPED
- 1 TABLESPOON BROWN SUGAR

- ¼ cup (55 ml) apple cider vinegar
- ¼ cup (55 ml) white wine
- 2 sprigs fresh thyme, leaves only
- ¼ teaspoon salt
- Freshly ground black pepper, to taste

PREPARATION

Heat the olive oil in a large saucepan over medium heat. Add the leeks and onions. Stir continuously for 4 to 5 minutes. Add the kale and stir for 1 to 2 minutes until lightly cooked. Add the sugar, and stir slowly to caramelize. Continue to cook for 10 to 12 minutes, until the vegetables are soft and have reduced in size. Add the apple cider vinegar, white wine, and thyme, and bring to a boil. Reduce heat to a simmer, and let cook for 30 to 45 minutes. Halfway through, add the salt and pepper. Continue to stir occasionally to prevent the mixture from sticking to the bottom of the pan. For a softer, smoother spread, once the mixture has reduced, use an immersion blender or food processor to mix to desired consistency. The spread can be served hot or cold and will keep in the refrigerator for one week.

YIELD

- 1 jar. (approx. 7½ ounces/207 g)

Chapter 28

I arrived back in Paris, without incident this time, not having packed any kale in my luggage. With the city still in shutdown mode and Philip able to escape office politics, we decided to take two weeks for ourselves to do *vacances* like the French do, and head down south. We rented an apartment in the small beach town of Le Canon, on Bai d'Arcachon, which is about a ninety-minute drive from Bordeaux.

But first I had to take care of something: my bikini line. I had not yet taken the plunge and gotten my first French bikini wax. Don't get me wrong; things had been trimmed, but it was summer, the time for tiny swimsuits, and I knew that if I didn't go for it now, I would spend another winter with razor burn.

Espace beauté, beauty spaces, are all over Paris. Many different companies each have multiple locations, with window signs that make promises of reducing cellulite, removing upper-lip hair, and leaving customers with silky, smooth skin. Somehow I was able to find an *espace* that was actually open amidst all the August closures.

"What kind of *épilation*, wax, would you like?" I was asked. The esthetician was young, with thick, dark hair pulled back in a ponytail high on her head and bright-red lipstick clashing with her purple uniform.

I had not prepared myself for this question. I had no idea what kind of wax I wanted. In America, it was easy to ask for a Brazilian but then, once behind closed doors, to talk through what I really wanted with the esthetician. Some here, not too much there, and so on. Here, for my *épilation maillot de bain*, there were choices. *Épilation intégral* sounded serious, and the *épilation américaine* made me realize that I actually had no idea how Americans waxed, or at least, how the rest of the world thought we waxed. And finally, there was *épilation sexy*. Were the other options *not* sexy?

I opted for *épilation sexy* and hoped for the best. The treatment room was bare with the faint scent of baby powder. I stripped down and waited for the esthetician. Sitting on the table, legs crossed, I wondered how I was going to explain what I wanted her to do. I had no clue what the vocabulary words for down *there* were.

She entered and closed the sliding door, leaving only the two of us for this intimate moment of sexy waxing. My back began to sweat, and I started swearing in my head at the person who invented the bikini wax in the first place. No matter how many times I've had one, it never becomes less painful.

"*Alors*," she said to me. "So, you want the sexy wax?"

"Umm, *oui*," I answered, straining my neck to look up at her. "*Si vous pouvez faire* something like this…" I started to motion with my hands where she should wax. "*Comme ça*? And like that," I continued, making various crisscross motions, hoping she was getting the gist.

The woman leaned in closer to me, making casual conversation, dripping the piping hot wax onto my skin. My brain, focused only on the pain as the hairs were ripped out, could barely form a coherent thought in English, let alone French. I struggled, stuttering out where I was from, how long we'd lived in France, and that we lived just down the street. I kept switching back and forth between the formal and informal conjugations. Because I didn't know this woman at all, I had to address her formally. Yet at the same time, as I struggled to conjugate my verbs in the *vous* form, her face was in my crotch doing a sexy wax. I couldn't think of anything less formal than that.

❧

A day later, feeling much sexier from my sexy wax, I packed up and headed off with Philip for *vacances*. The purpose of the trip was, of course, to relax and reconnect, but I still had a lot on my mind because the first season of my farmers' kale was about to begin, which meant I had to figure out what to do next with the project. Did I want to distribute the kale? Did I want to sell the kale directly to restaurants? Would Hermione and Sebastien even *have* enough kale to sell to restaurants? And could I really see myself driving a refrigerated kale truck through the dark streets of Paris at five o'clock in the morning to deliver it?

I decided to launch a kale subscription service. Modeling my service after community supported agriculture (CSA) in America (or AMAP as it's known in France), my plan was to buy kale directly from the farmers and resell it, delivering it to various drop-off points throughout the city. I called it "Kale Wanted," and within two weeks, I had twenty-five subscribers, all people who were waiting anxiously for their first taste of kale in Paris.

❧

Vacances did not disappoint. We jogged through the pine forests (in which we saw a lot of *gîtes*, my French camping vocabulary coming in handy). We took long walks on the beach, the waves crashing against our ankles and the sun shining on our backs. We inspected the German World War II bunkers that were settled into the sandy hillside dunes—now covered in graffiti and littered with cigarette butts and broken beer bottles—eerily popping out like medieval war helmets.

At the end of every day, we enjoyed *apéro* at the tiny oyster houses in Le Canon. Lined up along the bay like a village of their own, the houses were painted bright colors, like red, pink, blue, and yellow, and each offered fresh-from-the-water oysters with brown bread and butter, paired with a glass of chilled, local white wine. We watched the colors of the bay change from light blue to dark navy blue as the sun set to the west, turning the sky pink. Then we went home and cooked dinner together, listening to nothing but the cicadas outside our deck.

Le Canon had only one main road, and on it we found everything we needed. There was a *boucherie*, a *boulangerie*, a *fromagerie*, a small grocery store, and best of all, a fisherman who had set up shop in a deserted wooden shed in front of the oyster houses to sell his daily catch from earlier in the morning. His face was worn from years of salt and sunshine, and his gray eyes sparkled like the water behind him. When he spoke, his belly bounced, round with age. Visiting his shop one day, we admired the options of glistening sole, sawdust-colored turbot, and Atlantic cod. Every fish was whole. Choosing the turbot, we assumed that the fisherman would fillet it for us, like our local *poissonnerie* in Paris does.

He bellowed, immediately discerning that we city folk had no idea how to prepare a whole turbot. "*C'est facile!*" he said, launching into how easy it was to prepare the fish. Trying to keep up with his French and make mental notes of what to do, we left his shop willing to give it a try. He did make it sound easy, and a girl's got to learn how to fillet a fish at some point. What better place than right next to the waters where it came from?

Later that evening, sunburned and salty, I put my game face on, ready to tackle the fish. The kitchen was small, with a tiny counter space in between the sink and stove, reminding me of the little *cuisine* I had in Hell's Kitchen. Wanting to avoid getting any flying scales or escaping fish guts on my clothing, I stripped down to only my bathing suit and flip-flops and tied my hair away from the humid air. I had a feeling this would be an intimate affair.

As I stared into the sink, the fish looked less attractive and less glistening than I remembered. In fact, it looked downright ugly. I continued to stare. It stared back at me, with its tiny, lifeless glass eye. Its skin seemed rougher too. This was not going to be easy. I grabbed the sharpest knife I could find as I was about to begin and realized I didn't really know what to do. I started to scrape the scales off of one side. Not much was coming off, so I scraped harder. Small flakes like fingernails started to come off, flying every which way. Scales flew up in my face and eyes, they splattered all over my hands and forearms, and they fell onto the floor. There had to be a better way to do this. Why hadn't I ever paid more attention at our *poissonnerie* when they prepared my fish for me?

After five minutes of scraping, the skin of the fish felt as rough as it did when I had started. This was not going to be a solo job. Philip, watching me struggle, took a turn. Sweat soon formed on his brow. Scales kept flying everywhere, and the smell of turbot intensified as we hovered over the miniature sink, working closely with the fish.

I am an adventurous eater. I'll eat almost anything raw: clams, scallops, shrimp. I love eating things tartare. I dream of sushi. So why was this little creature freaking me out? As the knife hit the thick skin of the tiny, difficult *poisson*, my stomach started to churn. I knew if I scraped that fish one more time, I would throw up. I stopped, threw it into the sink, and ran into the bathroom, where I stayed put. Not able to admit that I had failed at this cooking milestone, I convinced myself it was a stomach bug, went to bed, and didn't surface until the next morning. I was a fish failure.

Unable to face the kitchen the following night, I made a reservation at Chez Hortense, where I knew they would fillet our fish for us. Practically an institution in Cap Ferret, Chez Hortense has been in existence in some form or another since the early twentieth century. It sits on the tip of the Arcachon peninsula, with a view of the impressive Dune du Pyla, Europe's largest sand dune, across the bay. It's a popular spot, frequented by celebrities like Marion Cotillard and Vanessa Paradis. Hidden from plain view off the small, sandy road that leads to it, the restaurant is unassuming. The outdoor terrace has wooden beams and a wooden floor, is enclosed by green plants and vines that sway with the conversation as guests devour the delicious, fresh seafood.

The ceremony of ordering a whole fish at a French restaurant is quite dramatic. It may be the simplest item on the menu, but it comes with the most pomp and circumstance. The server will bring out the whole, raw fish with pride, as if he or she were the one who caught it.

"Here it is, *monsieur*," the server will say, bending down and revealing the fish, telling you how many grams it weighs. With your nod of approval, the server will quickly rush the fish back to the kitchen. After being either grilled or baked, the fish is brought back out for a second reveal, this time with greater fanfare. Sometimes a second server will follow the first, as everyone gasps at how delicious the fish looks.

"Will you need us to prepare the fish for you, *monsieur?*" We always accept this offer, although I am always very impressed with how skilled the French are at filleting cooked fish at restaurants, leaving tidy piles of skin and bones. The official filleting begins, the waiter, using a flat fish knife and fork to work his way through the process of delicately pulling the tender white flesh away from the skin and off the bone, working meticulously enough to ensure that nothing goes to waste.

I went to Chez Hortense expecting to order a whole fish, but we saw from every other table that the thing to order there are the *moules*, mussels. The light aroma of white wine, garlic, parsley, and parmesan filtered through the terrace as pot after steaming pot of mussels and small bowls of *frites* were delivered. Voices hushed as the clicking sound of empty mussel shells hitting metal pot lids overtook the conversation. When our last mussel was finished, we dipped each *frite* into the remaining sauce, not leaving a drop behind. I wanted to eat here every night—anything to never have to fillet a fish again.

·· PARSLEY MUSSELS ··

For a long time after our dinner at Chez Hortense, I could not stop thinking about their moules, *and I knew I was going to have to try to recreate them. Mussels were actually one of the first things I cooked on my own when I had my first apartment in college, probably because the idea of only having to add a sliced onion and white wine to something seemed easy enough. And now, one of my favorite things at our* poissonnerie *are the tiny mussels that come fresh from Mont-Saint-Michel in Lower Normandy. When trying to recreate the flavors from Chez Hortense, I vaguely remembered the taste of spicy chorizo but decided against adding it into this recipe because I prefer to keep the freshness of the parsley and sharpness of the garlic pure.*

INGREDIENTS

- 1 BUNCH (3 OUNCES/80 G) PARSLEY, WASHED, THICK STEMS REMOVED
- 1 HEAD (ABOUT 8 CLOVES) GARLIC
- 6 OZ (150 G) PARMESAN CHEESE, FINELY GRATED
- 3 TABLESPOONS OLIVE OIL
- 2 TABLESPOONS SALTED BUTTER
- 4 TO 6 SHALLOTS, THINLY SLICED
- 1 POUND (700 G) MUSSELS, CLEANED*
- 1½ TO 2 CUPS (360 TO 480 ML) DRY WHITE WINE

PREPARATION

Mix the garlic and parsley in a food processor, until the ingredients are finely chopped but not smooth. Remove and place in a separate bowl. Finely grate the cheese in the food processor. Heat the olive oil and butter in a large pot over medium heat. Add the shallots, and stir for 4 to 5 minutes until they begin to soften. Add the mussels and white wine, and stir continuously. Add the parsley mixture, and stir continuously until the mussels have opened. Serve with or without the excess sauce and a warm chunk of hearty bread.

YIELD

• 2 SERVINGS

It is recommended that you thoroughly clean the mussels before steaming. Soak in cold water and rub any shells that are dirty. Inspect each mussel individually, and debeard by pulling the sticky membrane away from the shell. Remove any mussels that have already opened. After cooking, do not serve mussels that have not opened up during the cooking process. Continuous stirring with heat and wine will help them cook and open.

Chapter 29

B efore I knew it, the leaves were crinkly, brown again, with more on the ground than on the trees. Autumn comes early in Paris. The leaves in Paris don't really change color, at least not like they do in New York. French trees, like French people, are not flamboyant. American trees are dramatic, as if they're trying to sell you something. French trees quietly change from green to pale mustard to brown, and then, once dry, fall to the ground. Piles of them collect in the corners of the grand boulevards, crunching beneath the passing bicycles and scooters.

C'est la rentrée—the return to Paris. The city came to life again. Like a bear coming out of hibernation, Parisians returned, ready for the new season. Mopeds whipped around street corners and annoyingly trailed pedestrians on sidewalks. The shops were all open, and once again there were more Parisians than tourists filling the café terraces.

This time last year, I felt like I was standing on the sidelines, watching as everyone else seemed to be doing something real, something important. This year was different. I too had a purpose and a responsibility of my own. I had promised twenty-five people, eager for their first bite of French kale, that I would soon be delivering the leafy green to their doorstep. The timing was ideal. Both Hermione and Sebastien had planted their seeds around the end of

June, which hopefully meant their kale would be ready by the beginning of September.

Before I had a chance to check with the farmers, I had a meeting with two women who had previously worked in fashion and were relocating from New York to launch a company that would bring aspects of Brooklyn to Paris. The "brand" of Brooklyn was becoming more and more trendy with Parisians, so the timing could not have been better. The first event was a pop-up dinner during the September Paris Fashion Week, to be cooked by a popular New York restaurant. And since they were coming from New York, it was no surprise that they were looking for kale.

The *rendez-vous* was at a new café on trendy rue Charlot in the Marais. They had already arrived when I got there, one brunette and one blond, casually sipping freshly pressed mango juice. I immediately loved their outfits. They were dressed in revamped penny loafers, high-waisted jeans, and soft, chambray denim shirts. I wished I had spent more time getting ready that morning.

"*Helloooo!*" they said to me in unison. "So *niiiice* to meet you. Isn't this café just the *cutest?*" They leaned in for the double kiss, because newly arrived Americans like to immediately adopt this custom. I'd been there. It makes us all feel a little more European.

We sat down at a small table, with even smaller chairs, and they spoke in their saccharine voices through sweet, petite smiles. I could tell they had only just arrived in Paris. They were still peppy. Energetic. They were fresh, not yet worn down by the day in, day out struggle with the French language and rarely being understood. For them, the sun in Paris was still shining every day.

My juice—"the *best* juice," they told me—arrived, and the brunette turned to me. "Well, we just *love* your project," she said. "We think it's *so* great. I mean, who would have thought that Paris has no kale?!"

I wasn't as accustomed as I once was to the friendliness and positivity of Americans.

"But do you make any *money?*" she asked. I was taken aback. I also wasn't used to the bluntness of questions like that. The French do not talk about money with strangers and many times not even with friends. I didn't have a very good New York answer. The project, not even six months old, was just that: a project. I didn't have a formal business plan. I was doing all of the legwork out of passion, in return for a sense of fulfillment and, if it was successful, it would fill a five-year gap on my résumé. I had a few thoughts on how to make money, but without any actual kale, they were difficult to execute.

Still trying to answer their questions, I said, "Well, my farmers should have their kale crops ready any day now. I'm going to see them both this weekend." They took notes in tiny, expensive-looking notebooks. "My plan is to start a small kale delivery service and bring kale to the people. Like a kale CSA."

The blond replied, "Well, that's perfect, because we need kale for our pop-up dinner. And we would *love* to work with you if possible."

The brunette quickly chimed in, between sips of her juice, which she held with long, slim fingers wrapped in rich, gold jewelry. "Well, we *are* working with Terroirs d'Avenir," she said, referencing the same local distributor that Laura had told me about at Verjus. "In fact"—she smiled again—"they told us they might have kale."

My heart started pounding, pushing through my chest. Did I really hear her correctly? Kale? From Terroirs d'Avenir? Perhaps I should have connected with them. I could see her eyes twinkle with satisfaction, waiting for my reaction. I did not want my panic to be obvious, and I tried to keep my cool. "We're meeting with them next week to review all the produce we need and to see if they really have kale. It would be great if we were the first to serve kale in Paris!" she finished, closing her notebook.

I was confused. What I thought was going to be a harmless "let's meet each other, we all came to Paris from New York" type of get-together had turned into something uncomfortable. At least for me. I had just spent the last five months working toward a very specific goal, and now, in one day, all that work might become pointless.

"Really? That's great news!" I said, still trying to hide my concern. "You must let me know how it turns out."

"Oh, we will. Absolutely. And please, tell us what happens with your farmer friends too," the brunette replied. "We have to jet now. Another meeting with a designer for our VIP invitations! The pop-up launches the first night of Fashion Week, you know."

Oh, I knew, and I wanted to be the one to supply the kale for the pop-up, which meant that I had to talk to Hermione and Sebastien as soon as possible.

❀

That Saturday, Philip and I went to see Hermione at the market. Since our first official meeting with her in April, we had gone back almost every weekend, even if only to say hello and buy herbs. She finally started smiling more at us, and I was so grateful and encouraged when she let Emily and I visit her farm.

But on this day, she was distracted and didn't seem to recognize either of us. Philip made small talk, asking about the kale. "Oh," she said, staring in a different direction. "Are you the kale man?"

I was crushed. Did she really not remember us? Even after my visit to her farm? I could feel tears forming in my eyes. Why was everything becoming so difficult? I started to shut down, ready to turn around, walk away, and give up. Screw it. This project was not going to work.

Philip sensed my frustration. He responded for me, "*Oui!* That is us! How is the kale growing?"

She shook her head. "*Les escargots*," she said sadly. "*C'est fini.*" Snails had eaten all of Madame Mustard's kale. "*Mais*, but," she continued, "I am not giving up. I am going to try again. I should have time in the next few weeks to replant it, but there will not be any kale for at least a few months."

One farmer down. Two to go.

Since Hermione wasn't going to come through, Philip and I immediately called Sebastien. He had good news. He had planted the seeds and felt confident the plants were growing well.

"Come out to the farm! On Sunday, after the Vincennes market will be best," he said, garbling the address to Philip over the phone. "I will call you when I leave the market so we can confirm." I rented a car, to be picked up at the Gare Saint-Lazare train station, for the following Sunday.

But when the day arrived, Sebastien's phone call never came. We waited and waited. We called him, but he didn't answer or call us back. Much to the confusion of the rental car company, we pushed our pick-up time back.

"*Mais, monsieur*, changing the time, *ce n'est pas possible*," the rental car agent said. "It is just not done. I do not understand why you would want to change the time." Philip pushed back, trying the trick that so many of our French friends have told us—keep asking and, after a few tries, the "it is not possible" will eventually become a "yes." On his fourth explanation that it was, in fact, completely normal to slightly move the pick-up time for a car rental reservation, the woman begrudgingly moved it. But we never heard from Sebastien.

Philip called him again a few days later, confirming a Sunday visit for the next weekend, and I reserved the car again. It was beautiful September day, perfect for an afternoon in the countryside. The blue sky was never ending, without a cloud in sight, and the sun shined down at an angle, keeping off the chill. We arrived at the address for the rental car office at the train station, but the office wasn't there. We searched and searched, walking circles around the train station. Finally, I saw the tiny sign for the office tucked behind a window. Right next to it was another sign: *Fermé*. The office was closed. Not open for business—at all.

"Shit!" I screamed, throwing my bag onto the pavement. I could feel tears forming in the corner of my eyes again. Of course the car office was closed on Sunday. Practically everything in France is closed on Sunday. Even the corner café called Le Week-End is closed on the weekend. How could I have made such a rookie mistake? Not taking Sunday closures into account was a Year-One mistake, but Year Two? I was disappointed in myself, and Philip, understandably, was annoyed. He'd given up two Sundays in a row to go with me to what was now a mythical farm where a mythical farmer was growing mythical kale. He called Sebastien, embarrassed and apologetic, to inform him that we would not be making it. And for the third time, we confirmed the next weekend.

This time, it was cold and pouring down rain, the complete opposite of the weather the previous weekend. Sebastien didn't call when he was leaving the market, and we didn't call him. Philip was putting his best foot forward for me, but I could tell he didn't want to go. It was the kind of day meant for curling up under the duvet on the couch, not for trekking around kale fields in the rain. We stayed home. Two farmers down. One to go.

Already distraught and disappointed, I scrolled through Instagram, and a photo posted by the New York fashion girls caught my attention. The blond was walking down the street, hair blowing in the wind as if she were in a magazine shoot, carrying a crate of kale. To make matters worse, the caption read, "First Kale in Paris." I was crushed. They knew that my entire project was about reintroducing kale to Paris. It was my sole objective. Even if it wasn't their intention, why did they have to make kale *their* thing? I couldn't stop staring at the photo.

What I had feared the most was happening. Failure. Looking stupid. Not living up to the promise I had made to twenty-five loyal kale hopefuls, or whoever the people were following the project. I had returned to Paris convinced that there would be kale ready from *my* farmers. And now Hermione had to start over, I had all but lost contact with Sebastien, and the New York fashion girls were going to bring kale to the people first. I was jealous and annoyed but mostly disappointed.

I sat down at the computer and stared at the screen, trying to write a new blog post. What was I going to say? Somehow a race for kale in Paris had begun, and in my mind, I was losing. There was only one farmer left. I had to go see Joël.

·· KALE PESTO AND SPELT ··

The New York fashion girls' pop-up dinner turned out to be a fun and beauti-
fully done event, and their kale dish, spelt with kale pesto, was excellent. There
are two things about this easy recipe that I like. The first is that it uses spelt,
a grain that is gluten-free and not always a go-to grain like brown rice and
quinoa are. The second is that the recipe can be done with either parmesan
cheese or miso paste. Like the vegetable itself, kale pesto is versatile and can top
pasta, grains, fish, and roasted vegetables, and it also works nicely as a dip for
happy hour. Make enough for the week, and enjoy it a different way every night.

INGREDIENTS

- 3 CUPS (150 G) KALE, WASHED AND ROUGHLY CHOPPED
- 1 CUP (200 ML) OLIVE OIL
- 1 CUP (75 G) PARMESAN CHEESE, OR 1 TABLESPOON MISO PASTE
- ½ CUP (50 G) WALNUTS OR ALMONDS
- 1 CLOVE OF GARLIC, CUT IN HALF
- LEMON JUICE, FRESHLY SQUEEZED FROM 1 LEMON
- 1 CUP (175 G) SPELT
- 3 CUPS (720 ML) WATER
- PARMESAN, SHREDDED
- SALT AND FRESHLY GROUND BLACK PEPPER, TO TASTE

PREPARATION

To make the pesto, add 1½ cups kale, ½ cup of the olive oil,
½ cup of the cheese (or 1 tablespoon of the miso paste), ¼
cup of the walnuts, ½ of the garlic, and juice from ½ of the
lemon to a food processor, and blend. When well mixed,
add the remaining portions of the first 6 ingredients to

the food processor, and mix again, until well blended. Add salt, and set aside. To prepare the spelt, put it in a colander and rinse. Add the spelt and water to a saucepan, and bring to a boil. Reduce heat to a simmer, and cover the saucepan halfway with a lid. Cook for 50 to 60 minutes, stirring occasionally. To serve, mix in the pesto with the spelt. Add a small spoonful on top with salt, pepper, and parmesan.

YIELD

• 2 SERVINGS

Chapter 30

T ying up my running shoes, I hit the pavement, knocking out my frustration with each stride. I had a boss once who would come into work in the morning and tell me that he'd had a million good ideas in the shower—it was where he did his best thinking. I've learned that I do my best thinking while I'm running. Building up my pace, I took a mini-tour of Paris. I passed the Grand Palais, the French flag flying gallantly in the wind. I crossed the Pont Alexandre III and, seeing the Eiffel Tower out of the corner of my eye, cut down to run along the Seine. Watching cyclists whizz by and Bateaux Mouches boats pass along the river, I knew I needed to do my best thinking right now. What was next for the Kale Project?

Things were taking an unexpected turn, and I had only myself to blame. I should have worked harder to find more farmers. I should have worked harder to speak better French, so that I could do more on my own instead of relying on Philip or Emily. I should have examined all angles and exhausted all possibilities. But I hadn't done that, and now there was a chance the project was going to end unsuccessfully.

I crossed over the Seine again from the Left Bank to the Right Bank and ran up a side street next to the Palais de Tokyo until I reached Marché Président Wilson, where Joël sells his produce on

Wednesday and Saturday mornings. I hadn't seen Joël since we first met in May, so I wasn't sure what had happened. Just another thing I *should* have done.

Marché Président Wilson is one of my favorite markets, and I often recommend it to visitors. With every visit, I always feel as if I'm wrapped up in a cornucopia of the best France has to offer. At the flower stands, tightly arranged roses and peonies give off a sweet scent. The grocer on one end stacks bunches of green and purple grapes, spilling them out onto the table, a few always rolling down onto the ground. Sausages hang from the butcher's stand, and terrines sit displayed in the glass case below. Fishmongers lay out their *rouget barbet* (red mullet) and fillets of sea bass in tidy rows, the scales shining against the shaved ice. Farm fresh eggs, some with a few tiny feathers still attached, sit in half-dozen cartons. Blue-and-white-striped shirts hang from a canopy across from a stand dedicated entirely to apples. Joël's stand is right in the middle, and, as I knew from my first visit, the line starts forming early.

Today, I reached the market around one o'clock in the afternoon, so it was emptying out. The change in season was obvious. Summer squash and ugly, lopsided heirloom tomatoes, while still in abundance, were pushed to the side by fall cabbages, like the bright, greenish-yellow, cone-shaped, alien-looking *chou romanesco*. I continued to survey Joël's tables, walking from one end of his stand to the other, peering over and between the heads of customers in line.

That's when I saw it. Kale! There was only one bunch, but it sat proudly at the front of the table. Joël had planted the seeds after all. My heart began to race. My stomach flipped. I felt like I was about to go on a first date. I didn't know what to do or say. The excitement was too much for me.

Joël appeared from behind his truck. "Joël!" I exclaimed. "I'm

Kristen. We met in May. Kale! You planted the seeds! This is great! Thank you!" I gushed, stuttering and spitting out what French I could manage over my giddiness.

"You're welcome," he said, smiling at me as he gathered piles of gold and pink radishes into his hands.

"Could I come visit your farm one day? To see the kale fields?" I asked him, not sure how he would feel about this overeager, American kale lady popping by for a farm tour.

"Of course," he agreed. We set a date for the following weekend.

Running home (without the kale, since go figure, I hadn't brought any money with me), I started thinking hard again. What was my next move? Joël's operation was too big for me to use his kale for Kale Wanted, so I would have to put that on hold. People could go to his market stand to buy it in the meantime. As for Terroirs d'Avenir and the New York fashion girls, they were going to do a dinner with kale. What if I did a dinner too? I could announce kale in Paris. Perhaps Laura and Braden would be interested in hosting it at the Verjus wine bar? It seemed like the perfect spot. I only hoped that Laura and Braden would agree.

I called Laura the minute I got home. After I explained the situation, she checked the Terroirs d'Avenir produce list to see if they were already offering kale to restaurants.

"Oh, here it is," she said to me. "They're calling it *chou noir de Toscane*, Tuscan black cabbage." That was exactly what I had seen in the photo.

"We would be happy to do something here," Laura said. "It will be fun! A kale party!"

The event was set for later that week. We wasted no time in planning it, and Braden and his team, who were literally knee deep in kale the day of the event, revamped the wine bar menu so that every dish included the green. "It has a vegetal and clean taste. Almost in line with parsley," Braden said as he described the dishes they were preparing. The menu was creative, innovative, and guaranteed to be delicious. He was even incorporating kale with their famous fried chicken dish. Instead of the normal napa cabbage slaw, they would use a chiffonade of the kale with jalapeño vinaigrette. "It's a slightly acidic contrast to the chicken," he told me.

I wasn't sure how many people were going to attend, but I waited patiently by the door with a vase filled with a kale bouquet, wrapped in blue, white, and red ribbons. For party favors, I made envelopes filled with kale seeds and a recipe for kale salad.

The doors opened at seven o'clock, and an hour later, the wine bar was packed. More than one hundred people attended; guests were spilling out into the street. Laura played upbeat music and poured glasses of white and red wine as the dishes were brought out from the kitchen. The menu included artichokes with a lemon, kale, and chipotle mayo; a burrata salad with kale, fennel, and tarragon, dressed with a warm brown-butter vinaigrette; and arancini with Taleggio cheese, wild greens, and a bacon-shallot balsamic jam. My favorite was the kale and farmer's cheese ravioli, with candied kumquats, pickled grapes, hazelnut oil, and shaved foie gras. And of course, the fried chicken.

I met people who had been following the Kale Project since the beginning and had been eagerly awaiting kale. There were Americans, English, and even a lot of French people. One woman told me, "It's so exciting because I am a *Parisienne*, but I live in the States, so coming back to Paris and not having kale has been tough. I'm so happy the Kale Project organized this event with so many delicious dishes." She brought her wineglass up to toast the evening, "So long life to the Kale Project."

·· KALE FRITTERS ··

Contributed by Braden Perkins and Laura Adrian, Verjus restaurant

Verjus is a favorite of mine, and it's not only because they hosted the first kale evening. Laura greets everyone with a sweet and upbeat smile, eager to tell you about the wines that are available by the glass that evening. Braden scours the marchés *for the freshest produce to create their seasonal menus. You can enjoy casual plates to share at their sister restaurant, Ellsworth (just down the street), or splurge for the tasting menu, with or without wine pairings, at Verjus's upstairs restaurant. These fritters are great for bite-size hors d'oeuvres or as a main dish.*

INGREDIENTS

- 3 TABLESPOONS OLIVE OIL
- 1¼ POUNDS (500 G) KALE, WASHED WITH STEMS AND LEAVES SEPARATED, FINELY CHOPPED
- 2 TEASPOONS FINE SALT
- 1⅓ CUP (160 G) ALL-PURPOSE FLOUR
- 3 LARGE EGGS
- ½ TO ¾ CUP (20 G) CHOPPED PARSLEY
- ½ CUP (80 G) RED CORN POLENTA
- ½ CUP (220 ML) WHOLE MILK
- ¼ CUP (25 G) GRATED PARMESAN
- ¼ CUP (10 G) CHOPPED SAGE
- 1 MEDIUM SHALLOT, MINCED
- 1 TABLESPOON BAKING POWDER
- 1 TABLESPOON LEMON ZEST
- 1 TEASPOON FRESHLY GROUND BLACK PEPPER

- 1 TEASPOON CARAWAY SEEDS, TOASTED
- 2 CLOVES GARLIC, MINCED
- ½ TEASPOON RED CHILI FLAKES
- ¼ CUP (25 G) GRAPESEED OIL FOR FRYING

PREPARATION

Heat the olive oil in a large saucepan over medium-high heat. Add the kale stems and fine salt, and sauté for 4 to 5 minutes, until soft. Add the kale leaves, and continue to cook for 7 to 8 minutes, until the water has left and the leaves are wilted. Squeeze the kale stems and leaves between paper towels to remove excess moisture. Allow the cooked kale to cool to room temperature. In a large bowl, mix the cooked kale with the flour, eggs, parsley, red corn polenta, milk, parmesan cheese, sage, shallots, baking powder, lemon zest, black pepper, caraway seeds, garlic, and red chili flakes. Fry the mixture in a saucepan at medium heat in small spoon-fuls. Test 1 fritter, and adjust for seasoning as needed. Fry additional fritters from the remaining mixture. Serve warm.

YIELD

- 12 TO 15 MEDIUM-SIZE FRITTERS

Chapter 31

The day after the kale party at Verjus, I slept in late and woke up to a flood of emails and messages. People had taken beautiful photos and written lovely blog posts about the evening. At the very least, I could say that it was a success and that kale in Paris was just getting started.

Since it was a Friday, Philip and I arranged to meet for dinner at a wine bar and restaurant called Au Passage that is hidden away on passage Saint-Sébastien in the Eleventh arrondissement, not far from the Marché Bastille. I arrived early to secure a table and waited for Philip at the bar.

The lights grew dim and the restaurant started to fill up, the height of Friday night *apéro* commencing. "How is my kale queen?" Philip asked, squeezing my shoulders and kissing my cheek. "What a success last night was, darling!" he continued. "I'm so proud of you. Can you believe all the people that came? And how tasty the food was! That fried chicken—I thought about it all day today."

While waiting for our table, I heard the woman next to me speak English. Within a few minutes, we'd struck up a conversation, and within no time, I learned she had relocated to Paris from England because her boyfriend was the sous-chef of the restaurant. Then it was my turn to explain what I was doing in Paris.

"Wow! There's no curly kale here?" she said. "I can't believe it.

What a fun idea!" As she was about to ask me more questions, her boyfriend and the head chef came out of the kitchen to greet her.

"Shaun," she called to the head chef, "you have to hear about this!" After I explained the project, he'd agreed to serve kale at Au Passage the following week.

"I'm heading out to Joël's farm next weekend, so we can use his kale if you want," I offered.

"Absolutely," Shaun replied, retreating back into the kitchen. "I love his stuff. Good choice in farmer."

I was determined not to screw up the visit to Joël's farm like I had with Sebastien. Since I was dragging Philip to yet another farm, I told him to go have a morning coffee while I retrieved the rental car. Driving toward the place du Maréchal-Juin roundabout near our apartment, I called him. "I'm almost there. Where are you?" I asked. "Which café?"

"Hello, darling! I'm at…hold on…I'm at Cafés Richard," he said over the voices of waiters hollering orders of *petite dejeuner* and *café allongé*, espressos with water.

"Cafés Richard?" I questioned him, confused. I knew the area well, and there was no Cafés Richard. Entering the roundabout, I started to panic, trying to place Cafés Richard. There was the La Place café and the Royal Pereire brasserie. I knew the small *tabac* and the flower shop right next to it, but there was no Cafés Richard. Circling the roundabout for the third time, I called him again. What café was called Cafés Richard?

That's when I realized what Philip was thinking. "Sweetheart? Are you reading the inside of your coffee cup?" I asked.

"Yes. It's labeled right underneath the rim. It's the café's name, right?"

As I circled one more time around, I said, "No! That's not the café! That is the coffee *brand* you are drinking. Practically every café in Paris uses Cafés Richard and the same labeled coffee cups."

I pulled over next to the Royal Pereire. "Well, at least we found each other!" he said, climbing into the front passenger seat. "Okay, where to?"

Joël's farm is located twelve miles northwest of Paris in Carrières-sur-Seine. Luckily the beautiful weather from the first two times we were supposed to visit Sebastien's farm had reappeared; the sky was clear blue and the bright sun took the edge off of the chill in the air. We wrapped our necks in big scarves and wore Wellington boots to combat the mud. We arrived at a nondescript yellow warehouse with open overhead doors. Wooden pallets were stacked off to the side and piles of boxes and crates, all filled with vegetables, sat near the entrance. Joël, dressed in a blue jumpsuit and knee-high brown boots, greeted us with a jolly *bonjour*, then immediately launched into a story about one of his fields. Joël always speaks so quickly that I still sometimes have a difficult time understanding him, and I never know where he's going to go with the conversation.

"*Bon*, are you ready to see the kale?" he asked, starting off behind the warehouse, beckoning us to follow. The land has been in Joël's family since the fourteenth century and has been used in many different ways over the centuries, from vineyards and orchards to Joël's vegetable farm. I could feel its history and heritage beneath my feet, the years and years of crops and harvests that have gone into the city to nourish French families. Our boots crunched over mulched leaves and squished into trenches of mud made deep by tractor wheels. We hopped over cauliflower, the white, purple, and yellow heads tucked away underneath thick, palmlike green leaves that protected them from the sun, harsh winds, and pests.

Spanning more than fifty acres, Joël's farm is enclosed by ancient stone walls, covered in graffiti, and crumbling from centuries of inclement weather. With train tracks running right at the edge of the farm and a view of La Défense, the large, suburban business district northwest of Paris with tall, unsightly skyscrapers, in the distance, the farm was more urban than I'd imagined and nothing like the large commercial farms I'd seen in America—which, given Joël's output every week, was what I had expected.

Passing broccoli, bok choy, alien-looking kohlrabi, and uniformly shaped red and green cabbages that opened up toward the sky, we arrived at the kale fields. Right in front of me were rows and rows of thin kale stalks, like little green trees, the top leaves fanning down toward the ground, with fresh dew drops hidden between the curly edges. Joël reached down and pulled off a few leaves, handing them to me. "*Voilà!* Your beloved *chou*," he joked.

"So is the kale selling well?" I asked.

"*Mais oui*," he responded, leading us through the kale field and across the street to another section of the farm. "A lot of foreigners are buying it—Americans—and even a few chefs. Some French people too," he winked. "I think I will plant the Tuscan variety next year." We walked down a wide, dirt road, Joël leading us through his kingdom, proud as a peacock marching ahead. He exuded passion for vegetables.

"It's just been in the past ten years or so that vegetables have really come into their own again," he said. "The younger generation is more interested in trying them. Chefs are more interested in cooking with them." His arm extended to the row of greenhouses filled with endless vines of tomato plants, near the end of their life cycle. "Chefs encourage me to try to plant new and different things."

We arrived back at the warehouse, and Joël grabbed a few wooden crates for the kale, throwing in a bunch of golden beets and large red radishes. I was set for the lunch at Au Passage.

"You know," he said to us, looking out into his fields that glowed golden from the morning sun and dew, "I don't know what's going to happen to my land or to the farm." He put the crates, filled to the top, with kale leaves spilling out, into the trunk of our rental car. "I have two children, and I am not sure if they are interested—at least right now—in continuing the operation." I sensed sadness in his voice over the uncertainty of what might happen to his land, his farm, and his legend. Then, snapping out of his thoughts, he pepped up again, smiling and waving good-bye, his mind already thinking about the next task of the day. We drove back toward the city, crossing the Seine, the car brimming with Paris kale.

A few days later, I went to Au Passage before their lunch service, bags of kale in hand. The late-morning light poured through the restaurant's red, wooden door, onto its gray-and-red-tiled floor, criss-crossing over the worn-in wooden tables and chairs. Servers were setting each table with simple napkins and silverware. Shaun met me at the bar, where I handed over the kale, keeping a few leaves to place in a vase at the front window, like I had done at Verjus.

This would be different from Verjus as it wasn't an actual event but an everyday lunch service for people who most likely weren't expecting or craving cabbage. The diners would be people coming from work, taking their usual hour (and sometimes longer) break for the regular lunch *formule* of *entrée, plat, dessert*—the set menu of a starter, main course, and dessert. Just as Chris from Northern Spy and Shanna from Back Forty had recommended, we were going to serve the vegetable in a familiar setting and with familiar food.

"The plan is to serve the kale with our main plate options of *mulet noir*, black mullet, or *magret*, duck," Shaun said. "It will be nicely marinated in white wine and butter with shallots and lardons," he continued, showing me the chalkboard in the back of the restaurant with the day's lunch menu. Pointing to an empty space on the board, he asked, "What should I call it? What did you say the name is in French?"

I still was not sure what to say since there still was not a common way to reference the vegetable. I took Thomas's advice that he gave me during our meeting together at Google. "Just say *chou kale*," I said, answering quickly.

"I change the menu daily," he said. "So people are accustomed to seeing something new up here," he finished, writing it out. Stepping back, looking at the chalkboard against the distressed, mirrored wall, I thought *le chou kale* didn't look too bad.

A little past noon, businesspeople started filing into the restaurant, placing their coats on hooks and scooter helmets on shelves. The kitchen grew warm and busy, and steam drifted out with the first course of *moules*, mussels in a cider sauce. Then came the main course, the moment I was waiting for. One after another, plates of fish and duck with a side of sautéed kale—the leaves still a deep green, a sign that it was cooked perfectly—were set on tables. I watched intently, enjoying my own serving of mussels, dipping crusty bread into the sauce and cutting small slivers of *Crottin de Chavignol*, a popular goat cheese with a nutty flavor from the Loire Valley. I watched everyone eat their meals and saw a few inquire, "What is this *chou kale?*"

The servers gave the perfect response: "It is a cabbage, a *légume oublié*, but now it is being grown again." It was a simple, truthful answer. People nodded, smiled, and kept eating until there was very little green left at all.

SAUTÉED KALE WITH WHITE WINE,
·· SHALLOTS, AND LARDONS ··

My best advice for this dish is to make it right before you're ready to serve, so that the kale doesn't soak up too much liquid. Make sure the kale retains its vibrant green color—it's a fine line between sautéed kale and overcooked kale.

INGREDIENTS

- ¼ CUP (50 G) LARDONS, OR BACON CUT INTO BITE-SIZE PIECES*
- 3 SHALLOTS, THINLY SLICED
- 6 CUPS (200 G) KALE, WASHED AND CHOPPED
- 1 TABLESPOON OLIVE OIL
- ¼ CUP (120 ML) WHITE WINE
- SALT AND FRESHLY GROUND BLACK PEPPER, TO TASTE

PREPARATION

Place the lardons or bacon in a saucepan, and heat over low heat. Cook for 10 to 15 minutes, until well done. Remove from the pan, and set aside on a plate lined with a paper towel. Add the shallots to the pan, and cook them in the remaining grease for 4 to 5 minutes, until translucent. Add the kale and olive oil, and continue to stir for 1 to 2 minutes. Add the white wine, and stir. Cook for 2 to 3 minutes, until the kale soaks up the liquid. Season with salt and pepper, and serve.

YIELD

- 2 SERVINGS

This recipe can easily be made without meat. Simply skip the first step, and start by cooking the shallots, using 2 tablespoons of olive oil.

Chapter 32

S unday mornings are, for me, the best part of every week. Growing up, they meant Johnny Eggs, a recipe passed down from my stepfather John's Italian grandmother.

John was one of my cross-country coaches, and he and I would return from a long morning run and gather around the kitchen island with my mom. The air filled with the smell of hot oil as he sliced onions, reminding me to put the bread in the toaster, timing it so the toast would be crisp and hot right when the eggs were ready. When I left home for college and eventually moved to New York, my Sunday mornings changed, and one of the things I missed the most were Johnny Eggs and the Sunday family rituals that went with them.

Sundays became about sleeping in, long runs in Central Park, or day-long brunches with friends. Now, as autumn continued in Paris, my weekends—including Sundays—were consumed with searching for kale or verifying a location where someone told me they had spotted kale. It was only a handful to start, but I took it upon myself to spread the word.

I found kale at the Marché Bastille, grown by a producer from Normandy, Serge Baudry. His green-and-purple kale was always fresh, picked at just the right moment when the leaves are big enough for a hearty meal, and never when they're yellowed and too old and tough to enjoy. The kale was a welcome addition to his stand filled with squash, cabbages, colorful carrots, and mushrooms in shades of brown, yellow, and cream. And above it, written in white on a small, green sign: "*chou kale.*"

Kale was also at the Marché Monge in the Fifth arrondissement, not far from the Jardin du Luxembourg. Marc Marcsetti, who grew it, called his kale *chou hollandais*, since his seeds came from a farmer friend in the Netherlands. He picked the entire plant instead of just the leaves, arranging it into a forest of small kale trees.

In each case, it was the first time the farmer had grown kale, and it was always by accident. Even if it was a coincidence that their first time growing kale happened to be the same year I started the project, it seemed that kale in Paris was meant to be.

The project was always taking unexpected turns, and I found myself quickly turning into kale's publicist. I was giving people a reason to talk about kale in Paris—or, should I say, the *lack* of kale in Paris. Before, no one had ever questioned the difficulty of finding the vegetable. When Joël grew kale years ago, I'm sure someone was excited to find it, but that was probably the extent of it. There was no real reason to talk about finding kale in Paris and no way to truly spread the news. The Kale Project was changing that.

In October, I received an email from Omid and Alannah, the American couple behind Emperor Norton. They had spotted kale too, by way of a relatively new start-up company. *La Ruche qui dit Oui!* (The Hive that says Yes!) is a cross between a farmer's market and a weekly CSA box. They source everything—produce, meats, cheeses, breads, and more—from local producers, and their customers preorder their purchases online, customizing them to include only the specific goods they want to buy. This system means there is less waste for the farmers, who only harvest what they need to fulfill the orders, and customers aren't dealing with issues that are common complaints with CSAs, like being left with too much of one vegetable or receiving produce they don't really want. In 2012, only a year and a half after it started up, La Ruche had grown the number of *ruches* in France to more than seventy—and today, they have ten times that number in several countries throughout Europe. Their model would be innovative in any country, but especially for a country like France, it is hugely instrumental in ensuring that local producers in every region are supported. The Ruche farmer who'd grown the kale that Omid and Alannah spotted, Nicolas Thirard, was calling his kale *chou plume*, or feather cabbage—yet another name.

Eager to check out La Ruche and meet this producer, I called Emily to see if she wanted to meet me there. This *ruche*, located in the Tenth arrondissement, right off of the Canal Saint-Martin, fits right in with the hipster, on-the-verge-of-gentrification vibe that's happening in the area.

Emily and I met up next to one of the iron, graffiti-covered, green bridges that crosses over the canal. Kicking aside trash, most likely from a canal-side picnic the evening before, with her foot, Emily greeted me with *la bise*. We entered Le Comptoir Général, a restaurant/bar/event space, and walked through a long, dark hallway toward the back room, which was illuminated by skylights. Earlier in the week, Emily had joined the *ruche* and now was picking up her orders, directly from the producers, striking up a conversation with each of them. It was nice to see that the *ruche* fostered a sense of community between the producers and customers. Nicolas's stand was the last one, and behind him were dusty, yellow crates filled with kale.

Emily introduced us. Nicolas, a thin, small-framed man with short, brown hair and glasses, was dressed in simple blue jeans that I could tell had been pressed, a bulky beige coat with a lot of pockets, and knee-high rubber rain boots caked with dried mud.

"I received the seeds from my nursery thinking they were going to be another type of cabbage," Nicolas explained. I had heard that one before. "I had to look up what this cabbage was online, because I had never seen it before. I didn't even know its name!"

I began to explain my project, but within twenty seconds, it was obvious that he was confused, so Emily took over. Nicolas, like most of the farmers I spoke with, was mystified as to why in the world I would dedicate an entire website to a vegetable and why I was even doing this project at all.

"This?" Nicolas asked, pointing to his kale and grinning in disbelief. "This is popular? Really?" Emily placed her kale into a canvas bag, offering to share half with me. Nicolas and I promised to keep in touch. Later that day, I compiled all of the recent kale sightings into a Google Map titled "Kale Spotted," to help people find it easily. And I wrote about La Ruche, Nicolas, and his *chou plume*. Almost every weekend after that, his kale sold out.

❦

Our neighborhood is always filled with Sunday-morning action. Racing against the clock, shoppers go into overdrive to complete their errands by one o'clock in the afternoon, when practically everything will close for the day, many places not reopening until Tuesday. People go crazy buying what they need, emptying shelves as if we're all going to be snowed in for weeks. I tried to buy toilet paper once on a Monday and had to go to *three* different supermarkets to find it.

When the clock strikes one, shops shut their doors, and the city goes quiet. The courtyard noises subside, and the streets are devoid of cars and scooters. Parisians head to parks or museums or enjoy a long Sunday lunch. Just as I used to do with my mom and John, they spend time together with family.

On the Sundays of kale searching, I would return home and Philip and I would do Sunday brunch together. As the coffee brewed, I spooned the hot olive oil over Johnny Eggs, keeping the yolk intact, slicing an avocado and taking out homemade lemon rind jam. Paris was finally starting to feel more and more like home.

·· SUNDAY JOHNNY EGGS ··

Although I make Johnny Eggs, I don't make them nearly as well as my stepfather, so when I'm visiting Pittsburgh, I'll eat Johnny Eggs almost every morning for breakfast, or at least when John is home to make them for me. Our Sunday morning rituals are similar to when I was growing up. I run less and stretch more, and the coffee has gotten a little better, but we still sit around the kitchen island while John chops the onion. He still tells me when it's time for me to put my bread in the toaster, and my mom still tells him to go light on the oil. It's nice that some things never change.

INGREDIENTS

- 4 TO 5 TABLESPOONS OLIVE OIL (*As John says, "Don't be afraid to use a lot of oil!"*)
- 1 MEDIUM YELLOW ONION, CHOPPED (*"The more, the better!"*)
- 2 LARGE EGGS
- 1 TO 2 SLICES BREAD, FOR TOAST (OPTIONAL)
- SALT AND FRESHLY GROUND BLACK PEPPER, TO TASTE

PREPARATION

Heat the oil and onions in an 8-inch (22-cm) cast-iron skillet over medium-high heat. Sauté for 2 to 4 minutes, until the onions start to soften. Add the eggs, being careful not to break the yolks. Mix the onions into the eggs, keeping the yolks intact. (*"This is a good time to put the toast in."*) Season with a pinch of salt and pepper. Let the eggs sit for 1 to 3 minutes, to solidify. Continuously tilt the skillet, and, using a spoon, scoop the oil and the onions onto the eggs, until the eggs are cooked to your preference. (*"Less time for runny yolk, more time for solid yolk.*") Grind more fresh pepper on top, and serve. As with most egg dishes, Johnny Eggs pair well with cheese, tomato slices, avocados, or even a few pieces of smoked salmon.

YIELD

- 1 DELICIOUS BRUNCH SERVING

Chapter 33

I didn't know it when I started the project, but Paris was poised for a green, healthy detox revolution. Up until 2012, options for healthy eating in restaurants were slim. Marc Grossman started Bob's Juice Bar in 2006 and soon after opened a sister restaurant, Bob's Kitchen, in the Marais. Sol Semilla in the Tenth arrondissement specialized in South American superfoods. Pousse-Pousse in the Ninth arrondissement was a good option for raw food.

There were not any cold-press juice bars yet and eating out meant either choosing to eat somewhere that was labeled "healthy" or assuming that your meal would come with very few vegetables. Brasseries had *salade composée*, which is basically the French term for larger, mixed salad. These big salads had a lot of lettuce, unripe tomatoes, and, depending on the restaurant, various toppings like ham, hard boiled eggs, or smoked salmon. You would find potatoes. Maybe leeks. Spinach was like striking gold.

Vegetables in general weren't always the most important part of the meal—at least, at restaurants. One time, while dining at a nice restaurant in Normandy, I asked for *une petite salade verte* on the side, to accompany my fish, and the waiter came back to tell me that the kitchen didn't have any lettuce. *Or any green vegetables at all.*

Around 2013, French magazines started to write more articles about the detox craze that was taking place in America. More information was becoming available on going vegetarian or vegan. As luck would have it, the Kale Project and the reappearance of kale in Paris were happening at exactly the same time, which meant that it was in a prime position for publicity.

I wasn't proactive about press for kale or the project; in fact, it was hugely important to me that press happened naturally. I wanted journalists to write about kale in Paris because they had heard about it on their own, through a friend or from visiting somewhere where they had tried the vegetable. I wasn't going to send out a press release for a cabbage. I did, however, have a hunch that once the first piece of French press *did* come out, more would follow.

I was delighted when Clotilde Dusoulier asked to meet for coffee. It was if she knew what an inspiration she had been, when I'd read her blog post mentioning kale. She said she might write an article for *ELLE à table*, a bimonthly magazine under the *ELLE* fashion magazine brand that focuses on all things food.

Meeting over soy chai lattes at a new coffee shop in the Eighteenth arrondissement, I immediately felt at ease with her, like I was chatting with an old friend.

"Kale is considered more of a northern French vegetable—a cheap vegetable or a 'poor man's vegetable,'" she started telling me, speaking in perfect English. Clotilde, who had first tried kale at a vegetarian restaurant in New York City called Angelica Kitchen, knew what I was up against.

"Unfortunately, there are many things that are physically wrong with *chou*. It can be bitter. It gives off unpleasant smells when you cook it. Many people might even associate it with crowded tenement buildings and the smell of cooked cabbage wafting through the hallways. People do not find *chou* to be something exotic or desirable," she said, listing reason after reason why kale had fallen out of favor in France.

"My hope is to change that," I said, smiling at her. "At least a little."

"Well, it's not only kale that is a problem," she continued. "You know, I think the French, and many people really, have a complicated relationship with vegetables. You buy them and they're dirty. You put them away and they have such a short shelf life." She was right. It's easy to be discouraged by all the work involved with vegetables, especially when you're coming home after a long day at work to a cold, dark kitchen.

"It seems like that's just another obstacle to reintroducing kale," I said.

"Well, yes and no," she answered. "It really depends on a person's upbringing and whether or not their parents persevered to get them to taste and eat vegetables. My mother is a really good cook and always served a lot of vegetables. We were always told to try everything. She believed that even if we didn't like it at first, we would *eventually* like it."

So perhaps France *was* the perfect place to reintroduce a vegetable. Although they have a reputation for being averse to change, the French are also raised to try new things at the table, giving them a broader palate. Kale could be the latest new thing for them to try.

Clotilde continued, "In my family, it was all about seasonality. I was raised walking through the Sunday markets, and we only bought from the local producer, so we were never buying strawberries in November—even though I could see them at other stands."

I thought about my own relationship with vegetables. I always knew a lot about the importance of eating what grew in the ground around me from my mother's experience with macrobiotics, but I was usually more concerned with getting dinner on the table than I was with whether my kale was from California or Florida, in season or out of season. But France was changing me, and I had relearned how to shop, gravitating toward the local producers' stands and working with what they sell each week.

It wasn't always easy. As Clotilde remembered, "At the time, I felt a sense of deprivation from not being allowed to eat strawberries in the winter, but in the long run, of course, it provided me with a much better understanding of what I should be eating and when. My mother always had us make a wish when we took the first bite of the new fruit of the season."

As she wrote down a few final thoughts in her notebook, Clotilde looked up and asked, "Should I call it *le chou kale?*"

"I don't know. What do you think?" I responded.

"Works for me," she said, smiling.

❧

Although there were now a handful of places selling kale, Clotilde had reminded me that just because it was available didn't mean that people were actually buying and trying it. My next challenge was to encourage Paris to *taste* kale. A few restaurants had already used it, but not enough to show how versatile and easy it is to cook with. I knew how important it is to consumers to be able to sample a new product before they buy it, so I decided that a *dégustation*, a tasting/sampling was the next step toward debunking the terrible myths about cabbage.

Thanks to Omid and Alannah, I met someone who worked for Yelp Paris and was organizing a winter food festival and agreed to let the Kale Project be part of it, along with a variety of other food businesses and vendors. Set for mid-December, it was projected to bring in around five hundred people who would experience what different food businesses and vendors had to offer. The festival would be the perfect venue to showcase, talk about, and have people taste kale. I planned to serve kale chips, lightly seasoned with sea salt, and kale pesto on pieces of baguette; I also wanted to make kale, apple, banana, and almond milk smoothies on-site.

The plan was set except for one tiny problem: *Where* was I going to prepare kale for five hundred people? I couldn't handle that volume in my kitchen. I would be drowning in green leaves. Who did I know that had a bigger kitchen? I thought through my options. There weren't any restaurants that would be able to lend me their kitchen for an entire day. One option was my friend Jane and her cooking school, La Cuisine Paris. I had met Jane through Bryan, the journalist who wrote the first article about the project back in June. If the timing was right, I might be able to use one of their kitchens.

Over the phone, I was honest with her, telling her that I didn't have the money to pay her, as I wouldn't be selling anything at the event. Jane, with her bubbly voice, told me it was not a problem. "Of course you can use a space. I think our basement kitchen is free that day. The bigger question I have is how are you going to do this for five hundred people?"

That was a good question. Now that I had a space, I had to figure out how I was going to secure enough kale. By mid-December, the first season was coming to a close. The farmers were either running out or done harvesting it for the year. There was only one option that had the quantity of kale I needed, and would deliver it right to me—Terroirs d'Avenir. I debated this in my head. Did I want to order from them? It would've been so much better to use one of my farmers, but it was either use their kale or don't do the event. I swallowed my pride and ordered twenty-four bunches—three crates.

The delivery was scheduled for my apartment the day before the event, so I could get a head start on washing, drying, and storing the leaves in plastic bags. I could keep them cold by hanging them outside our bedroom window. In Paris, because of the limited kitchen space in most apartments, window ledges and balconies frequently do double duty as additional refrigerators during the colder months. I always have a bag or two of leafy greens hanging outside my kitchen window. I also planned to make the pesto the day before the event, to at least cross one thing off my list.

Then, the day of the event, I planned to arrive at La Cuisine early, use their multiple ovens to make the kale chips, then go to the festival with plenty of time to set up. I even scheduled an extra French lesson with Marion to practice a few key phrases I would need for the event. We role-played, with Marion pretending she was at the table sampling the kale.

The day before the Yelp festival came, with all the plans in place. The kale was scheduled to arrive at eighty thirty in the morning. I waited and waited. Eight thirty turned to nine, and then to ten, and by one o'clock in the afternoon, there was still no kale. I called Terroirs d'Avenir. No answer. I left a voice mail. No one called me back. I peeled the garlic and shredded the cheese for the pesto while I waited, trying to think of anything else I could do so more time wouldn't be wasted. Finally at four o'clock, I called again, angry but also very anxious that I wouldn't have any kale for the event.

"Ah, *oui*," was the nonchalant reply on the other end of the phone. "It is almost the end of the season and the farmer did not harvest any kale yesterday, so we could not deliver it today. We will have it tomorrow. I think."

They could have at least called or emailed me with this update. I was not reassured. I reconfirmed the order, asking for the kale to be delivered directly to La Cuisine. I was going to have to do all of the prep and cooking in one day.

I awoke early the next morning, having slept very little, to frost on the windows. Schlepping three big, plastic containers, a rolling suitcase, and a shopping caddy that held a blender, a food processor, olive oil, garlic, cheese, baguettes, apples, bananas, almond milk, bowls, platters, napkins, business cards, and recipe handouts into a taxi, I left for La Cuisine, my fingers crossed that there would be three crates of kale there to greet me.

La Cuisine is located along the Seine, not far from the Hôtel de Ville in the Fourth arrondissement. When I arrived, the early morning light was peeking into the large glass windows of the school. Jane, always peppy, greeted me, her thick, beautiful red hair swinging behind her in a ponytail. "It's here! The kale arrived!" she exclaimed.

Sure enough, in the corner of the school's basement kitchen sat three big crates of...red Russian kale. Not what I had ordered. I had never even cooked with the red Russian variety before, and I was going to start now? For five hundred people? I could have sworn that I'd ordered curly green or Tuscan kale. The red Russian variety's leaves aren't as curly, so I wasn't sure if it would bake well into chips, and I already knew I would have to spend time tweaking my pesto recipe. But what choice did I have? It was red Russian kale or nothing.

After thanking Jane profusely for letting me use her kitchen, and apologizing in advance for the mess I was about to make, it was showtime. I washed, destemmed, and dried the kale. I blended leaves into garlicky pesto and baked them into crunchy chips. It took a few tries to get the oven temperatures right, resulting in some burned batches, but eventually the leaves baked to an ideal crispiness.

After cleaning up what seemed like hundreds of kale stems and baby leaves all over the floor, I changed into a nicer outfit (one that wasn't stained with olive oil and kale pesto) and headed to the event. My table was small, set off to the side, and unassuming. I felt intimidated. I couldn't compete with the actual businesses that were there. I wasn't a big chain with a marketing budget and a graphic design team. I didn't have fancy flatbread pizzas or locally brewed beer. My shtick was giving out something green.

But people loved it.

Clotilde was right. People did have a negative perception of *chou*, but that night, the Kale Project started to change opinions. With my blender churning away, I told people about the project, recipes, the new Kale Spotted Google Map, and, of course, all about kale—in French. I could hear Marion coaching me in my head, as if she were whispering in my ear all the right things to say. And it was a huge success. The kale was devoured, and the reviews the next day were even better.

"THE discovery of the evening was the Kale Project," read one.

Another read, "I only knew of this vegetable by name but the woman who had us taste it was welcoming and kind. And the vegetable was fresh! Chips, pesto, and a kale-apple smoothie. All surprisingly good!"

Kale was a stinky, boring old cabbage? Not anymore.

·· SIMPLE SMOOTHIE ··

When I first moved to Paris, a lot of people had never had a smoothie before, so I thought it made sense to share a simple green smoothie recipe for Clotilde's article in ELLE à table. Like Hermione's Fresh Market Juice (pg. 169), this recipe is a base and is meant for experimentation. Try different liquids (like coconut water, soy milk, or homemade cashew milk) and fruits (depending on what's in season at the market). I like to keep my smoothies fresh and simple and normally find that less is more.

INGREDIENTS

- 1 HANDFUL KALE, WASHED AND DESTEMMED
- 1 CUP (240 ML) MILK
- 1 APPLE, SEEDS REMOVED
- 1 BANANA
- ½ (120 ML) CUP WATER
- 1 TO 2 DATES, PITTED (MORE DATES WILL MAKE THE SMOOTHIE SWEETER)

PREPARATION

Put all the ingredients a blender, and blend until smooth. If you prefer a lighter drink, add more liquid.

YIELD

- 1 LARGE JAR (ABOUT 2 SERVINGS)

Chapter 34

I exited the Grands Boulevards *métro* station and was surrounded by cheapness. Corner Irish pubs reeked of last night's vomit mixed with bleach, chintzy shops tried to rip off tourists with any and every kind of plastic souvenir, American chain restaurants oozed with greasy fried foods, and it was all tied together by the loose trash that lined the streets. Paris is not always *macarons*, peonies, and balloons by the Eiffel Tower. Real life happens here too. I double-checked the address of my *rendez-vous* and turned off the main boulevard. Wrapping my coat tighter around my body and pulling my bag closer to my chest, I tried to dull the damp, chilly January air.

Clotilde's article about the Kale Project hit newsstands in early January, and, as I'd suspected, more journalists started to contact me. *Glamour* was next. They were doing a Top Ten list of trends for 2013, and *le chou kale* was on their list. The journalist from *Glamour* had also contacted someone from La Ruche qui dit Oui!, and apparently he wanted to talk more with me about growing kale. I was on my way to meet with him.

I arrived in front of a typical French apartment building. I was early, so while I waited, I reviewed the one page of notes I'd put together the night before outlining how the Kale Project could work with the producers connected to La Ruche to grow kale on a national

level. Yes, a national level. I couldn't believe it myself. It hadn't
even been a year since the project had launched, and I was about to
head into a meeting to discuss a national growing plan. Or at least
so I thought. I wanted to work with and support local producers,
like Nicolas, and La Ruche had the contacts and connections. I had
visions of traveling to different regions of France to run kale infor-
mational sessions and *dégustations* like I had organized for the Winter
Food Festival.

I felt confident about the meeting. To me, collaborating seemed
like a no-brainer. Since I was willing to do most of the legwork, why
wouldn't La Ruche want to partner? Nicolas's kale sold out every
weekend, and I was willing to do the collaboration for free. I wasn't
expecting a cut of the sales—it was all for the mission and the good
of the project. As I practiced French phrases and sentences in my
head, Emily arrived—of course she was going to help me through
the meeting.

"Hey, honey," she said warmly. "Are you ready?"

"As ready as I'm going to be," I responded, shivering as I punched
in the code and entered the large front door and adjoining courtyard.
"I have no idea how this is going to go."

We walked up the steps and rang the bell at the door. In Paris,
it's common for businesses and organizations to have their offices in
apartment buildings. I've been in doctors' offices that look like rooms
out of Versailles.

The moment the door opened, it was everything but Versailles,
and a stench of fried fast food irritated my nostrils. The foul odor hit
me in the face as I surveyed the open, fluorescent-lit office space. It's
not like I was expecting an actual farm to be behind the door, but
lunches of McDo? The people sitting at the five or so desks didn't
look up, nor did they smile. Posted to the wall was a map, which

looked like something from a 1980s school textbook; pins marked every *ruche* location throughout the country. I started to imagine all the kale fields in my head.

Taken to a small room around the corner, we waited. Five minutes and then ten minutes passed as Emily and I grew more nervous. Finally, a man entered and sat down.

He stared at us, clearly not interested in making an effort to commence the conversation himself. Emily stared at me, and we shifted uncomfortably. The air in the room quickly felt stale. The lights flickered like those of a cheap motel bathroom. Emily began with a short stutter, "Hi. This is Kristen, and I'm Emily, and I help Kristen, who started the Kale Project. Are you familiar with it?" she asked, assuming, as I did, that he had at least heard of the project from his conversation with *Glamour*.

Jerome, whose name we knew only from his emails, since he never formally introduced himself, answered her, without making eye contact, "Eh. *Oui. Un peu.*" Yes, a bit.

Emily continued, "Well..." She swallowed, crossing and uncrossing her hands. "We wanted to speak with you about the potential to work with your local producers to grow kale for other *ruches* in France. It seemed to sell very well this year at the *ruche* in the Tenth arrondissement with Nicolas Thirard. And—"

Jerome cut her off, saying in French, "Kale. That is an English word. What is the name in French?" Here we go.

I decided to try to join the conversation in French, slowly answering, "Well, there are many names in French, so it is difficult to know what to call it. There is *chou frisé non-pommé* and *chou plume*. Now some people are calling it *le chou kale*—"

"*Non. Chou plume*," he interrupted me. "That is what it is and that is what we will call it. It is better than the American word." He straightened his cargo capri pants and ran his hands through his slick salt-and-pepper hair.

Ok. *Chou plume.* Not a problem. One little nomenclature hiccup wouldn't stop us. Emily began again in French, but as Jerome gazed in every direction but ours, she stopped and asked if we could continue in English, so that I could more easily participate. Jerome, finally making eye contact with us, responded curtly, "*Je pourrais, mais non. Français.*" I could, but no. French.

Emily, being the tough woman she is, wasn't ruffled. Continuing where she left off, she said, "Well, you had great sales of *chou plume* this fall, and we believe that interest and demand will continue to grow as most people become aware of the *légume oublié.*"

Jerome looked unimpressed. He rolled his eyes, yawned, shook his head *non*, and crossed his legs, revealing footwear that looked to be a take on bowling shoes, with thick laces and block colors. "Why would I give you any of my contacts? Why would I help you at all? The last thing I would want to do is ask any of my producers to grow something for which there is no demand."

I could feel my frustration growing. What was this all about? *Jerome* had sent an email to the *Glamour* journalist saying that *he* was interested in kale. *He* was the one who had initiated this meeting, which it was now obvious he didn't want to be having. Or at least that's what I thought. At least that's how the *Glamour* journalist positioned it. The past ten minutes had been one big, pessimistic French *non*. I wanted to stand up and yell, "But how can there be demand if people don't know what kale is? And how can people find out what it is if there is no supply?"

Instead of taking that route, which I knew I would regret, I took my only other option: English. "Yes, Jerome, I understand that you would not want to put any farmers at risk, but this could be a trial period. Perhaps you could pick a few of the more populated *ruche* communities and have one producer cultivate just a few plants as a starter. A test."

He continued staring at the ceiling, tracing the design of flowers and plants in the molding that, ironically, resembled kale. His silence made me more nervous, which led me to keep talking, but I tried not to ramble.

"Also, there has already been press in *Glamour*, *ELLE à table*, and *Grazia*, with more to come, so the buzz about the vegetable is only going to increase—and, with that, so will the demand."

Jerome remained silent.

Finally, I played my last card, one that I hoped would hit home for him, the cofounder of a company that prides itself on supporting local producers.

"The last thing I would want is for suppliers to source kale from Germany or the Netherlands when our own *local, French* farmers can easily grow it in this climate. Why not support local production if we can?"

Still no response.

I was desperate at this point. "I'm not asking for a financial arrangement," I said. "It's all about the mission. We are asking only for connections with local producers."

Jerome let out a long, loud exhale, thought for a few seconds, shrugged, and responded in rapid-fire French, "You're welcome to join each of the *ruches* individually and find the producers yourself. Or you can post something on our Facebook page. But do not think I'm going to help you any more than that."

Both his feet touched the floor and he stood up, his bunched-up cargo capris stopping midcalf. "*Merci et au revoir*," he said as he pivoted in his bowling-style shoes and walked out of the conference room.

Emily and I weren't sure what to do. Was the meeting over? Were we just supposed to get up and leave? Quickly gathering our things, we hurried out, speechless, barely able to process what had just happened. Here was a small start-up organization, barely eighteen months old, that believed in supporting local food, and Jerome had basically spat in our faces. I was raging on the inside and a jittery mess on the outside. My hands and legs were shaking as we walked down the steps to the street. The hive that says yes had just delivered a big, fat *non*.

·· KALE CHIPS THREE WAYS ··

My meeting with La Ruche qui dit Oui! came about because of an interview I did with a journalist from Glamour magazine. It was ten o'clock in the morning when she interviewed me, but she loved the kale salad and kale chips that I brought for her to taste, and they turned out to be a big hit at the office. I kept imagining all the French fashionistas munching on le chou kale as they discussed the upcoming February Paris Fashion Week. They featured my chips and the Kale Project logo in their article. One basic tip for preparing kale chips is to wash, destem, and pull apart the kale into medium-size pieces. You don't want to have thick stems in your chips, because they won't bake all the way through, and they'll become chewy. Here are kale chips three ways.

·· TRADITIONAL ··

INGREDIENTS

- 6 CUPS (200 G) KALE, WASHED, DESTEMMED, AND PULLED APART INTO MEDIUM-SIZE PIECES
- 2 TABLESPOONS OLIVE OIL
- FRESHLY GROUND SALT, TO TASTE

PREPARATION

Preheat the oven to 225°F (100°C). Line two baking sheets or oven trays with parchment paper. Set aside. Put the kale in a large bowl. Drizzle 1 tablespoon of the olive oil, and use your hands to mix, lightly covering the kale with the oil. Add the remaining olive oil, and repeat. Place the kale pieces onto the baking sheet, face up or face down. They shouldn't touch, but you don't need a lot of space in between each piece. Sprinkle salt over the pieces. This is best done with a salt grinder, as larger salt grinds don't stick to the chips and are too concentrated. Bake in the oven for 10 to 20 minutes, until crispy but not burned.

YIELD

- 2 SERVINGS

·· CASHEW & GINGER ··

INGREDIENTS

- ½ CUP (75 G) CASHEWS
- 1½ TABLESPOONS LEMON JUICE
- 1½ TABLESPOONS SESAME OIL
- 2 TABLESPOONS SOY SAUCE OR TAMARI
- 1-INCH (2½-CM) PIECE FRESH GINGER
- 6 CUPS (200 G) KALE, WASHED, DESTEMMED, AND PULLED APART INTO MEDIUM-SIZE PIECES

PREPARATION

Preheat the oven to 160°F (65°C). Line two baking sheets or oven trays with parchment paper. Set aside. Put the cashews, lemon juice, sesame oil, soy sauce or tamari, and ginger in a food processor, and mix until somewhat smooth. There will still be smaller chunks of cashews, which is fine. Put the kale in a large bowl, and add half of the sauce on top. Mix with your hands, lightly and evenly covering the kale with the sauce*. It's best to avoid having large chunks of sauce on the piece, so that they cook evenly. If needed, add more of the sauce (although this recipe makes enough for extra). Spread out kale evenly on two baking sheet or trays, face up or face down. They shouldn't touch, but you don't need a lot of space in between each piece. Bake in the oven for 80 to 90 minutes, until pieces are crispy but not burned. Pieces may appear to slightly be wet around 80 to 90 minutes but once removed will crisp nicely when they dry.

YIELD

- 2 SERVINGS

*There will be leftover sauce to make another batch later on if desired.

·· ALMOND & COCONUT ··

INGREDIENTS

- ½ CUP (75 G) ALMONDS
- 2 TABLESPOONS COCONUT OIL, MELTED
- 1 TABLESPOON HONEY
- 1 TABLESPOON SHREDDED COCONUT
- 6 CUPS (200 G) KALE, WASHED, DESTEMMED, AND PULLED APART INTO MEDIUM-SIZE PIECES

PREPARATION

Preheat the oven to 160°F (65°C). Line two baking sheets or oven trays with parchment paper. Melt the coconut oil in a small pan if not already soft. Put the almonds, coconut oil and honey in a food processor, and mix until somewhat smooth. There will still be smaller pieces of almonds, which is fine. Put the kale in a large bowl, and add half of the sauce. Mix with your hands, lightly and evenly covering the kale with the sauce. It's best to avoid having large pieces of sauce on the piece, so that they cook evenly. If needed, add more of the sauce (although this recipe makes enough for extra). Spread out kale evenly on two baking sheet or trays, face up or face down. They shouldn't touch, but you don't need a lot of space in between each piece. Sprinkle the shredded coconut over the kale leaves. Bake in the oven for 80 to 90 minutes, until pieces are crispy but not burned. Pieces may appear to slightly be wet around 80 to 90 minutes but once removed will crisp nicely when they dry.

YIELD

- 2 SERVINGS

*There will be leftover sauce to make another batch later on if desired.

Chapter 35

The first season of kale in Paris mostly finished by the end of 2012. It had been short but successful. The small amount of plants the farmers had grown were picked over, and as the days became longer and lighter again, the plants would go to seed, their life cycle complete.

The winter markets were crisp, filled with squashes, parsnips, celery roots, and rutabagas. Leafy green *blette*, Swiss chard, was lined up in bunches next to sweet potatoes, onions, and dried heads of garlic. The market may not have had all the options of summer, but it certainly didn't lack for variety, and on this February day, I was in for a surprise.

Shivering underneath a big coat and heavy sweater, I looked up and saw that the sky looked ready to snow, the gray clouds blending into Sacré-Cœur. At the market, the green-and-white-striped tarps were pulled overhead, creating even more darkness, the naked lightbulbs strung along the top providing the only illumination. Underneath, it felt like a festive Christmas tree. Everyone was cold, shopping quickly, white clouds of breath forming with each exhale. I quickly scanned the market to see which producers had also braved the cold.

Hermione, faithful as ever, was there, dressed in the same chunky wool scarf that she wore the day we took her to coffee. She moved slowly behind her stand, organizing the few crates of petite endive and radicchio. I took my place in line and, once her produce came into clearer view, did a double take. She had a small sign that read: "*Chou Kale* 2,50€/250 grams." Hermione had harvested her kale! After weeks of checking in with her and waiting and waiting, I wasn't sure if it would ever be ready. This was the kale she had planted in October, germinating and growing it in cold weather. Her love and patience was clearly what had kept these little plants growing and safe from a second round of snails. The leaves were not big, having been picked young and tender. Not only did Paris have kale, but it had baby kale now too.

While I'd been ecstatic about Joël's kale and all of the kale spottings that project followers had posted, *this* moment was everything. Hermione was my first farmer and the first person who had agreed to work with me. She was the first person I gave seeds to, and she tried not once but twice to grow the vegetable. She could have easily given up after the first crop was eaten, but instead, she'd taken a risk with her small plot of land to grow something she wasn't even sure she could sell.

I had to prove to her that I was as good as my word. I wanted to make sure that, like the other farmers, Hermione would sell every leaf. I didn't think it would be too difficult, because her kale couldn't have come at a better time. With every other vendor sold out until a new crop was ready, which I anticipated would be in May or June, Hermione was the only person in Paris selling it. And sure enough, people came from all over the city to buy "Madame Mustard's" baby kale.

When I returned home from the market, my hands cold and red from carrying the heavy bags, Amelia cornered me. "Kreesteen," she said, pushing her face close to mine, a stale smell on her breath.

"Monsieur Sinclair...he is not nice. He is trying to force me to move!" I could tell she was upset, scared. Her normally frizzy hair was even frizzier, and thick, oily pieces fell down from her bun. "They are not happy with me anymore! I have lived and worked here for twenty years. I am the heart and soul of the building! I keep this place moving and breathing! Please, tell your landlord not to vote against me at the meeting next week."

Amelia was campaigning to save her job and her home. I had no idea that things had gone sour between her and Monsieur Sinclair. They always appeared to have such a harmonious relationship. I made a mental note to tell Philip to find out more. For a building with so many elderly tenants, there sure was a lot of drama.

I found myself at another crossroads. The Kale Project had come a long way, but I had a desire for it to be more. I was always on the lookout for new farmers, and I was contacted by one from Lyon and put in touch with a few others, which was exciting because it meant more people were interested in growing kale. But I still wanted to find a way to get more people to try *eating* it as well. And then I met Channa Galhenage, a rising figure in Paris's coffee scene.

Since we had arrived, more and more craft coffee shops were opening up, offering a space to enjoy freshly roasted beans, filter coffee, and locally baked goods, such as those provided by Emperor Norton. Channa was set to open Café Loustic in March 2013. We first met at the Yelp Winter Food Festival event, and because he was raised in London, he was familiar with kale and wanted to offer it as part of his lunch special.

We met up in the Marais, near the space where his coffee shop would be, to discuss—over coffee, of course—how we could work together. Smartly dressed in slim jeans, a checkered shirt, and what I'd find out is his trademark paperboy cap, Channa told me about how he'd been working on his business plan, saving money, finding the perfect location, and finally commencing construction. The shop would be located in a narrow but long storefront on rue Chapon in the Third arrondissement.

"The area is changing," Channa told me. "There are new things moving in: galleries, design firms, smaller shops, and cafes. It's the right time for a place like Loustic. Bob's Kitchen is one block over. Kale will fit in perfectly in this neighborhood."

We easily decided that I would do a few simple dishes for Café Loustic, like kale chips and a kale salad. "And your kale pesto," Channa added. "I want to offer it as an *à tartiner*, a spread. I love that pesto!"

It was a great opportunity. Channa was providing me with a kitchen to prepare kale, a place to sell it, and, most important, a platform I could ultimately use to expose more people to it. No one was doing kale salads in Paris yet, so the timing was right to jump in and claim the dish as the Kale Project's own.

To legally work with Channa, I had to register myself as an *auto-entrepreneur*, a freelance status allowing me to charge by invoice and be paid like a consultant. I had no idea how to actually go about doing this, but given my past experiences with everything bureaucratic in France, I wasn't expecting it to be easy. Government workers in France are known to be difficult, repeatedly saying *non* over and over again. I'm convinced they like to see people squirm, informing them that even though they had brought with them the forty-five documents—including originals and three photocopies of each—that are necessary to do anything, just last night, at 10:47

p.m., a new required document was added to the list. Or so the stories go.

I could at least attest that when Philip and I first moved to Paris, even the simplest things were complicated. We couldn't open a bank account without an electricity bill as proof of our residency, but we weren't able to register an electricity account without a bank account. We claimed to live with Emmanuel and Léonie, using their electricity bill; after temporarily using their address, when it came time for us to change our information, it took nearly two months to process our new address with the bank.

We spent four hours trying to purchase a cell phone contract, going around in circles with the salesperson, not understanding what the issue was, only to finally be told that we needed...an electricity bill. The same went for joining the gym. I started carrying our electricity bill around in my wallet, just in case, making sure to switch it out with a recent bill every three months (otherwise it wouldn't count).

I had to wait nine months to receive my renewed *carte de séjour* because, as the *préfecture* told me, they were too busy to process it. By the time I finally received the new card, it was only valid for three months, and I had to start the reapplication process for the following year the very *next* day.

I was far from the only expat who found navigating the French system complicated, and there are actually people who have made a micro-industry out of helping clueless, language-challenged people like me handle these sorts of things. Figuring out how to become an *auto-entrepreneur* was daunting. So I hired Olivier. He had the magic touch. He swiftly navigated the mounds of paperwork, knowing exactly what I needed and when. He flirted with the woman behind the desk at the *préfecture*, complimenting her turquoise sweat suit and matching Ugg boots, as she questioned why I needed to be registered to work with…cabbage. I don't think she ever really understood what I was doing, but Olivier was a top-notch charmer, and within a few hours, all my paperwork was processed.

Everything was set except for one *tiny* issue. I had no kale. Hermione's kale was beautiful and selling well, but she didn't have the supply I needed for the café. Besides, I wanted to leave her kale for the kale lovers. And when Emily and I contacted all the other farmers to see when their next harvest would be ready—which I anticipated would be in the late spring, like it is in the northeastern United States—we were met with laughter. "Kale is a cold-weather vegetable. We won't have any new plants until at least September," all the farmers said. Kale was *hors saison*, out of season.

Fortunately, as had been happening with the project since the beginning, someone knew someone who knew someone else who would be able to help. Olivier knew Simon, and Simon grew kale.

Olivier lived in Normandy and, by chance, knew two English brothers, Simon and Theodore Painter, who had left the UK one year earlier to pursue their dream of farming in France. I immediately called Simon and told him my situation. Finding the whole thing somewhat bizarre, he said he wasn't sure if he could help me, but he could hear on the phone that I was desperate.

"Come out to visit. We can talk more, and you can see the kale plants," he offered. And so began my weekly journeys toward the Ger region, an almost three-hour train ride from Paris, to see Simon and his kale plants.

I met him at the train station, so he could drive me to their small farmhouse. The air was fresh, still smelling of the morning rain. Up and down the hills we drove, through the town and past barns, stone farmhouses, and field after field of empty land.

As soon as we parked, I could see stalks of kale—in multiple varieties—growing tall into the sky. They were nearly ready to go to seed because they hadn't been heavily harvested. There were kilos of leaves in the Painters' fields. They had saved the day.

Permaculture, which is the way the family chose to farm, encourages cultivating vegetables to enhance natural ecosystems. Plants are treated holistically, and farmers observe what happens naturally as the plants work together in harmony to organically eliminate pests and maladies. Brassicas, for instance, thrive next to aromatic herbs, potatoes, and onions, but they don't do as well next to strawberries and tomatoes.

Week after week, I would rush to the Gare Montparnasse train station, my feet pounding the concrete floor as I ran to catch the 7:45 a.m. train, which I'd always just barely make. Three hours later, I would arrive in Flers sleepy and hungry. Simon would pick me up, and we'd head to the farm to pick kale. Simon was fiercely dedicated. "I was up at four in the morning, picking slugs off the leaves. Brassicas really are a magnet for pests," he would tell me, marching through the rows of kale in the firefighter suit from his previous job in the UK that he always wore. He made sure I was taking back only the absolute best-quality leaves. We clipped kale, leaf by leaf, for hours, until I had at least two full garbage bags, which I then schlepped back with me on the train. I looked bizarre, weighed down by the bags, waddling through the train station, taking the walking escalator at the Châtelet *métro* to change trains, and waddling home.

❧

When I finally did make it home, my shoulders burning, the real work would begin. I became an expert at washing kale. With all the events I was signing up for and my dishes for Loustic, I spent a lot of my evenings washing, destemming, and drying the green. The whole apartment would be filled with the salty smell of baked kale chips. Philip would come home to stems and leaves all over the kitchen floor; he'd joke that I was running a secret drug ring and the kale was just a cover-up. "It's all a little too *Breaking Bad* in here for me," he'd say, grabbing a big handful of kale chips before leaving me to do more kale washing. When he opened the fridge, plastic bags of washed kale would fall out, covering his feet. "Everyone gets kale but me! I would love a kale salad!" he'd moan, complaining that because I was making kale for everyone else, we never ate it at all.

One morning at Loustic, while I was mid-kale-massage, my hands covered in chopped greens and olive oil, the phone rang. Channa answered and, after a moment, he covered the receiver and, laughing, asked me, "Kristen, if someone wanted to buy kale from you, what would you sell it for?"

This was a strange and difficult question. I had no idea what to charge. "Why?" I asked, curious as to who wanted my kale. "I don't think I have enough to sell. I need it for this week. I won't be heading back to Normandy until next week."

"It's a posh hotel. A VIP guest is demanding a kale salad, and the hotel knows you're the only person who has access to it," Channa told me.

Thinking quickly, I tallied up the costs in my head. The train ticket plus what I paid Simon, divided by the approximate amount of kilos I dragged home with me, came out to around twenty euros per kilo (about twenty dollars for just over two pounds). Steep. Surely the hotel wouldn't pay that much just for some cabbage.

"Done," Channa said. "The concierge will be here in half an hour. Get the bag ready."

Less than an hour later, a young man, clearly an errand boy, showed up, dressed like an antique solider in a thick, navy-blue wool suit, as if he were fighting a war a hundred years ago.

"Who is this for?" I asked, eager to know why they needed kale so desperately.

"I cannot say," the man told me, as he carefully placed the bag of kale under his arm. He paused, considering how much information he wanted to divulge, then said, "All I can say is that it's for a singer who is in town tonight performing. And her name is that of a color," he finished, turning briskly to leave.

Channa and I looked at each other. "Pink!" we both cheered. I had just sold a bag of Painter Permaculture kale from Normandy to Pink?! I desperately wanted to be in the kitchen with the hotel's chef, helping him prepare it for her. I never did find out how he prepared it.

After the excitement from my celebrity sale died down, the next few weeks went well. I made kale salads and stacked containers of fresh kale chips every morning, and they always sold out quickly. I made sure to highlight the farm where the kale came from with a photo and a sign on the counter next to the bowl of salad. Customers came for good coffee and left having learned about a new vegetable. I loved my role at the café, being able to interact and talk with people about the vegetable.

The Kale Project was taking on a life of its own. After Clotilde's article and the Glamour piece, other French magazines and even newspapers followed. There started to be a lot of interest and buzz around the vegetable.

One of the photographers I met from a magazine photo shoot invited me to his *vernissage*, photography exhibition opening. Upon arriving, I immediately learned that the event was being held in one of Picasso's old *ateliers*, studios, near Montparnasse. It had big windows and high ceilings. As I sipped on a glass of champagne and looked at the photography, it was exciting to think that such a legendary artist had been in the exact same room, working away.

Startled out of my trance, an American woman interrupted me. "You! Aren't you the woman who is doing the project with kale?" she asked me. I wasn't used to random people approaching me, but the expat community in Paris can become very small very quickly, and I was excited that someone who I didn't know had heard of the project.

"Yes," I replied to her, smiling. "Nice to meet you." She quickly continued talking. "Well, I've had an idea after living here for years and years—something that France needs and is also impossible to find. But it's a secret! You can't tell anyone because I know I will get rich off of this!" Over the past few months, a lot of people had written to me about food or items that they wish I could help reintroduce or bring to France. Frozen strawberries, collard greens—the list goes on and on. I was prepared for anything. Well, almost anything.

She looked me straight in the eyes and said with the utmost confidence, "Turkey basters."

❧

It seemed that the media and many of the farmers had concurred on a name for the vegetable, and by summer's end, as we entered our third year in Paris, the green was coined *le chou kale*. And after months of kale gathering, prepping, cooking, and *dégustations*, I'd become too busy to even realize the empty feeling I had when we first moved was no longer there. And it was all because of a leafy green.

·· KALE AND CURRANT ··
EARLY MORNING MUFFINS

When I lived in New York, heading to an early morning meeting (even though I'm not a fan of getting out of bed earlier) was never a big deal, because there was always an open bodega around the next corner where I could grab hot coffee and a bagel and cream cheese for breakfast. But in Paris, my weekly kale-picking trips to Normandy were so early in the morning that almost nothing was open yet, so I had to bring my own breakfast. I needed something simple for the train, and these savory muffins—made with Painter Permaculture kale, of course—worked perfectly.

INGREDIENTS

- 2 TABLESPOONS GROUND FLAX SEEDS
- 6 TABLESPOONS WARM WATER
- 1½ CUPS (170 GRAMS) WHOLE WHEAT FLOUR
- 1 TEASPOON BAKING POWDER
- ½ TEASPOON BAKING SODA
- 1 TEASPOON GROUND CINNAMON
- ½ TEASPOON GROUND GINGER
- ¼ TEASPOON SALT
- ⅓ CUP (80 ML) OLIVE OIL
- ¼ CUP (60 ML) HONEY
- ½ CUP (120 ML) RICE OR SOY MILK
- 1 TABLESPOON APPLE CIDER VINEGAR
- 1 CUP (30 G) KALE, PUREED*
- 1 SMALL APPLE (ABOUT 4 OUNCES/120 G), SHREDDED
- ¼ CUP (60 ML) WATER
- ¼ CUP (35 G) CURRANTS
- 2 TABLESPOONS SUNFLOWER SEEDS

PREPARATION

Preheat the oven to 375°F (190°C). In a small bowl, combine the ground flax seeds and warm water. Let sit for about 10 minutes, or until the flax seeds have congealed. In a large bowl, mix together the dry ingredients. In a separate bowl, whisk together the congealed flax seeds, olive oil, honey, apple cider vinegar, and rice milk until smooth. In a food processor, puree the kale and water, until the kale pieces become tiny flecks. Add to the wet mixture, and add the shredded apple. Pour the wet mixture into the bowl of dry ingredients, add the currants and sunflower seeds, and stir until well blended. Spoon the batter into paper or silicone muffin liners and bake for 18 to 25 minutes, or until the tops are a deep golden brown.

YIELD

- 12 MUFFINS

*Puree the kale in 1 tablespoon of water, which will produce the perfect consistency for this recipe.

Chapter 36

I spent a lot of my time emailing and talking to journalists and I did the interviews in English. I was being cautious, scared, or, as Philip would say, lazy. He'd ask me how I would ever know if I could do it in French if I never tried. He had a point, but it always *seemed* easier to stick to English. So when I was asked to be interviewed by *Rue89*, a more liberal news website with articles for millennials about culture and politics, I approached it like any other interview. I spoke slowly in English, giving the same answers I always gave.

In every interview, I made it a point to remain humble and cautious. I wasn't in my home country and had to be respectful of France, the French, and their culture—specifically their food culture (even more so since I was coming from a country that doesn't really have a food culture). When I was asked why I felt a need to do something about the lack of kale, I chose to play off of a famous quote by Napoleon Bonaparte, "*Le mot impossible n'est pas Français.*" The word "impossible" is not French.

I answered, "I'm American. Nothing is impossible." I didn't mean that I was exceptional in any way. It was meant to be playful. The journalist didn't have a surprised reaction. We ended the interview, and I went about my day.

Two days later, without realizing the article had been

published, I started to receive hateful emails, blog comments, and Facebook messages.

> "Hey, poor girl!!! I will teach you the French culture! In our country, what you name "Kale", is a "chou frisé"! We ate it from centuries, you can find it in a lot of French personal gardens, and in a lot of supermarket. Why are you trying to let us pass for a silly people??? Go back to America, perhaps if you can really study French culture, you will be able to give them a real gastronomy culture!!!"

That was one of many. Clueless as to where the sudden rush of negativity was coming from, I checked my website traffic. It was the *Rue89* article. I clicked on the link and gasped when I saw one of the highlighted quotes, "*Je suis américaine, on ne peut pas accepter un 'non' comme réponse. Pour nous, rien n'est impossible.*" I am American, we cannot accept "no" as an answer. For us, nothing is impossible.

The quote, which was nowhere near accurate to what I'd said, was placed above a photo of me in a greenhouse full of kale. Comments were mean-spirited, saying that I worked for Monsanto and was importing GMO kale from America. (GMOs are illegal in France.) They said I was taking over Brittany with pesticides. People asked if I was going to invade the Middle East with kale next. I was crushed. I had been so diligent and careful to never say anything too controversial or too pro-American. It didn't matter now. This article, of course, went viral and was picked up by two more sites, including Yahoo France. I was humiliated, I felt stupid, and I could not stop crying as I read hateful comment after comment. As soon as possible, I posted a reminder of the project's mission on my blog. I could only hope it would help.

The Kale Project supports French farmers. They are outside of Paris, in Flers, Lyon, Tarascon, and many more. Not one is outside of France. I do not import kale from any other countries—even European countries. I do not support Monsanto, and I am not trying to take over Brittany. There is not a multinational company backing this movement. While I work with both organic and conventional farmers, I encourage everyone to eat organically when possible.

The Kale Project began as a passion project because I could not find this specific variety of cabbage in Paris markets. I asked farmers, distributors, restaurants, French food bloggers: most did not know what it was. Is it a type of cabbage? Yes. Is it *chou frisé*? Yes & no. *Chou frisé* is also savoy cabbage. They are in the same family but different.

After spending two months researching the history of kale and cabbages in Europe and *how other cultures eat kale* (like Germany, the Netherlands, Italy, and such) and realizing that it was very difficult to find in France, I launched the project. I launched it with no money and without making any money. There is not a big media campaign behind the movement. It's a poorly designed blog with a Facebook page. That is all.

I did it because I love a vegetable I have eaten my entire life. I do not make a living from this but have enjoyed making lovely French friends throughout the journey. And while Americans do not like to take no for an answer, it was after all Napoleon who said, "Impossible is not French."

I hoped that would explain everything to my loyal readers, but especially to the people who had stumbled upon the blog from the negative article.

A few days later, I was scheduled to do a *dégustation* at a nightclub called Silencio. A private club, Silencio also has a movie theater and organizes cultural events for their members with art, music, and food. They'd invited the Kale Project to serve and discuss kale. Feeling down and upset about the article, I had no choice but to pick myself up, put on a smile, and talk kale. I had kale salads, chips, and pesto to prepare. I was afraid that members of the club were going to arrive at the event having read the article. I walked on eggshells the entire evening, waiting for someone to say something. No one did.

The next day, I received an email from a top television station. Still feeling paranoid about the article, knowing that it had only been twenty-four hours since it was published, I was convinced they wanted to interview me because of the negative press. After all, controversy brings more traffic. I was hesitant, asking a lot of questions about what they wanted to do. Their deadline was tight, and they wanted to come to our apartment that night and talk to me.

"You should do it in French," Philip said to me as I cleaned and organized our kitchen, washing a bunch of kale.

"Hah," I said. "Yeah right." As I stood at the sink, the cold water trickling through the leaves, removing dust and dirt, I thought more about it. Perhaps I should try to do it in French. If I failed, they could always dub over me. At least it would show that I was making an effort. Perhaps it would make up for my earlier *bêtise*, mistake.

And that was how I found myself, on a Sunday evening in our kitchen, narrating a kale massage in French. I rarely did interviews in English again.

·· KALE BLOODY MARY ··
Contributed by Rob McHardy, Silencio

Who doesn't love a good Bloody Mary? Especially after a very fun and long night out. This Kale Bloody Mary recipe, from Silencio bartender Rob McHardy, is just what you'll need to recover the next morning. All specialty ingredients can be purchased at fine liquor stores.

INGREDIENTS
Kale Shrub
- ½ CUP (120 ML) KALE JUICE
- ½ CUP (120 ML) WHITE BALSAMIC VINEGAR
- ½ CUP (100 G) SUPERFINE SUGAR

Kale Bloody Mary
- ¾ SHOT* (30 ML) KALE SHRUB
- 2 TABLESPOONS KALE JUICE**
- 4 TABLESPOONS CARROT JUICE
- 4 TABLESPOONS CELERY JUICE
- 4 TABLESPOONS AMONTILLADO SHERRY
- 3 TABLESPOONS LIME JUICE
- 3 DASHES THAI BITTERS
- 3 DASHES TABASCO
- 3 SPRIGS CILANTRO
- 1 SMALL TEASPOON HORSERADISH
- 1 SLICE BELL PEPPER, FOR GARNISH
- 1 LARGE PINCH SMOKED SALT

PREPARATION

Kale Shrub

In a small saucepan, bring the vinegar and sugar to a simmer. Stir until sugar is dissolved. Remove from heat and let cool. Then, add the kale juice, and store in a jar.

Kale Bloody Mary

Muddle the ingredients, and mix. Roll over ice, and transfer from one container to another over ice, without shaking. Add the bell pepper slice and a large pinch of salt, and serve.

YIELD

· 1 DRINK

This is based on the American shot glass size, where 1 shot is equal to 1½ ounces or 45 ml.

**For a sweeter version, use 1½ shots (60 ml) kale shrub and ¼ shot (20 ml) kale juice.*

Chapter 37

"Meet me at Gare de Lyon at five o'clock," I told Philip over the phone. "I have everything planned. All you need to do is show up."

"*Parfait, ma chérie*," he sang back to me. It was our second wedding anniversary, and we had train tickets to Avignon to meet with a new farmer. I was trying to make the weekend special, but I wasn't sure how special Philip thought *another* farm trip was going to be. Yet he had been so helpful and patient since I had started the project by helping me with translations, phone calls, farm visits, and marketing advice. I felt lucky to have him by my side.

We both arrived early and took seats in Le Train Bleu, the ornate *Belle-Époque* restaurant on the train station's second level. Large windows gave travelers a peek at gold-plated ceilings, crystal chandeliers, and walls painted with murals of angels, cherubs, and flowers. Clinking his glass of champagne against mine to celebrate the start of our anniversary weekend, Philip bit into an olive and asked, "So how did you meet these farmers again?"

"I haven't met them…yet. The wife, Françoise, emailed me a few times. She was very persistent and interested in growing kale. She was adamant that we visit them to see the farm," I responded, checking my watch to make sure we wouldn't miss our train.

The journey to Avignon was a little under three hours and, while the train sped along quickly, we wouldn't be arriving until close to nine o'clock at night. I hoped we'd still be able to find somewhere to eat dinner together at that hour. By the time we arrived and picked up the rental car, it was dark. The drive from the station to the old town of Avignon was easy. It was once we entered the town that things got complicated. The GPS couldn't find a signal, nor could our phones. The robotic British voice that kept telling us to make turns where turns were forbidden was no match for the narrow, medieval streets of Avignon.

Hungry and tired, we kept driving in circles, exiting and entering the stone city walls hoping that *this* time, we would make the correct turn toward our hotel. "Google Maps says to make a right," Philip said, pointing to another road that was much too small for a car to drive on.

"I can't make a right there," I answered, my frustration growing by the second. "That road is a one-way, and look, the road that leads to our hotel is blocked off to traffic." There was no way for us to actually drive to our destination, and I didn't see any parking spaces anywhere. I'd forgotten to ask the person at our *chambre d'hôtes*, our bed-and-breakfast, where to park the car. And now the clock was ticking: 10:00 p.m. 10:15 p.m. Restaurants were shutting down for the night and grocery stores were closed. At this rate, I wasn't even sure if we'd be able to go to a street-side *crêperie*. Finding nowhere to park, we had no choice but to leave the city center, park the car outside the old city, and walk back.

Thumping along in our rain boots for the mile-long journey to the *chambre d'hôtes*, I apologized. "I'm sorry. What a crappy way to spend our anniversary."

"It could be worse, you know," Philip said as we walked into the B&B I'd reserved. "I'm happy as long as we're together…in this…hostel." Right as Philip was trying to make me feel better, we walked into our accommodations. Don't get me wrong. I'd stayed in and loved hostels all over Europe, but a hostel was definitely not what I'd imagined for our anniversary. The lobby was deserted, and our room keys were in an envelope taped to the front desk. A lone computer sat on a small table, surrounded by tourist pamphlets and brochures about Provence. A sign above the computer advertised a weekly happy hour with one-euro beers for backpackers.

"Quick," I said, ignoring the fact that there was nothing less romantic than a hostel. "It's 10:50 p.m. If we have any chance of finding somewhere to eat, we have to go now." Grabbing Philip's hand, I pulled him into our room to dump our stuff; then we rushed out of the hostel and into the street. The food (if not the foodie) gods were looking over us, and right as we turned the corner, I saw the glow of a Chinese restaurant with a red sign flashing, "*Ouvert.*"

France isn't known for good Chinese food, but at this point, we were happy to eat anything. As our steaming wonton soup arrived several minutes later, we sipped our chilled beers and dug in, starving from the last two stressful hours.

"Well, we managed to park the car without an argument. That's a success to me," I said to Philip. Looking at my handsome husband, the same jitters of excitement surged through me, like it was the very first day we'd met. "I know this wasn't how you imagined spending the weekend, eating random, bad Chinese food and talking about kale for me, but I just want to tell you how much it means to me."

"Pleasure treasure," he teased. "It could be worse you know. Think how much we've been through in the past two years. Think about how far we've come—together."

Springtime in Paris is a myth. March and April (and often May and June) are as gray and rainy as December, January, and February. The only way to see the sun this time of year is to go south. And here we were in the south! So I was hugely disappointed when we woke up the next morning to pouring rain and cold air. After nearly flooding our hostel room with a broken shower, we bundled up, checked out, and walked the mile back to the car.

Françoise Jullian was a cute, petite woman with bangs and shoulder-length brown hair. She met us in her town of Tarascon, forty-five minutes away from Avignon. With a bright smile, she welcomed us both and motioned for us to follow her white SUV. Deep in French farm country, we saw little else but field after field of new corn plants, greenhouses, and young sunflowers that, in a few months, would be basking in the bright summer light. Driving down a long gravel lane, small rocks spitting at the sides of our rental car, we pulled into a carport that stood out front of a large, but inconspicuous, house.

"*Voilà*," Françoise said casually, as we jumped out of the cars into the garage, dodging the rain. She led us into a large, warm kitchen, where we were greeted by a giant sheepdog with fur the color of cream. A shorter, tan man with salt-and-pepper hair followed the dog. He wore a gold chain, expensive-looking jeans, and a shirt unbuttoned to his midchest.

"*Bonjour*! I'm Frédéric!" he said, presenting himself. He surely didn't resemble the other farmers I'd met so far. Introducing ourselves, we removed our wet boots and sat at the kitchen table next to a potbellied stove.

"We brought kale for you," Philip said. "Kristen would love

to show you a few of the ways she prepares it." I never would've thought that making and eating kale chips would be an icebreaker. Imagine if I'd served that at our first French dinner party. I asked Françoise for a bowl, olive oil, and salt and talked her through the steps of preparing the chips. While we cooked at the counter, Philip took the lead on telling the story of the Kale Project and why in the world I began it in the first place.

"I read about your project in *ELLE à table*," Françoise said— another connection made from Clotilde's article.

After talking through the basics of kale, how to grow it, and who they could sell it to in Paris, Frédéric asked a question that seemed most important to him: "What are people paying for this vegetable? What's the price per kilo?"

"Nine euros per kilo for *bio* and around six or seven for conventional," I answered, distinguishing between the price for kale that is grown organically and kale that is grown conventionally, with pesticides.

He put his hand to his heart, grasping his gold chain. "*Mon Dieu!*" he said, My God! I could see euro signs springing into his eyes.

The price of kale in France had been a point of contention for many people. Most thought it much too expensive for a cabbage and believed the price had been hiked up because it had become *tendance*, trendy. I had no idea when or how the price had been decided but also tried to remind people that a kilo of kale is *a lot*, 2.2 pounds—practically a large plastic bagful that can last well into ten days.

"The chips are ready," Françoise said. I pulled the baking tray out of the oven and poured the chips into a wooden bowl on the table. Frédéric, still hesitant about the vegetable itself, took a chip and crunched it between his teeth. His eyes lit up again, "*Ah, c'est bon!*"

Licking his fingers, he finished the bowl, and although I doubted that it was the chips that did it, I could tell he was hooked.

There was a knock at the door and a tall, lanky man with wavy, grayish-blond hair rushed in, kicking off muddy boots. "*Bonjour!*" he bellowed.

"Ah *oui, bonjour*, François!" said female Françoise, rushing to take his raincoat. François was a French-American friend of the Jullians, raised in America, and recently retired in France. In the 1980s, he founded a well-known aerobics-wear company, and he now spent his time refurbishing homes with sustainable hemp walls. He'd been telling the Jullians for months about kale, how popular it was in the States and how they should start growing it too, but they were unconvinced that they should grow something they were unfamiliar with. It wasn't until Françoise saw the *ELLE à table* article that they knew François was onto something.

François was interesting, outspoken, and quirky. Without knowing anything about Philip and me other than our names, he began to talk, making it very clear that if the Jullians grew kale, he already had plans of his own for it. "Kale, yeah, man," he said to us in English. "It is such a big deal in the States. I kept telling Fréd"—he shortened Frédéric's name—"'You need to start growing this. Big money!' But no one here knows what it is, so how can you sell it when no one knows it?"

Philip and I tried to interject, but François kept talking. "Apparently there is this woman in Paris who is trying to do something—a project or something. I read about it in a magazine."

"Umm, yeah." I finally spoke up, loudly enough to get a word in. "That's me. Hi!"

François's eyes bugged out. "Oh, it's you!" he exclaimed. "Wow! Interesting! And you came all the way down here to talk to the Jullians?" I nodded. François grew quiet. I could see him trying to rework the plan in his head. Would he have to split the profits three ways now?

Frédéric, sensing the tension, suggested that we go see the farm. Piling into their SUV, François included, we drove back down the lane and onto another long driveway toward their land. "The farm was my father's," Frédéric said. "And I happened to be the son who took it over. We have thirty greenhouses full of lettuce, melons, and tomatoes."

We walked past the greenhouses and I could see hundreds of heads of lettuce, row after row of rosettes, hypnotizing in shades of green and dark red.

"Do you have seeds?" Frédéric asked me.

I nodded, pulling out a packet of Tuscan kale seeds I had grabbed at the last minute. "You should plant them soon to avoid the hot summer months," I said, handing them over.

Frédéric poured the seeds into his hand to examine the size of each grain and said, "This sounds great. I'm going to do a test first with just a few plants."

"And I will email you with updates!" Françoise added, promising to keep me informed of the progress.

Leaving their farm, I was excited. The Jullians' operation was no joke and much bigger than any other producer I was working with. This could be a game changer.

When we returned to Paris, the lobby of our building smelled of bleach and lemon-scented floor cleaner. The lace curtains on Amelia's front doors were removed, and I could see through the window that the room was empty. Having lost the battle with Monsieur Sinclair, Amelia was gone, and she had taken all of Philippa's things with her.

Around the same time as our visit to the Jullians' farm, I received an email from a food writer, Bruno Verjus, who recently opened his own restaurant, Table. He wrote me, "We now cook kale. Almost every day. You're welcome.—Bruno."

Having a chef reach out to me of his own accord was new territory, but I wrote back, asking if we could meet.

Bruno, a tall, burly man with curly hair, who is never without a thin scarf tied tightly around his neck, greeted me at the door. "*Bienvenue à Table*," he said with a big grin, fanning his arms to show me his restaurant. He seated Philip and I at the front bar, which overlooks the modern, open kitchen, so I could see all the action.

From a refrigerator, Bruno pulled out two large shells that were the size of his palm and the color of sand, as if they'd been plucked out of a mermaid's hair. Cracking them open, he revealed fresh, shiny *coquilles Saint Jacques*, scallops.

"I was raised near Lyon, and my uncle grew kale in his garden," he told me. He took the scallops, still locked in their shells, and shucked them, setting the shells to the side, then thinly sliced each scallop, arranging the raw slivers on a plate. Using a small cheese grater, he shredded cauliflower, the white flakes landing lightly on top of the scallops, like a dusting of snow. Adding a squeeze of lemon juice and a sprinkle of *fleur de sel*, sea salt, he placed the dish in front of us.

"Near Lyon," he said, his eyes glowing, watching us as we took our first bites, "you need three things: *chou, cochons, et pommes de terre*." Cabbage, pigs, and potatoes. He sliced an orange in half, carefully squeezing the juice from high above into a pan filled with kale, sautéing it and adding another sprinkle of finishing salt—reminding me that Chris from Northern Spy also loves to sauté kale with freshly squeezed orange juice. As Bruno cooked, he smiled and laughed a lot, making his kitchen staff and diners feel comfortable. The produce was fresh, and the dishes were simple and delicious.

"*Chou d'aigrette* is what I grew up calling it," he said. This version of the name, another new one for me, references the plumes of feathers that grow at the back of egrets' heads. "But I like *chou plume* too," he added, pulling more leaves out from a box and placing them into a fan shape behind his head. "It's like the feathers of a peacock!"

As Bruno continued to cook, plating dishes for diners, we ate charcuterie, sliced from the dried meat hanging in the window, and vegetables roasted in olive oil. The menu at Table was never large, meaning it was truly seasonal, inspired by whatever vegetables Nicolas Thirard—the farmer I'd met at the *ruche* with Emily—brought in the mornings. "I love his kale," said Bruno. "Just wait—in two years, you are going to see kale everywhere!"

As we were getting ready to leave, Bruno added one last thing, "You know, the most important thing I can do here is nourish people. It is my duty!"

I hadn't heard from the Jullians since our first visit, but finally, in mid-July, after a few unanswered emails, Françoise replied with a few photos. They had planted the kale in June (not avoiding the summer months), and the test had gone well; the kale was big. Almost too big and I had a fear we were already too late.

By chance, for our second year of *vacances*, Philip and I had decided to rent a summer house in a protected forest located between Avignon and Tarascon, only twenty minutes from the Jullians' farm. My parents were going to join us for walks in the woods, cooling off in the pool, and cooking Provençal dishes.

In the countryside, it is possible to do all your shopping—produce included—at large *hypermarchés* like Intermarché, but I wouldn't recommend it. The roadside produce stands offer much better options, and they often do double duty as small *épiceries*. We frequented Le Jardin de Frédéric (no relation to our Frédéric), which sold plums, peaches, nectarines, summer tomatoes, striped white-and-purple eggplant, dark green zucchinis, yellow squash the color of cornmeal, and green, red, yellow, and even small purple peppers. It was everything the region had to offer. That, in addition to their selection of cured meats, cheeses, anchovies, olives, and fresh pastas, meant that we had a crate filled with enough fresh things to cook for a week.

"We're set to visit the Jullians on Wednesday," I told my parents on the train ride to Avignon. After the email from Françoise, I knew we had to visit and assess the situation and whether the kale was already too big. They also invited us over for dinner at their house *à la terrasse*. François and his wife, Sophie, who grew up in the Netherlands, would also join us.

Like a group of explorers, we set out to see the kale. I was expecting to see a few rows of kale in one of the greenhouses, but when Frédéric, bronzed from a morning of deep-sea fishing, pulled aside the plastic flap, he revealed an *entire greenhouse* of kale. I gasped at the jungle in front of me. There was row after row after row of tall, fully mature Tuscan kale stalks. I was stunned. Why hadn't they told me they'd planted more than two hundred plants? Better yet, why hadn't I asked them? I never thought a "test" would be an entire greenhouse. They were obviously proud, but I was worried. How in the world was I going to be able to sell all of this kale…in August? Restaurants were closed. No one was answering phone calls or emails. Distributors were on *vacances*. Paris was shut down, *fermé*.

I began to panic, and Philip could sense my anxiety. He stepped in. "It would have been helpful to have seen photos of the kale as it was growing, so Kristen could have done some legwork before it was already almost too late to harvest."

John, my stepfather, who is an accomplished gardener, whispered into my ear, "I have no idea what everyone is saying, but I do know that this kale is already overgrown. It should have been harvested a few *weeks* ago."

To make matters worse, Sophie joined in. Referencing the Dutch tradition of waiting to harvest kale until after the first frost has sweetened the leaves, she said, "It has not been through a frost. No one will eat it."

The Jullians' pride was quickly melting into panic as well. My energy was sour and stressful. Sophie said outright that no one would eat it in both English and French. And my parents were completely clueless as to what was going on, trying to keep smiles on their faces. Philip was the only person who could keep this situation together.

"Listen—should we have been told about the kale a few weeks ago? Yes. Kristen is going to try to see what she can do with the people in Paris that are actually at work right now, who might want to buy it. But for the time being, why don't we grab a bunch, and Kristen can make a kale salad for our dinner," he suggested, starting to pick the leaves off the plants in the front. I stood there, motionless, staring at greenhouse of kale. How was I going to help them sell this? I pushed the dilemma out of my mind. I would deal with it tomorrow.

Despite the unfortunate miscommunication, which it seemed was probably going to result in an entire greenhouse of kale going to waste, the dinner went well.

Françoise, outfitted in a cute blue-jean dress, cut up tomatoes for a fresh salad, dressing it with basil and oregano. Frédéric, who had caught fresh tuna, earlier that morning, sliced the fish into paper-thin raw slices and marinated it in a paste of ginger, garlic, diced cornichons, and salt. I showed their daughter, whose tan was deeper than both her parents' put together, how to do a kale massage. After all, there was plenty of kale to practice with!

François and Sophie talked with my parents, eating slow-roasted cherry tomatoes and fresh goat cheese on toast and sipping champagne for *apéro*. As I dished out the kale salad, everyone oohed and aahed, except for Sophie, who announced, "I cannot eat this salad. The kale is *too* bitter. It's *so* raw." I ignored her.

The sun dipped down behind the trees, and Françoise lit candles all around the table. The only sounds were the cicadas humming and the English and French chatter on the patio. Curious about Françoise's slow-roasted tomatoes, I asked her if she had any secrets to making them without preservatives. The conversation stopped—everyone went silent. The Jullians' two teenage children stifled their laughter.

"Umm, darling," Philip quickly whispered to me, "It's *conservateurs*, not *préservatifs*." I'd made the classic French mistake that so many English speakers do and asked Françoise if she makes her tomatoes with condoms. Before everyone could erupt into laughter at me, I corrected myself, "*Non, non*," laughing at myself, "*sans conservateurs*."

The wine bottles were empty, the fish was eaten, and there were only crumbs of dessert and droplets of candle wax left on the tablecloth. We left (each with a huge bag of kale to take with us) and I promised to send over a few contacts to Françoise in the morning with hopes that we could sell at least a little bit of the kale. As everyone was leaving, I could hear Sophie whisper noisily to François, "When we get home, I will be putting this kale in the freezer before *we* eat it."

·· SLOW-ROASTED TOMATOES ··

I have very little to say about slow-roasted tomatoes, except that they make every bite of food a little brighter. They are summer sunshine, dirt, and fragrant vines exploding in your mouth, and if you freeze them like Françoise Jullian does, you'll have some to enjoy later in the year.

INGREDIENTS

- CHERRY, COCKTAIL, OR GRAPE TOMATOES, WHOLE OR HALVED
- OLIVE OIL
- FINISHING SALT, TO TASTE

PREPARATION

Preheat the oven to 225°F (100°C). Put the tomatoes in a roasting dish, spreading them out evenly. Pour the olive oil into the dish, making sure to coat each tomato. Roast for 2 hours, until well cooked. Sprinkle finishing salt on each tomato, and enjoy. To preserve, pour the tomatoes into a jar, and fill it with olive oil to the top. Seal the jar with its lid, and freeze.

·· CARPACCIO DE FRÉDÉRIC ··

Contributed by Françoise Jullian

Although things didn't work out with the Jullians, and we left Provence unsure whether we'd see them again, when I contacted Françoise for this recipe, she replied immediately and was very excited to share it. We even spoke over the phone about the book, the project, and, of course, the dinner we enjoyed together at their home. While the Jullians might never grow kale again, I feel that Françoise's recipe contribution was a nice ending to our story with them.

INGREDIENTS

- 1 POUND (500 G) FRESH FISH FILLET, THINLY SLICED*
- 2 MEDIUM ONIONS, FINELY CHOPPED
- 2 TABLESPOONS CAPERS, DICED
- 12 CORNICHONS (SMALL PICKLED GHERKINS), CHOPPED
- 4 TABLESPOONS OLIVE OIL
- JUICE FROM 2 LEMONS
- SALT AND FRESHLY GROUND BLACK PEPPER, TO TASTE

PREPARATION

Prepare 2 to 3 hours before serving.

For the marinade: Chop the capers, cornichons, and onions, and add to a large bowl. Add the lemon juice and olive oil, and mix. Let the fish marinate for 1 hour in the refrigerator. Mix around the bowl every 15 minutes. To serve, place slices of fish on a serving platter, and place the remaining marinade on top. Season with salt and pepper.

YIELD

- 4 SERVINGS

*If using tuna, freeze the tuna and remove from freezer 1 hour before preparation. It will be easier to slice.

Chapter 38

Only a week after returning to Paris from Provence, I received an interesting email. It was from Elaine Sciolino, author of *La Seduction*, the book that had been my guide during our first few weeks in France. Had she emailed me by accident?

From: Elaine Sciolino
Subject: Seeking Information

I write for the *New York Times* and am interested in your project. Who is/are the organizer/s and is there a chance to chat by email or phone?

I thought back to seeing her speak at the expat day two years earlier, her confident voice ringing throughout the American Church, making us laugh as she told the story about trying to find her first Thanksgiving turkey. I blinked twice, not sure that I'd read the email correctly. Was she really interested in writing a story about kale in Paris? For the *New York Times*?

All I had imagined for the Kale Project was to find a farmer and grow kale. I had never envisioned getting so much French buzz about the project or any of the American press—let alone the *New*

York Times. It was the beginning of September and we had only just returned, so I had no idea what the state of kale in the city would be as its second season commenced. I only hoped there would *be* kale for Elaine to write about. I told her I needed a few days to look around the markets first. If the second year would be anything like the first, the green would be out on market stands.

I had a fear that kale's debut season had been a fluke, that it was a one-time thing. Even though I'd confirmed with each of the farmers that they'd be growing it again, I knew I wouldn't believe it until I saw the leafy greens with my own eyes. And sure enough, day by day, farmer by farmer, and market by market, kale started to reappear. Joël, Nicolas, Terroirs d'Avenir, Serge at Marché Bastille, and Marc at Marché Monge all began to sell it again. Hermione had a new harvest as well. I was receiving new Kale Spotted tips on a daily basis. Even middlemen distributors were finding it at Rungis, which meant larger producers were growing it, which meant there was now an established market for it. I told Elaine we were good to go. Paris was flush with kale.

"Perfect," she replied. "It really is a fascinating story. I need a farm, a market, a restaurant, and an event to tie it all together," she told me. I rattled off my ideas, suggesting a trip to Hermione's farm and inviting her to a tasting event I had coming up. I told her about my kale chips and salads at Loustic. I informed her that the first-ever celebration of National Kale Day was going to be on the first Wednesday in October, and that people in Paris were planning to celebrate as well with another kale party at Verjus.

Elaine has lived in Paris since 2002, and as the *New York Times*'s Paris correspondent, she had become friends with Jean-Claude Ribaut, the acclaimed French food writer and critic for the newspaper *Le Monde*.

"Kristen. I have big news," she told me over the phone as we discussed the schedule for her research. "Alain Passard has agreed to prepare a kale tasting menu…with Hermione's kale."

I was speechless. I'd obviously heard of Alain Passard and his three-star Michelin, L'Arpège, and a few people had actually suggested that he would be perfect to approach, but I didn't have the nerve to speak to him or any chef of his stature.

"It's because of Jean-Claude," Elaine continued, ecstatic. "He knows everyone in the food world. He is a friend of Alain Ducasse, Guy Savoy, Joël Robuchon! And, of course, Alain Passard," she said. I couldn't have asked for a better top chef than Monsieur Passard. He is known for bringing vegetables back into the limelight. He even grows the majority of the vegetables for his restaurant on his own farms. The one vegetable he had yet to grow or cook with? Kale.

Since Elaine wanted to highlight one of the farmers I worked with for her story, we took a trip to Hermione's farm—with Jean-Claude. We also planned to pick up a crate of her kale to take to Monsieur Passard's kitchen. We piled into his tiny Twingo and headed east to Terre d'Émeraude. Hermione welcomed us while Tiloup and Reglisse jumped up and down, greeting us.

"I've been picking a crate of kale for you this morning." Hermione smiled at me, pointing to the wooden crate she had layered with brown paper. Carefully placed on top was leaf after leaf of baby kale. Elaine had told her over the phone that we were going to use her kale for a special kale-tasting menu. "I hope it is enough."

I don't think Hermione had any idea to whom we were actually taking the kale or that *her* kale was going to be cooked by a famous chef. Or if she did know, it probably hadn't sunk in yet. It still hadn't really sunk in for me yet.

Elaine, with her characteristic journalist's curiosity, talked with Hermione for well over two hours about her life, farm, land, vegetables, dogs, and, of course, the kale she was growing. We all sampled Hermione's kale, its tender leaves perfect for a raw bite.

Back in Paris, we parked in front of L'Arpège and Jean-Claude, with his VIP status, waited in front of the side kitchen door. With the wide crate in his arms, the door opened, and he sidled in, as if he were entering a secret speakeasy. Only gone for a few minutes, he popped back out again, his forehead perspiring from the kitchen heat. He walked back to the car, leaned into the window, and said, "He was too busy to talk but said he would experiment over the weekend and be ready for the tasting menu for lunch on Monday." Alain Passard was going to prepare Hermione's kale.

Monday could not arrive fast enough, and I made sure to show up for our reservation hungry. L'Arpège, located in the Seventh arrondissement, is an elegant and classic restaurant, with modern furniture, crisp white tablecloths, and woodwork accents throughout. The tables were decorated with the in-season vegetables of the moment; ours had a centerpiece of golden, red, and dark purple cherry tomatoes and small green gourds of autumn squash. Aside from these few touches, it was a no-fuss dining room, putting all the attention on the food (and then, when the meal is finished, on the price tag, as Monsieur Passard's fixed tasting menus do not come cheap).

Once we were seated, a tall, thin, handsome man with wavy gray hair glided over to the table. Dressed in chef's whites, with an air of affluence, he greeted us. Jean-Claude immediately stood up and said, "*Bonjour, Alain. Ça va?*" They grasped hands and greeted each other with *la bise* on each cheek. Elaine and I followed.

"*Et vous êtes la femme du chou?*" Alain asked, staring right at me, his eyes twinkling with charisma, asking if I was the cabbage woman.

"*Alors, le chou kale,*" Alain said, pronouncing "kale" slightly off-kilter, like "kahl."

"For the first of six courses, we will serve a light pastry fill with kale, onion, and turnip," he said, walking backward and disappearing into the kitchen.

Jean-Claude ordered three glasses of *sauvignon blanc*, and we waited for the first dish. "So where do you see the project going?" Elaine asked me. "Do you have any new challenges or endeavors?"

It was a good question, and one that I didn't have just one answer to. I was playing with the idea of launching a kale chip company. I had been in conversation with someone about possibly launching a juice brand. But I didn't really know *where* I wanted the project to go or *what* I wanted it to be. I wasn't sure if kale chips or juice were where I saw myself in the future.

The second course came out. A small silver bowl held four ravioli stuffed with kale. They sat in a light tomato bouillabaisse, with a dash of fresh pepper. Alain strode out of the kitchen, wiping his hands on his spotless apron, and came up to the table again.

"*Bon appétit*," he said with a large grin. We carefully broke the ravioli and ate small pieces with spoonfuls of the peppery broth, which added a spicy kick to each bite.

The third dish arrived soon after and was a thin gratin, almost like a fritter, half-kale and half-zucchini, topped with finely diced chives. Alain, standing next to our table again, said, "I found that the acidity of the chives was a great balance with the alkaline taste of the kale." I made a mental note to include chives in my next raw salad.

Each time a course arrived, Alain came out of the kitchen to tell us about the dish and to visit with the other guests. The dining room was filled with Parisians having business lunches and tourists splurging on an extravagant meal, but he paid equal attention to everyone, making them feel special, one of a kind.

Our next course was a kale and zucchini *velouté* topped with *crème de speck*, a cream made from pork.

"This soup, it is delicious," Jean-Claude said, eagerly tasting another spoonful. "It is *paysanne* and rustic. Perfect with a crusty piece of country bread."

When the fifth course came out, Alain told us, "This to me is the most unique of the dishes." Pointing to the miniature sausage, he said "It is a vegetarian onion, kale, and zucchini sausage accompanied with a red pepper purée and celery root and turnip foams." Set between a tricolor of green, red, and cream foam, the sausage simmered on the plate.

We ordered three glasses of Côte de Beaune wine for the last course, a take on *chou farci*, stuffed cabbage. Alain's version was vegetarian and used kale instead of traditional savoy cabbage. A sauté of kale and finely chopped onion and potato was wrapped in the green leaf and marinated in a green tomato and matcha broth.

"Spectacular," Elaine gushed as she took her first bite.

I grew quiet, savoring my last few bites of the meal, doubting I would ever eat a lunch like this again. Everything was top-notch and prepared with craft, attention to detail, and the aim to serve only the most delicious and beautiful food. I also grew quiet because I couldn't believe how far the project had come, from my first blog post, which I wrote for no one, to enjoying an all-kale tasting menu created by a famous chef.

At the end of the meal, while we were sipping fresh mint tea and eating *macarons* made in-house, Alain came out one last time.

"*Alors?*" he asked, wanting to know what we thought.

"Incredible! Excellent! We have no words," Elaine and Jean-Claude said in unison. Alain Passard had cracked *le chou kale*.

I was still speechless.

"What a vegetable!" Alain said to us, pulling up a chair next to me, making sure he was in the right light to smile for a photo. "It is like an algae," he continued, taking a bite of one of his *macarons*. "It captivates almost all the senses. Touch, taste, smell, and visually, it is stunning!" I could tell that *le chou kale* had captured his heart.

As lunch came to a close and I thanked Jean-Claude for arranging the tasting and Alain for cooking it, he whispered in my ear, "I want to grow this *kahl*. Please! Will you bring me some seeds?"

Two weeks later, the article was published on the front page of the Sunday *New York Times* (it must have been a slow news day). Hermione was the star, the heroine of French kale, and I couldn't wait to show her. She loved it, smiling as she saw her photo in print.

Walking up and down the market's rows, I realized that the vegetable was *everywhere*—even more so than it had been just a few weeks earlier. Almost every produce stand was selling *le chou kale*, their square-shaped black signs all written out with the same name.

As if it had always been present, the kale fit in perfectly next to the lettuce, the spinach leaves, and the long bunches of chard, just as I knew it would. I overheard one *vendeur* tell someone, "It is the *légume* of the year!" People were looking for it, asking questions about it, wondering how to prepare it. If I happened to be standing next to someone asking a question, I would answer, in French, with a short explanation and recipe ideas. People were buying bags of it, thrilled when they saw that it was available. *Le chou kale*, once lost and forgotten, had been found again. Who knew a simple green could bring so much joy?

But it did. For them, for me, for us.

·· KALE AND COURGETTE SOUP ··

There is something about green soups that can be very striking. First, of course, is the color. Soups aren't normally green. Second, the green screams healthy. I was delighted when L'Arpège served a green soup, and I've created my own version with a little extra spice. Philip says it's "moreish," which is British speak for "Yum, I want more!"

INGREDIENTS

- 3 TABLESPOONS OLIVE OIL
- 1 MEDIUM ONION, CHOPPED
- 2 ZUCCHINIS, SLICED
- 1 MEDIUM POTATO, CHOPPED (PEELED IF NOT ORGANIC)
- 1 TEASPOON CUMIN
- 6 CUPS (200 TO 250 G) KALE, WASHED AND CHOPPED
- 3 TO 4 CUPS (720 TO 960 ML) WATER OR VEGETABLE BROTH
- GROUND CORIANDER SEEDS, FOR GARNISH
- SALT AND FRESHLY GROUND PEPPER, TO TASTE

PREPARATION

Heat the olive oil in a large pot over medium heat. Add the onion, and cook, stirring frequently, for 3 to 4 minutes, until translucent. Add the chopped potato, and cook, stirring frequently, for 3 to 4 minutes. Add the zucchini, and stir for 5 to 6 minutes, until it begins to soften. Add the cumin. Add the kale, cover the pot with a lid, and let the ingredients cook on low heat for 4 to 5 minutes, stirring every minute. Remove the lid, pour in the water or broth, increase temperature to medium heat, and bring soup to a boil. Reduce heat again, and simmer for 5 minutes. Blend the soup in a blender (or use an immersion hand blender in the pot), until it is a smooth consistency. If you want a thinner soup, add more water or broth. Season with salt and pepper. Garnish with ground coriander seeds before serving.

YIELD

- 4 SERVINGS

·· *CHOU KALE FARCI*, ·· STUFFED KALE IN TOMATO BROTH

Contributed by Alain Passard, L'Arpège

This kale dish from our kale dégustation *is a take on an old French cabbage recipe,* chou cabus farci, *which is said to be a medieval Belgian dish traditionally made with ground meat, eggs, and spices. Monsieur Passard adapted his kale version to be vegetarian.*

INGREDIENTS

- 12 LARGE KALE LEAVES, WASHED (STEMS INTACT)
- 2½ POUNDS (1 KG) GREEN ZEBRA TOMATOES, OR ANY COMBINATION OF RIPE HEIRLOOM TOMATOES, HALVED AND CORED
- 3 TO 4 BAY LEAVES
- 2 MEDIUM NEW POTATOES (ABOUT 10 OUNCES/300 G)
- ¼ CUP (55 G) SALTED BUTTER
- 6 TO 8 MEDIUM KALE LEAVES (1 PACKED CUP/50 G) THINLY SLICED
- 1 SMALL ZUCCHINI, FINELY CHOPPED

- ½ SWEET ONION, MINCED
- ¼ CUP (30 G) UNROASTED PISTACHIOS, CHOPPED
- 2 TO 3 SPRIGS FRESH THYME, LEAVES ONLY
- 1 FRESH HYSSOP BRANCH (OPTIONAL)
- A FEW DROPS OF PISTACHIO OR WALNUT OIL
- FRESHLY GROUND BLACK PEPPER, TO TASTE

PREPARATION

Bring a large pot of salted water to a boil. Blanch the large kale leaves for 30 seconds, drain, and transfer to an ice bath, or run under cold water to stop the cooking. Set aside. Heat the tomatoes in a medium saucepan over high heat. Bring to a boil, and let soften for 2 to 3 minutes. Crush the tomatoes with a potato masher. Reduce heat to a simmer, and continue to cook for 10 minutes. Remove from heat, and cool. Strain the tomato water into a bowl through 2 layers of cheesecloth. (Don't force the extraction.) When all liquid has drained, discard the cheesecloth and pulp, add the bay leaves, and let stand for 15 minutes. Discard the bay leaves, and set aside the tomato water.

Meanwhile, bring a large pot of salted water to boil, and cook the potatoes for 10 to 15 minutes, until tender when pierced with a knife. Drain, peel, and cut into small cubes, about ¼-inch squares. Place a medium saucepan over medium-high heat, melt the butter, and add the sliced kale leaves, zucchini, and onion. Cook for 15 minutes, stirring occasionally. Add the cooked potatoes, pistachios, thyme, and hyssop (if using), and stir gently, until just combined. Do not mash. Remove from heat.

Lay a 10-inch square piece of plastic wrap on a clean work surface. Place 1 large kale leaf in the center of the plastic, and spoon about 2 tablespoons of the filling into the center of the leaf. Gather up the edges of the plastic wrap, and twist to form a ball with the kale leaf at the bottom; tie the plastic tightly at the base of the ball. Repeat with the remaining kale and filling. Bring a steamer to a boil, reduce heat to a low simmer, and add the plastic-wrapped kale. Gently steam the bundles for 5 minutes. (Be careful— if the heat is too high, the plastic will melt.) While the kale is steaming, divide the tomato water into 4 serving dishes. Remove the bundles, carefully untie, and serve, seam-side down, in the warm tomato water. Drizzle with the oil and sprinkle with pepper.

YIELD

· 4 SERVINGS (3 STUFFED KALE LEAVES PER SERVING)

Epilogue

A few weeks after the kale *dégustation*, I delivered seeds to Alain. With the same twinkle in his eye, he eagerly took the seed packet from my hand and winked, thanking me for bringing them to him. Months later, I saw on Twitter that L'Arpège had *le chou kale* on the menu, this time for everyone.

❧

It is September again, our fourth in Paris. Another *rentrée*. I am no longer surprised by the early chill in the air or the fact that the sun doesn't rise until late in the morning. I'm also no longer surprised that there are still times when I order a *café crème* and no one understands me or when I wear exercise clothes and someone stares. I gave up trying to be French long ago.

I think about how it is the start of another kale season. There are many farmers now, both young and old, from farms big and small, growing kale. There are many *marchés*, *supermarchés*, and now even a few *hypermarchés* selling it, too many for me to even keep count. I continue the Kale Spotted map, always trying to support local, French producers. Juice bars juice with it, a kale-chip company makes chips with it, restaurants cook with it, and, funnily enough, it's even served at the airport. And while people are aware of kale's American superfood status, just as Marc-Antoine predicted, the French have embraced the vegetable because it was always theirs. Someone just needed to grow it again.

I think about the girl I left behind in New York, the girl who followed her heart to a city and a job, only to fall in love and into a life that made her rethink and relearn, which helped her grow up. I think about leaving that New York life. The comfort of it. The routine of it.

I think about how everything in Paris was upside down but how now I understand. I finally feel the magic from living in the most beautiful city in the world.

I also think about Philippa. I think of her at the hospital château, sick but pretending she was going to be all right. I think of Philip and how we've learned to be more compassionate and respectful. More than we ever knew possible.

❧

September 23 is Philippa's birthday, and it turns out to be a day meant for a postcard, so Philip and I decide to go to Versailles. We visit *le Potager du Roi* again and while walking through the quadrants of vegetables, I see a gardener, digging and loosening the ground around him, pulling, curly, green leaves off of a tall, stoic kale plant.

"How long has the garden grown this cabbage?" I ask him. Wiping the sweat from his forehead, leaving a smear of dirt, he responds, "Oh for around two years now. Since 2013." I tell him about my project and he removes a small plant from a seed tray. "Do you want this plant? I'm happy to give it to you." I graciously accept it, excited to plant the king's kale outside our window ledge.

Leaving the garden, we walk toward the Grand Canal and reach the spot where we put Philippa to rest four years earlier, and we tell our baby girl, Grady, about her *grand-mère*. Wherever Philippa is, I hope I have made her proud. I hope she feels that her son is happy, taken care of, safe, and loved. I hope she knows we think about her every day.

This autumn is also when Hermione surprises me. It was a weekend like any weekend. A walk with Grady to the market, a green juice at Hermione's stand. But this time when she sees me, her smile is bigger, and her icy-gray-blue eyes light up. She whispers, *"Bonjour,"* and takes my hand, squeezing it.

"Kreesteen. My daughter—she translated it all for me. Everything. Your website, the kind things you wrote. What you have done. You said you were going to sell the kale and you did. What a *belle histoire."* A beautiful story.

I return the squeeze. *"Avec plaisir,"* I say. My pleasure.

Pulling a sprig of rosemary from her baskets, she hands it to me. "For you, Madame Kale. *Merci beaucoup.* From me, Madame Mustard."

Acknowledgments

Without the involvement of many people, the Kale Project would never have become what it is today. The same goes for this book. I want to express my thanks and appreciation (and give a big American hug) to all of you.

Liz, my first friend in Paris.

Lisa, Mary Kay, Lindsey Kent, and Sylvia, for making my first year much happier.

Grant and Helen Parker, for the brilliant logo idea.

Lucy Williams, for your beautiful illustrations.

Without the Paris online community, the word of kale would have been a lot harder to spread. To David and Clotilde, for the inspiration to go forward with this crazy idea—and for supporting it. To Bryan, Lindsey, and the Paris blogging world, for bringing your enthusiasm with beautiful photos and kind words.

Without very special friends, the project would have been stuck in a rut many times. Mariana Keller, for giving me ideas and pushing me to try new things. Jane and Olivier, for lending La Cuisine Paris and always being open to helping out. Elke Seyser, for the use of Superfoods Café in time of need. Channa, for letting kale shine at Loustic. Virginie, for being my first kale ambassador. Caitlin Riley and the Dark Rye team, for producing and telling the story so well. Maggie Schmerin, the unofficial

Kale Project cheerleader. Elaine Sciolino, for taking things to a whole new level. Marion Aubert, without you, my dear friend, so much of what I accomplished would never have been possible. Thank you for teaching me to find my French tongue! Emmanuel Heimann and Léonie Gwerder, for family dinners and your endless translation help.

My agent Bridget Matzie, for visualizing a book and working with me so patiently to the end game (and beyond!). Shana Drehs, my editor, for her thoughts and encouragement during the writing process. To the team at Sourcebooks for your attention to detail and hard work.

A big American hug to my dear friend Emily Dilling, for her constant kale companionship at the market, with farmers, and everywhere in between. I raise a mug of *café filtre* to my Paris girlfriend book lunch club: Emily, Anna Brones, and Jessie Kanelos-Weiner (and the Holybelly crew for keeping our stomachs full and our spirits bright). Your encouragement, listening, recipe testing, talent, and insight is unparalleled.

Without the chefs, kale would never have been cooked. To Chris Ronis, for my first kale salad. Omid and Alannah, for your friendship. Alice Quillet, Bruno Verjus, Shaun Kelley, Alain Passard, and most importantly, Braden Perkins and Laura Adrian, for giving a crazy girl and her leafy green a chance.

And of course without the farmers, there would never have been any kale at all. Joël Thiebault, Michèle Françoise, Gérard Essayan, Nicolas Thirard, Frédéric and Françoise Jullian, and Palmer Permaculture. Suzanne Newman, who is my vegetable fairy godmother. And of course to Hermione Boehrer, the kale pioneer.

I would be nowhere without my parents. My mom and John have never stopped believing in me or encouraging me. I am who I am because of you both.

Lastly, to my wonderful Philip. You, darling, are my best friend, and I can't imagine doing life without you. *Heureux, heureux, heureux.*

About the Author

Photo credit: Caitlin Riley

Kristen Beddard is the American founder of *The Kale Project*, a successful initiative to reintroduce kale to France. Through her work with local French farmers, *le chou kale* can now be found at various outdoor markets and supermarkets. She is the author of *Savez-vous manger les choux*, a French book about Brassicas, and she is a contributing author of *We Love Kale: Fresh and Healthy Inspiring Recipes*. She currently resides in Paris with her husband and daughter.